Cultural Relativism in the Face of the West

Cultural Relativism in the Face of the West

The Plight of Women and Female Children

Bret L. Billet

First published in 2007 by
PALGRAVE MACMILLAN™
175 Fifth Avenue, New York, N.Y. 10010 and
Houndmills, Basingstoke, Hampshire, England RG21 6XS.
Companies and representatives throughout the world.

PALGRAVE MACMILLAN is the global academic imprint of the
Palgrave Macmillan division of St. Martin's Press, LLC and of
Palgrave Macmillan Ltd. Macmillan® is a registered trademark in
the United States, United Kingdom and other countries. Palgrave is a
registered trademark in the European Union and other countries.

ISBN-10: 0-312-22131-2
ISBN-13: 978-0-312-22131-7

Library of Congress Cataloging-in-Publication Data

Billet, Bret L. (Bret Lee)
    Cultural relativism in the face of the West: The plight of women
and children / by Bret L. Billet.
        p. cm.
    Includes bibliographical references and index.
    ISBN 0-312-22131-2 (alk. paper)
        1. Human rights. 2. Cultural relativism. 3. Women—Social
conditions. 4. Children—Social conditions. I. Title.

JC571.B542 2007
323.3'4—dc22   2006049143

Design by Macmillan India Ltd.

First edition: April 2007

10 9 8 7 6 5 4 3 2 1

Printed in the United States of America.

"The great danger for family life, in the midst of any society whose idols are pleasure, comfort, and independence, lies in the fact that people close their hearts and become selfish."

"As the family goes, so goes the nation and so goes the whole world in which we live."

Pope John Paul II

Many cultures regard the concept of "family" as a fundamental unit of social structure. Although its exact meaning is controversial and differs on the basis of temporal and cultural distinctions, it invariably performs functions such as reproduction, social and economic well-being, and education. Moreover, it is predicated on the idea that the whole remain strong in the face of individual adversity.

For me the essence of family has always been somewhat distant and removed from daily life. At the same time, however, it is by far the most important aspect of my existence. I regard *family* as the chief component of our lives that is responsible for *f*ostering, *a*dvancing, and *m*entoring the *i*magination, *l*earning, and *y*earnings of its members. The triumph of family comes only at the defeat of selfishness. My hope is that members of all families experience some measure of this success in their lives. However your culture has come to understand the concept, this book is dedicated to the *family*, both yours and mine.

CONTENTS

LIST OF TABLES

Acknowledgments

As an undergraduate student one of the first significant works that I read was Plato's *Republic*. I remember one particular discourse on education, between Socrates and Adeimantus, which resulted in Socrates declaring that "the direction in which education starts a man will determine his future life." Remembering this has given rise to the realization that what I have become is a testament to both my early education and its continual evolution. Consequently, I am forever indebted to the many members of my family who, in a manner sometimes unbeknownst to them, have influenced my imagination, furthered my learning, and left me yearning for more.

More specifically, I am indebted to my wife, Paula, and my son, Brandon. Paula continued to encourage me during the emotional highs and lows associated with the writing of the specific case studies. Being an academic also allowed her great insight into the stumbling blocks that I encountered. For this I am forever appreciative of her patience and understanding. In his own unique way, Brandon provided me with timely loving reminders that my writing was far from on schedule. Watching his devotion to education and commitment to overall excellence provided me with the impetus necessary to complete the manuscript. Indeed, his actions have taught me a lesson on desire and perseverance. I only hope that my actions will have served him likewise.

Beyond family I am indebted to my many students over the years who have at times provided a spark for a fiery idea, a keen insight, or an impassioned look of excitement. It is at these times that I know my learning has made a difference in yours. As usual, all errors of omission and commission rest entirely with me. To all my family, friends, and colleagues, Godspeed.

ABBREVIATIONS

CLDA	Child Labor Deterrence Act
DEBT	foreign debt
ECPAT	End Child Prostitution, Child Pornography and Trafficking of Children for Sexual Purposes
EI	Child Labor Education Initiative
FDI	foreign direct investment
FEMPOP	total female population
FGM	female genital mutilation
FMR	female to male sex ratio
FMRBIRTH	female to male sex ratio at birth
FMRGENPOP	female to male sex ratio in the general population
GDI	Gender-related Development Index
GDPPC	gross domestic product per capita
GENPOP	total general population
HDI	Human Development Index
IAC	Inter-African Committee on Traditional Practices affecting the Health of Women and Children
IBESR	Institute for Welfare and Research
IBRD	International Bank for Reconstruction and Development (World Bank)
ICJ	International Court of Justice
ICLP	International Child Labor Program
IFC	International Finance Corporation
ILO	International Labour Organization
IMF	International Monetary Fund
INTERPOL	International Criminal Police Organization
IPEC	International Programme on the Elimination of Child Labour
MALEPOP	total male population
MOLSA	Ministry of Labor and Social Affairs

ODA	Official Development Assistance
PEACE	Protecting Environment and Children Everywhere
PREDA	People's Recovery, Empowerment and Development Assistance Foundation
PROTECT	Prosecutorial Remedies and Other Tools to End the Exploitation of Children Today
SAP	structural adjustment policy
STEP	Support to Employment Promotion
STOP	Support to Atrocities Prevention
TOTBIRTHS	total births
TOTFEMBIRTHS	total female births
TOTFEMPOT	total number of females potentially affected on annual basis
TOTMISSFEM	total missing females
TOTPOP	total population
UNDP	United Nations Development Programme
UNFPA	United Nations Population Fund
UNHRC	United Nations Human Rights Commission
UNICEF	United Nations Children's Fund
USAID	United States Agency for International Development
WCACSEC	World Congress against the Commercial Sexual Exploitation of Children
WHO	World Health Organization
WTO	World Tourism Organization
WTO	World Trade Organization

1

Introduction: Universal Human Rights versus Cultural Relativism

The General Assembly Proclaims this Universal Declaration of Human Rights as a common standard of achievement for all peoples and all nations, to the end that every individual and every organ of society, keeping this Declaration constantly in mind, shall strive by teaching and education to promote respect for these rights and freedoms and by progressive measures, national and international, to secure their universal and effective recognition and observance, both among the people of Member States themselves and among the peoples of territories under their jurisdiction.

> Excerpt from the Preamble of the 1948
> Universal Declaration of Human Rights

Although the idea, if not the practice, of universal human rights has been part of global consciousness since 1948, its content is still under discussion. Even some of what was once thought settled is under increasing attack, especially with respect to rights of dissent and the rights of women and indigenous peoples.

> Nagengast & Turner (1997, p. 270)

All Human Rights for All.

> United Nations motto for the 1998 Year of Human Rights

The idea of universal human rights was perhaps the most contentious concept of the twentieth century. Originally presented as a response to the atrocities of the past and an attempt to stifle the potential ills of the future, the concept has been under heated assault by adherents to the concept of "cultural relativism." Although this concept, too, has been under fire in recent years by cultural feminists, it was sanctioned by the American Anthropological Association in 1947 and continues to influence the work of social scientists and specifically anthropologists (Nagengast & Turner, 1997, p. 270).

The basic conflict between these two extreme perspectives lies in the degree to which either should be the chief underlying consideration when dealing with the great diversity of peoples worldwide. The importance of this conflict was reflected by a panel presentation on the theme during the 1995 annual meeting of the American Anthropological Association.[1] On one extreme, adherents to universal human rights strongly believe that there is a fundamental group of human rights that are applicable to all members of the world society regardless of the diversity of cultures, values, and beliefs that exist. This belief is portrayed splendidly in both the Preamble to the Charter of the United Nations and the 1948 Universal Declaration of Human Rights. The Preamble to the Charter of the United Nations unequivocally states:

> We the Peoples of the United Nations determined to save succeeding generations from the scourge of war, which twice in our lifetime has brought untold sorrow to mankind, and to reaffirm faith in fundamental human rights, in the dignity and worth of the human person, in the equal rights of men and women and of nations, large and small, and. . . (United Nations, 1998)

The other extreme on the continuum is the notion of cultural relativism, which considers virtually every society to be "distinct" from others. The chief implication arising from this is that while some human rights may be applicable to perhaps a few societies, there can never be a universal human right that is uniformly applicable to people worldwide. The outright suggestion of such a standard is viewed as ludicrous to the majority of cultural anthropologists whose doctrine involves a steadfast commitment to ethnic diversity and the belief that any concept that purports to be universal has but limited utility (i.e., application). Many maintain that the introduction of such "universal" concepts, which are in reality not universal at all, is only a biased, ethnocentric effort by the West to "stretch" concepts that are derived from the Western experience (Sartori, 1970; Wiarda, 1981). Adherents to cultural relativism claim that the rich variety of practices among different cultures does not make the uniform application of universal human rights feasible.

To their credit, cultural relativists are primarily concerned with achieving a greater degree of understanding, usually in functionalist terms, of the diversity of cultures worldwide. Unfortunately, the uniform application of universal human rights often conflicts with this objective. What is often lost in the debate between these two extremes is the substantive practices of these very numerous cultures. In many debates about universal human rights, a particular practice, such as female circumcision, is invoked, but it is not fully understood in terms of what functions it performs in society or from what history it is derived. It is routinely the case that uncommon behaviors are summarily dismissed without its cultural relevance having been fully explored. Conversely, to their credit, those who adhere to the concept of universal human rights are proceeding in their quest of uniform application with the best of intentions. They seemingly strive to produce an outline of behaviors, born out of a preconceived notion of human nature, that is in sync with the notion of liberty and justice for all. Moreover, some adherents to this school explicitly indict cultural relativism for its apparent inability or desire to criticize those cultures whose practices are often construed as flagrant violations of fundamental human rights.

This overarching conflict between the uniform application of universal human rights and the specific understanding provided by cultural relativism is the primary focus of this book. Much of the literature regarding these ideas, however, is written on a very superficial level. As is typically the case, the debate is introduced, the foundations (sometimes theoretically based, sometimes not) are presented, and an opinionated summary is provided by the author. What is often not well presented is the cultural relativism side of the equation. Case studies, presented within the context of the discussion of universal human rights, are not typically introduced. Alternatively, many writers will make vague reference to an uncommon cultural practice, such as female circumcision, without providing a fuller picture of how the practice may be functional, indeed even desired, within the practicing society. While the debate between the uniform application of universal human rights and cultural relativism must be fully developed in order to lay a foundation for further inquiry, there must also be a detailed understanding of the cultural behaviors that the uniform application of universal human rights implicitly finds questionable.

This book examines the debate between the uniform application of universal human rights and cultural relativism. In so doing, it will present the foundations for both schools of thought as well as outline a brief evolution of the debate. On completion of this overview, several case studies of cultural practices that involve either women or children and are typically viewed by the West as violations of fundamental human rights will be presented. These presentations, in juxtaposition to the aforementioned criticism regarding vague references to obscure practices, will be quite detailed. Each case study is presented in accordance with a sixfold framework that includes (1) the history of the practice, (2) specifics of the practice, (3) cultural relevance, (4) the clash of cultures, (5) implications for foreign relations, and (6) potential resolutions. The presentation of several cases, via this framework, will provide readers with a fuller account of the practice's value to the culture in which it is practiced. Moreover, an attempt is made within each case study, under the heading "Potential Resolutions," to assess the merit of those who argue for the uniform application of universal human rights as well as those who adhere to the doctrine of cultural relativism. In sum, it is argued that the extremes are overdogmatic and that in most cases a middle ground can be found that, while not entirely satisfying to either extreme position, may represent a compromise that all cultures involved can accept.

THE FOUNDATIONS OF UNIVERSAL HUMAN RIGHTS[2]

On December 23, 1994, the General Assembly of the United Nations passed resolution 49/184 announcing that the period between January 1, 1995, and December 31, 2004, would be the United Nations Decade for Human Rights Education. Moreover, the United Nations High Commissioner for Human Rights then defined human rights education as

> training, dissemination and information efforts aimed at the building of a universal culture of human rights through the imparting of knowledge and skills and the moulding of attitudes and directed to:
>
> (a) The strengthening of respect for human rights and fundamental freedoms;
> (b) The full development of the human personality and the sense of its dignity;
> (c) The promotion of understanding, tolerance, gender equality and friendship among all nations, indigenous peoples and racial, national, ethnic, religious and linguistic groups;
> (d) The enabling of all persons to participate effectively in a free society;
> (e) The furtherance of the activities of the United Nations for the maintenance of peace. (United Nations, 1996)

It is curious that the decade for human rights education did not seem to include laying the foundation on which the concept of universal human rights is based. The report implicitly suggested that this concept is not open to debate, or at the very least, it has been decided applicable to all. Contrary to this apparent oversight, it *is* important to understand the foundations underlying the concept of universal human rights.

Zechenter (1997, pp. 320–322) suggests four different bases of support for the existence of universal human rights: natural law theory, the theory of rationalism, the doctrine of positivism, and human capabilities theory. Natural law theories typically take one of two forms: classical or modern. Classical natural law theory is mostly concerned with the imposition of human conventions and laws on what is considered to be a system of justice that is not unique to a few groups in society, but rather is commonplace for all human beings. Modern natural law theory holds that all human beings possess a certain degree of sovereignty with regard to such lofty ideals as freedom and honor and that all human beings have equality in the sense that they possess this sovereignty. If an externality were to impose a restriction on the sovereignty of a particular entity, then the externality would be committing a wrong. It is unlikely that inequality, with respect to sovereignty, could be construed as a right unless there were an agreement by all entities involved, including the entity that would have its sovereignty curtailed, to forge such an agreement.

Ultimately, both classical and modern natural law theory are concerned with universality, as the gist of the theory deals with what is *good* and *bad* for all human beings (Perry, 1997, pp. 478–481). For both classical and modern natural law, there is a theological bent with respect to what is good and bad, as God is said to instruct all human beings that there should not be any deviation from our nature or any irreverence for the natural freedoms and equality that are inherent in all human beings.

Whereas natural law theories are more caught up with divine intervention, an external consideration, the theory of rationalism is more concerned with individual reason, an internal consideration. At first it might appear that rationalism would only serve to subvert the notion of universal human rights. However, the key concern here is largely with the *origination* of such rights. What is held as knowledge by natural law theories is externally derived, either with or without divine intervention. Conversely, knowledge, according to the theory of rationalism, is internally derived "due to the universal capacity of all humans to think rationally" (Zechenter, 1997, p. 321). In the end, the universalist position is supported by the implicit recognition that while all human beings hold these rights individually, the fact of the matter is that all human beings, *through their ability to reason*, hold these rights.

The doctrine of positivism, when invoked with respect to human rights discussions, is more accurately referred to as legal positivism. Unlike natural law theories, which suggest divine guidance, legal positivism presupposes that there is no higher authority than the sovereign power of a state. Only in discussions of *moral positivism* are divine intervention and the morality of laws of any consequence. Legal positivism suggests that as entities (i.e., countries) enter into agreements (e.g., the International Covenant on Civil and Political Rights and the International Covenant on Economic, Social, and Cultural Rights), they recognize the norms of behavior that signatories of the said covenants are expected to uphold. Moreover, the apparent global acceptance of these legalistic covenants is indicative of the desire for universal norms of behavior. As Zechenter (1997) notes, however, the application of universal human rights to indigenous peoples may not be justified because of their lack of representation (p. 321).

Human capabilities theory is a contemporary attempt to derive universal norms or standards with respect to fundamental characteristics of being human (Nussbaum, 1997). One might label this technique an anthropological approach to discern the common features among societies that lead to a certain state of *good* human existence. These commonalities, when adequately identified, would then give rise to a "baseline" of human rights that are appropriate for the universe of human beings. Examples of such common characteristics are the recognition of one's mortality; the need for food, drink, shelter, and mobility; and the capacity for pain and pleasure. These are among the several characteristics of all human populations (Nussbaum, 1995a, pp. 76–80). The basis of support for universalism is quite clear. If one can find those "qualities of life" that are present for all human populations, then one can create a set of universal human rights that seeks to ensure the continued existence of these qualities.[3]

It is quite easy to see how the concept of "universalism" finds support from any of the four aforementioned theories. Indeed, it does not take a good deal of insight to recognize how such documents as the Universal Declaration of Human Rights can find philosophical support or basis in each of these theories. Whether taken as a whole or independently of one another, these theories are the underlying foundations in support of the argument for "universal" human rights. Once individuals have been educated about these philosophical foundations, one can proceed with the aforementioned dissemination of human rights education.

There are, if you will, several visual aids that can be utilized in human rights education and that are each, although in their very different ways, proponents for universal human rights. It is important that each of these related visual aids be presented and utilized in the quest to promote the fullest understanding of "universal human rights" and how the concept has gained prominence throughout time. The first of these visual aids, the Preamble to the Charter of the United Nations, implicitly assumes that there is a constituent set of universally applicable "fundamental" human rights. Although this is boldly recognized, neither the preamble nor the charter itself specifically enumerates these fundamental human rights.

The task of specification was assigned to those who created the second key visual aid, the Universal Declaration of Human Rights. The United Nations, as is clear in Article 62, delegated responsibility for this task to the Economic and Social Council. The latter, as the charter indicates, is the main organ of the United Nations that is responsible for making "recommendations for the purpose of promoting respect for, and observance of, human rights and fundamental freedoms for all" (United Nations, 1998, Article 62). The 1946 creation of the Commission on Human Rights,[4] in accordance with Article 68, was then charged with the task of devising an international bill of rights. Led by Eleanor Roosevelt, the commission first produced the Universal Declaration of Human Rights and then proceeded to transform this nonbinding declaration into two separate visual aids (i.e., covenants) known as the International Covenant on Civil and Political Rights and the International Covenant on Economic, Social, and Cultural Rights.

Both covenants echoed the need for all people to respect and adhere to fundamental human rights. These covenants, adopted by the General Assembly in December 1966, did not enter into force until 1976. Although all three documents revolved around the notion of "universal" human rights, countries were quite reluctant to ratify the binding covenants as quickly as they could voice appreciation and support for the nonbinding Universal Declaration of Human Rights. The main point here is that the *idea* of universal human rights was readily acceptable to most members of the United Nations, but when it came time to enumerate just exactly what these fundamental rights would be (i.e., the two separate covenants), and subsequently adhere to them, several countries began to question exactly what a fundamental and universal human right entailed. Weigel (1995) states:

> Moreover, the endless piling-up of lists of "rights" that followed the Universal Declaration—in instruments such as the International Covenant on Economic, Social, and Cultural Rights and

> the International Covenant on Civil and Political Rights (not
> to mention such tracts for the times as the sundry international
> "conventions" on racial discrimination, discrimination against
> women, and the rights of children)—invited the suspicion that,
> if everything was a "human right," then nothing was, in fact, a
> human right in any serious sense. (p. 43)

In part the "piling-up of lists" might have been a necessity in order to allow the Western as well as socialist countries to come to some agreement. Arthur Schlesinger, Jr., for example, observed that the second set of human rights (i.e., the International Covenant on Economic, Social, and Cultural Rights) was "designed to please states that denied their subjects the first [set]" (quoted in Weigel, 1995, p. 43). This may be entirely correct, because when the resolution regarding the Universal Declaration of Human Rights was adopted by the General Assembly, the Soviet-bloc countries abstained from voting.

In the wake of these historic documents, several other visual aids (i.e., covenants) were devised that voiced sincere support for the notion of the universal application of fundamental human rights. Several instruments that specifically detail the universal human rights of women and children in this regard and also extend support for the uniform application of fundamental human rights include the 1979 Convention on the Elimination of All Forms of Discrimination against Women, the 1989 Convention on the Rights of the Child, and the 1993 Declaration on the Elimination of Violence against Women.

Moreover, several major conferences that have reviewed the status of universal human rights have also, in their final proclamations, favored the continued emphasis on "universalism." The 1968 Proclamation of Teheran, the 1993 Vienna Declaration and Programme of Action, and the 1995 Beijing Declaration and Platform for Action speak specifically to the concept of universal human rights. The Vienna Declaration and Programme of Action is indicative of these proclamations and states:

> The 1993 World Conference on Human Rights reaffirms the sol-
> emn commitment of all States to fulfill their obligations to promote
> universal respect for, and observance and protection of, all human
> rights and fundamental freedoms for all in accordance with the Charter
> of the United Nations, other instruments relating to human rights, and
> international law. The universal nature of these rights and freedoms is
> beyond question. (United Nations, 1993b)

CULTURAL RELATIVISM

Unlike "universal" human rights, the concept of cultural relativism is not easily traced back to a theory about human nature, natural law theory, and so on. Rather, the theory of cultural relativism finds it origins in the perceptions and understandings that experience can offer. Strictly speaking, cultural relativism can be defined as

> an intellectual doctrine that postulates a strict separation of ethnographic reporting from judgmental analysis derived from the cultural experiences of the scientist. Because every custom, even infanticide or cannibalism, is but one part of a whole culture, its true meaning can only be understood in its functional context. Therefore, any attempt to interpret ethnographic data in terms of values from a different cultural tradition distorts the reality of each people's way of life. (Lachmann, 1991, p. 74)

In essence, if one makes the assumption that cultures and their cultural practices (i.e., norms of behavior) are variable, then several further considerations might naturally follow. First, it is conceivable that what has meaning for one culture might not have meaning for another. Second, a cultural practice that is functional in one setting may not be functional in another. Third, one's understanding of what is an appropriate cultural practice will vary depending on the culture in which one finds oneself. Fourth, given the presumption of different cultural characteristics, it is inconceivable that any one characteristic, belief, value, and so on could be widely applicable to all other existing cultures. Fifth, one must be careful not to allow the values, customs, beliefs, and so on of an external culture to influence one's understanding of the culture under study or to influence one's judgment regarding the functions that various cultural practices perform. All of these considerations are, in part, chief ideas in the development of the theory of cultural relativism.

Although Renteln (1990, p. 62) suggests that the doctrine of relativism dates back at least to the Greeks, the modern "version" of the theory originates out of the disciplines of ethnology and ethnography in the late nineteenth and early twentieth centuries. Whereas ethnology is concerned with the overall pattern of culture and the structure of the social system, ethnography revolves around details and fills in the specific norms and behaviors of diverse cultures. As ethnography began to receive greater attention, there were those who recognized that there seemed to be an inherent bias, in that Western cultures were assumed to be superior, at the highest point in the evolution of culture to date, and that other cultures would (i.e., should) be judged in comparison to what Western culture finds to be acceptable norms of behavior. As a response to the inherent bias assumed in the evolutionary progression from savage to modern culture, the theory of cultural relativism was conceived (Renteln, 1990, pp. 62–63).

There are a host of related factors to consider when looking at any one particular culture and the norms of behavior incorporated. For example, one may wish to know, and attempt to understand, what the moral truths of any particular culture are. Moral truths are determined by one's own culture, custom, and the norms of society. Consequently, if one, as an investigator from another culture, wishes to study the moral truths of another culture, one would first have to lay down one's own cultural predispositions in this regard because one's own moral truths are culture bound. If one fails to do this, then one will be quite tempted to impose a moral judgment that is derived not from the moral truths of the culture under study, but from one's own culture. The result, according to cultural relativists, can be quite damaging, because one is basically asserting what types of behaviors *ought* or *should* be approved or accepted by another culture on the basis of what has been accepted or approved by one's own culture.

It is important at this juncture to state that a cultural practice that is approved of is not necessarily right or wrong. Alternatively, the cultural relativist would only remark that it is a functional practice that is existent in a particular culture. When a practice is morally approved of, it is also typically viewed as morally right in that culture. A practice that is morally right is one that can be defended by its adherents with moral reason. It is in this regard that the notions of ethical relativism and cultural relativism are related. Ethical relativism suggests that a practice that is right is one that is approved of by one's own culture, and that a practice that is wrong is one that is disapproved. The problem is that this is a typical belief of all cultures, so that unless there is a modicum of cross-cultural belief present, no two cultures will come to any agreement on what is, ethically speaking, right and wrong. It is for this reason that ethical relativism and cultural relativism maintain that it would be difficult to find a set of moral customs that could be universal in scope. This is no less the case with the notion of universal human rights.

THE CLASH BETWEEN UNIVERSALISM AND CULTURAL RELATIVISM

The conflict between universal human rights and a concept of human rights that cultural relativism would promote is somewhat clear.

At the center of the conflict, perhaps, are the concepts "value-free" and "tolerance." To be value-free is not the same as being valueless. Rather, to be value-free, or "objective," is to temporarily put aside one's own set of values and not let them either impact the manner by which one investigates another culture or predispose one into believing that the culture being investigated is to be judged on the basis of one's own values. For the adherent to cultural relativism, values radiate solely from the culture that is being studied. Adherents to universalism, especially with respect to human rights, suggest that values have *cross-cultural,* or universal, application. This is where conflict between the two extremes comes into existence. Let us say, for example, that one's own culture does not believe in the value of cannibalism and, therefore, suggests that other cultures should share in this belief. To do so would be tantamount to condoning cultural imperialism with respect to this issue, because what is valued, with respect to cannibalism or any other disparate behavior, must originate in the culture that is being studied. The lack of cross-cultural values, with respect to cannibalism, is illustrated very well in the following passage:

> Spix and Martius asked a chief of the Miranhas why his people practiced cannibalism. The chief showed that it was entirely a new fact to him that some people thought it an abominable custom. "You whites," said he, "will not eat crocodiles or apes, although they taste well. If you did not have so many pigs and crabs you would eat crocodiles and apes, for hunger hurts. It is all a matter of habit. When I have killed an enemy, it is better to eat him than to let him go to waste. Big game is rare because it does not lay eggs like turtles. The bad thing is not being eaten, but death, if I am slain, whether our tribal enemy eats me or not. I know of no game which tastes better than men. You whites are really too dainty." (Sumner, 1911, p. 331)

If one is to be judgmental, perhaps using one's own cultural standards to evaluate another culture, then it is highly unlikely that one has been value-free in one's assessment. Although the reality is that one can probably never be entirely value-free, the theory of cultural relativism necessitates that investigators be as value-neutral as possible. The promotion of universal human rights, however, attempts to impose a set of values that may not, in reality, either be value-neutral or have universal application.

Tolerance is a related concept that causes a good deal of friction between the two extremes. The theory of cultural relativism encompasses the ability to be not only value-free in one's appraisal of other cultures, but also tolerant of the practices of those cultures. Being tolerant is not necessarily the same thing as accepting a cultural practice that appears, on face, to be not only lacking a specific function, but also running counter to one's own sense of human rights. Tolerance, as it is now used, is more closely equated with acquired understanding of various cultural practices that heretofore were alien to one's own cultural norms of behavior (i.e., experiences). Unqualified tolerance of diverse cultures, however, does not allow one to enter into a serious discussion of human rights in the context of non-Western society (Zechenter, 1997, p. 326).

The challenge of cultural relativism, whether based on the notions of objectivity and tolerance or not, has made itself known in the dialogue regarding universal human rights. For example, when the executive board of the American Anthropological Association withdrew from discussions that led to the Universal Declaration of Human Rights, it did so "in the belief that no such declaration would be applicable to all human beings" (Fluehr-Lobban, 1995, p. B1).

Moreover, in preparation for the aforementioned 1993 World Conference on Human Rights, three regional conferences were held. Of the meetings in Tunis, San José, and Bangkok, the last produced the most contentious statement promoting the concept of cultural relativism over the uniform application of universal human rights. Inter alia, the 1993 Bangkok Declaration stated:

> Recognize that while human rights are universal in nature, they must be considered in the context of a dynamic and evolving process of international norm-setting, bearing in mind the significance of national and regional particularities and various historical, cultural and religious backgrounds. (United Nations, 1993a)

The Bangkok Declaration was viewed as an assault on the notion of uniform application of universal human rights. Although the expectation was that Vienna would be politically explosive (see Awanohara, Vatikiotis, and Islam, 1993), the reality was that the universal nature and uniform application of human rights won out over the Bangkok language of cultural relativism as the Vienna Declaration and Programme for Action did not use the aforementioned phrase.[5]

There are those who believe that while cultural relativism was once a very admirable position, it is now more important for anthropologists in particular to promote the well-being (i.e., development) and security (i.e., general safety) of those who live in the diverse cultures that are studied. Fluehr-Lobban (1995), for example, believes that "the time has come for anthropologists to become more actively engaged in safeguarding the rights of people whose lives and cultures they study" (p. B1). Moreover, she states that "we need to be sensitive to cultural differences but not allow them to override widely recognized human rights" (1995, p. B2). Feminists have also become quite alienated with the manner by which cultural relativism tends to "ignore" structural gender inequality in numerous countries. The latter, of course, often leads to gender-based violence (Gordon, 1993).

The sentiment to review the worth of the concept of cultural relativism is not just because of the need to ensure All Human Rights for All, but because of the concept's having a number of misgivings that, for some, make ongoing devotion to the position untenable. For example, there appears to be an inconsistency related to the concept and the field of culture studies in general. The concept itself appears to portray culture in a static manner rather than to concur with most who assert that the development of culture is evolutionary. Cultural relativism tends to provide justification for existent cultural practices even if they appear to be maladaptive (i.e., dysfunctional) in that culture (Zechenter, 1997, pp. 325–326).

It is also quite possible that proponents of cultural relativism have yet to overcome the argument that all cultures are ethnocentric, in that if given the chance to choose between their own cultural norms and those of other cultures, they would surely choose their own. This realization begs the question, Whose "cultural norms" should be used in the creation and uniform application of universal human rights? Obviously, this question is not to be reconciled easily. As Nagengast and Turner (1997) were quoted at the outset of this chapter as saying in reference to the concept of universal human rights, "its content is still under discussion" (p. 270).

For all of the apparent shortcomings of cultural relativism, it is this last indictment that can be used to protect the cultural norms, however dysfunctional, of non-Western societies. In brief, if it is not appropriate to universalize the cultural norms of any one non-Western society with regard to human rights, then it must be just as inappropriate to universalize the cultural norms of any Western country. In sum, it might be effectively argued that the ability to realize, in actual practice, a conception of universal human rights that is uniformly applicable to all societies is, in fact, impossible. This realization would, in essence, afford a standoff between the two dogmatic extremes of universalism and relativism.

Although the extremes rage on, it is quite possible to come to some middle ground. To arrive at this point, however, requires a reconsideration of what the concepts of universality and cultural relativism entail. Two points are in order. First, the notion of universality needs to be rethought in terms of whether human rights are to be viewed as *absolutes* or as *general guidelines* that are incorporated into different cultural settings without losing their intent. Second, the notion of cultural relativism would be better served if it rethought the notions of *tolerance* and *value-free*.

It is entirely possible that the uniform application of universal human rights, as they are outlined in the Declaration of Human Rights and the aforementioned covenants, represent absolutes that in reality have no hope of being applied uniformly to all societies. Alternatively, a universal is more general in terms of what is right and what is wrong. For instance, a universal with regard to theft may suggest the criterion on which to base the extent to which a crime has occurred. These standards, depending on the culture, may suggest varying degrees of punishment. An absolute, on the other hand, would allow you to state unequivocally that theft is wrong. Moreover, the penalties would be more uniform across cultures than might otherwise be the case. Perhaps Herskovits (1972) explains the difference between an absolute and a universal best when he states:

> *Absolutes* are fixed, and, as far as convention is concerned, are not admitted to have variation, to differ from culture to culture, from epoch to epoch. *Universals,* on the other hand, are those least common denominators to be extracted from the range of variation that all phenomena of the natural or cultural world manifest. (pp. 31–32)

In sum, the notion of absolutes, on which the uniform application of human rights is based, is perhaps less useful than the incorporation of universals that may serve to cut across cultures, hence the name cross-cultural universals. James (1994) also speaks to this distinction in speaking about how one should conceptualize human rights:

> Rejecting radical cultural relativism does not preclude flexibility in the conceptualization, interpretation and application of human rights within and between different cultures. Human rights are universal but not absolute (in the sense of pure, unalloyed, completely uniform) in their application to various cultures. In this way the relativist "truth" about enculturation can be accommodated. (p. 4)

The degree to which the concepts of being tolerant and being value-free are part and parcel of the cultural relativist credo are also in need of further deliberation. These two concepts have been interpreted as being at the heart of cultural relativism and, when speaking of the morals of a society, ethical relativism. The fact is, however, that these theories do not imply that one "be tolerant of diverse moral practices" (Renteln, 1990, p. 73).

Moreover, one must recognize that the theory of cultural relativism is based more on an understanding of how values are derived in a culture. The process of enculturation maintains that values are derived from within each distinct culture. Largely an unconscious phenomenon, enculturation serves to instill in individuals the notion that the values that they have become entwined with are far superior to the diverse values that exist for other cultures. This, obviously, is largely related to the aforementioned reality that, if asked, people would typically consider their own values superior to the values expressed in other cultures. The result is that a certain degree of ethnocentrism is prevalent in almost any culture. This, in reality, is what leads to the value judgments that diverse cultures typically make of one another (Renteln, 1990, pp. 73–78).

The reality is that the acquisition of *cross-cultural universals,* which have utility in diverse cultures regardless of the ethnocentric attitudes that are born out of enculturation, represents the middle ground between the two extremes. In order to realize this new conceptualization, on which more meaningful derivations and interpretations of international human rights can be based, one must transcend the absolutist nature of the uniform application of fundamental human rights while also reconceptualizing the basis for the theory of cultural relativism.

THE DESPERATE PLIGHT OF WOMEN AND FEMALE CHILDREN

The case studies that are addressed in the coming chapters focus exclusively on what many consider to be human rights abuses against women and female children. The noticeable exclusion of men and male children is deliberate. Throughout history it has been the women and children, particularly female children, who have disproportionately suffered societal abuse, neglect, and generalized violence. The United Nations recognized the continuing plight of women and children in the Universal Declaration of Human Rights, but until the 1970s it really failed to emphasize the desperate conditions that women and children face.

The First World Conference on Women, held in Mexico City from June 19 to July 2, 1975, was the first *substantial* attempt that the world body made to bring to the forefront the generalized violence and inequitable treatment that both women and female children suffer. The conference produced several documents, including a declaration of principles and a world plan of action. In the wake of these documents the General Assembly, on December 15, 1975, passed several resolutions (30/3519 through 30/3521) that, inter alia, provided for the United Nations Decade for Women, 1976–1985. It was this turn of events that led to the justifiable increase in attention that the world body was now going to give to the desperate plight of women and female children.

Of the several key events to have occurred during this decade, the Convention on the Elimination of All Forms of Discrimination against Women (adopted by the General Assembly in resolution 34/180 on December 18, 1979) was perhaps the most meaningful. Although it did not acquire the requisite number of signatures to enter into force until September 3, 1981, it explicitly stated the role of women with regard to issues such as violence, peace, development, and equality.

Soon after this resolution was adopted by the General Assembly, the Second World Conference on Women was held to assess the progress that was made during the initial years of the Decade for Women. The 1980 Copenhagen, Denmark, conference, although well intentioned, in reality did not accomplish much save continued recognition of the plight of women and female children and a prioritization of goals to be achieved during the last five years of the Decade for Women. The Third World Conference on Women that took place in Nairobi, Kenya, during July 15–26, 1985, was more substantive, as a total review of the progress achieved during the Decade for Women was undertaken. Moreover, this conference led to the establishment of a prioritized program for action to improve the status of women by the year 2000. The Forward-Looking Strategies to Improve the Status of Women was based upon the perceived progress (or lack thereof) achieved during the Decade for Women. As the Nairobi conference report makes clear:

> In some countries and in some areas, women have made significant advances, but overall progress has been modest during the Decade, as is evident from the review and appraisal. During this period, women's consciousness and expectations have been raised, and it is important that this momentum should not be lost, regardless of the poor performance of the world economy. The changes occurring in the family, in women's roles and in relationships between women and men may present new challenges requiring new perspectives, strategies and measures.

At the same time, it will be necessary to build alliances and solidarity groups across sexual lines in an attempt to overcome structural obstacles to the advancement of women. (United Nations, 1986, ¶ 34)

The Fourth World Conference on Women took place in Beijing, China, in 1995. It was here that an overarching evaluation was made regarding the progress that had been achieved and the goals that had yet to be realized both during the previous twenty years and since the Nairobi conference. Moreover, the Platform for Action stated explicitly their determination to:

> Intensify efforts and actions to achieve the goals of the Nairobi Forward-looking Strategies for the Advancement of Women by the end of this century. . . . Ensure the full enjoyment by women and the girl child of all human rights and fundamental freedoms, and take effective action against violations of these rights and freedoms. . . . Take all necessary measures to eliminate all forms of discrimination against women and the girl child and remove all obstacles to gender equality and the advancement and empowerment of women. (United Nations, 1995, ¶ 22–24)

Regardless of the positive influence of these conferences, one cannot deny the ever-present disadvantageous position that women and female children find themselves in throughout the diverse cultures of the world today. Patriarchy is typically the dominant mode of structured interaction in societies that are highly stratified. Relatively speaking, there are very few matriarchal societies whereby women enjoy the upper hand vis-à-vis men. Rather, in most stratified societies, males ensure that cultural practices ensure the dominance of the male in society. This implies that those who have the power to decide outcomes rule in favor of perpetuating their dominance (Butegwa, 1993).

This pattern of patriarchal relations that suppresses the value of being female throughout the world has served to further denigrate the objective position of women and female children. This proposition (i.e., fact) is illustrated time and again in the various statistics that are compiled annually for most countries. Female literacy rates are routinely lower than male literacy rates. Maternal mortality rates are unnecessarily high throughout the world. Moreover, the enrollment figures for females, at all levels of schooling, are typically lower throughout the world. All of these figures are biased in favor of being male when looking primarily at the developing world (United Nations Development Programme, 1995).

The disadvantage of being female is further illustrated in the numerous, seemingly repugnant, practices of many societies throughout the world. For example, molestation, rape, kidnapping, and wife beating are common practices. Women and, in particular, female children are prostituted into the sex trade; sold as wives in locations where traditional weddings have become cost prohibitive; forced to live in polygamous unions; made to produce "certificates of sterilization" in order to obtain employment; killed for "honor" to protect the status of a male partner or spouse; made to forgo the right to inherit; deprived of the opportunity for education that is afforded the male child; hated because of the cost of a dowry or their perceived inability to provide, economically, for the family or for the retirement of the parents; forced into altering their genitals in order to ensure high bride price; and not allowed to eat until the males in the family have eaten. The health and nutritional status of females in general is relatively low, and nearly three-fourths of all refugees are women and children. The list is seemingly endless.

From a universalism perspective, these practices justify the need to illuminate the desperate plight of women and female children. Perhaps no other specified group has suffered what many today label abuses of universal human rights as those who are the basis for the continued diversity of cultures in this world. The incorporation of a limited number of these practices provides a good foundation for applying the concepts of universal human rights and cultural relativism, but in no way serves as sufficient in terms of the education that is necessary for those who engage in the debate.

2

THE CASE OF FEMALE CIRCUMCISION

They flushed the wound with [hot] water, bound and strapped her legs with cotton cloth and lifted her from the ground to a low-lying *'angarib* (a low-lying wooden bed strung with cattle hide). Her mother held her head, comforting her as best she could. "Don't cry, don't cry," she said. But the girl wept and wept, for an hour or more. The flesh had since been buried and dampness on the ground was the only sign of the blood which had flowed so freely. . . . A little later I was pressed further about my thoughts on circumcision. But all I could say was that it was not something familiar to my own culture and that I was not sure I had understood what had happened. But just as I struggle to understand why it is necessary to remove a young girl's genitalia, so they appear mystified and astonished that the operation is not performed on girls in England . . . How can a girl find a husband and achieve the transition to womanhood if she has not been circumcised?

Parker (1995, pp. 509–510)

HISTORY OF THE PRACTICE

Female circumcision[1] is a long-standing practice of numerous traditional cultures around the world. It is believed to have originated in ancient Egypt during the rule of Pharaohs. The first confirmed instance of this practice dates back to female mummies in 484 B.C. (Slack, 1988, p. 444) and 200 B.C. (El Dareer, 1983, p. 41). The Greek historian Herodotus confirmed the practice of female circumcision in Egypt during his mid-fifth-century B.C. visit to the country. Nile Nubians circumcised nine- and ten-year-old girls with either sunna or pharaonic types (see the fivefold classification below) (Colón & Colón, 2001, p. 173). A Greek papyrus from 163 B.C. made specific reference to operations performed on girls in Memphis (i.e., the ruined capital of ancient Egypt located south of present-day Cairo) when they were of age to receive their dowry (Kouba & Muasher, 1985, p. 95). The Greek geographer Agatharchides of Cnidus also reported that the practice of excision was prevalent among tribes on the western coast of the Red Sea (Mackie, 1996, p. 1003). Moreover, the Greek geographer Strabo reported the ritual practice of female circumcision when he visited Egypt in 25 B.C. (Hosken, 1982). More specifically, Strabo distinguished "between the operations of circumcision and excision" (Bryk, 1934, p. 271).

It is important to emphasize that while the discovery of female mummies in 484 B.C. is the first confirmation of the practice, it is entirely plausible that the ritual actually predates the Egyptians. Moreover, this does not mean that the Egyptians originated the practice (Kelly, 1993, p. 46). For example, the Phoenicians, those occupying territory along parts of present-day Lebanon and Syria, also incorporated the ritual practice into their culture. Moreover, it also became commonplace in the Hittite culture in Asia Minor (i.e., the territory between the Black Sea and the Mediterranean Sea) and what is today northern Syria. Dorkenoo and Elworthy (1992) further suggest that there are two possible interpretations about its origins: it either developed in Egypt and spread or originated as an African tribal puberty rite that extended to places such as Egypt (p. 12).

The terminology used to classify the various types of female circumcision also indicates the extensive history of this practice throughout different parts of the world. For example, type 4 female circumcision (which is elaborated upon below in a fivefold classification scheme) is termed "infibulation" or "pharaonic circumcision." Obviously, the term "pharaonic" is a direct referent to ancient Egypt and the prevalence of the practice during the rule of the pharaohs (Abdalla, 1982).[2] It should be noted, however, that Egyptians refer to type 4 as "Sudanese" circumcision because of their belief that it began outside Egypt and subsequently spread (Dorkenoo & Elworthy, 1992, p. 12). It is a bit more difficult to uncover the historical origin of "infibulation," but it dates back to at least the Romans and a procedure they performed on slaves. "The Romans, to prevent sexual intercourse, fastened a 'fibula' or 'clasp' through the large lips of women" (Hosken, 1980, p. 15; Whitehorn, Ayonrinde, & Maingay, 2002, p. 162). This clasp was very similar to the one used to secure their togas. This allowed the fullest potential of slaves to be realized due to their inability to become impregnated.

Although female circumcision is a long-standing historical practice that has pervaded several cultures, there is ultimately no final consensus on where it originated. What is beyond contention, however, is that it has been substantiated as far back as 484 B.C. The rise of Christianity did not have any significant impact on female circumcision, as it continued throughout the early period of Christianity and up to the emergence of Islam. Perhaps the most mistaken idea about its history is that it originated as a Muslim practice, although the reality is that its origins predate both Islam and Christianity. Moreover, female circumcision is not explicitly or implicitly mentioned in any of the major (i.e., well-accepted) translations of the Koran (Momoh, 2004, p. 632). It is, however, possible that Islam is perhaps the one religion that has been mistakenly invoked in order to perpetuate the practice (Hicks, 1993). Moreover, Islam has "been instrumental in embedding infibulation into the structural nexus of marriage, family, and social honor" (Hicks, 1996, p. 6).

The reason for the undue influence of Islam stems from the *hadith* (i.e., the collected sayings of the Prophet Mohammed). The *ulama* (i.e., Islamic religious authorities) that condone female circumcision often invoke the sayings of Mohammed that suggest that mild forms of the practice are acceptable and sanctioned by the Prophet.[3] Moreover, this is typically why types 1 and 2 (see the fivefold classification below) circumcision are referred to as "sunna." The imperative to follow the tradition of the Prophet, and consequently the dictates of the Islamic religion, is a very strong basis for the perpetuation of female circumcision throughout the Islamic period. As will be seen later, many Islamic practitioners and followers of this prescription are mistakenly under the belief that the Islamic religion requires the practice.

One should be cautious not to overemphasize Islam's role with respect to female circumcision. Although circumcision is more prevalent among Islamic communities in African nations, followers of traditional religions, Christianity, and Judaism also practice it.[4] One should, however, note that similar to the Koran, no major text in the Christian faith or the Torah in the Jewish faith makes any mention of female circumcision. As with Islam, however, this has not totally prevented these religious communities from maintaining the practice.

The maligning of Islam that often occurs in the West is due in part to a lack of studies regarding non-Muslim groups' practice of female circumcision, whether on the African continent or not. Leonard (1996) points out that this is problematic precisely because of scholars' overemphasis on predominantly Muslim communities in the Sudan, Somalia, and Egypt. Most of their studies focus on the practice of "pharaonic circumcision" and implicitly indict the *ulama* for their promotion of more extreme forms of female circumcision. Leonard (1996), emphasizing Christian communities in the Moyen-Chari region of Chad, found that 96 percent of rural Catholics and 53 percent of urban Protestants among the Sara people had endured female circumcision (p. 256). Given that its origins predate Christianity, Judaism, and Islam, it is best to state that the practice is one that was incorporated into these religious communities by the members themselves, but for reasons other than religion.

The practice of female circumcision continued throughout Christianity and Islam until it began to be seen in other geographical areas of the globe. It is particularly ironic that the chronology of female circumcision indicates that it has been practiced in many countries of the West. Of particular noteworthiness is the long-standing association that the United States had with the practice during both the nineteenth and twentieth centuries. Wallerstein (1993) notes that "clitoridectomy was performed in England and the United States from the 1860s to about 1920 to treat what were considered 'emotional' problems of women" (p. 735). Slack (1988) maintains that it was undertaken to discourage masturbation and to "control female sexuality" (p. 461).

Burstyn (1995) contends that female circumcision was practiced in both England and the United States as recently as the 1950s in order "to cure nymphomania and melancholia in girls" (p. 32). Moreover, Dr. James E. Burt, the notorious "Love Surgeon," continued to practice the equivalent of types 1 and 2 female circumcision as recently as 1979 (Sarkis, 2003). There is also evidence that the practice was used in Germany to treat nymphomania, excessive masturbation, and insanity (Cutner, 1985, p. 438).

The scope of the practice of female circumcision today is considerably wide. It is currently present in numerous geographical locations stretching over a minimum of four continents. Moreover, it spans multiple religious affiliations and cuts across pastoral, rural, and urban divisions. It involves immigrant populations as well as peoples with more long-standing historical ties to a region. Largely grounded in culture and ritual tradition, it also transcends socioeconomic class and age. The age at which it is performed depends on the ethnic group, but it is known to be practiced on infants who are only a few days old (e.g., among the Falasha Jews) as well as on adolescents (e.g., among the Ibo in Nigeria) (Dorkenoo & Elworthy, 1992, p. 7). Moreover, to the alarm of many in the West, the practice continues today undisturbed, for the most part, by modernity.

There are no exact data regarding the number of women and girls affected by female circumcision. Various estimates of the total number of women affected by various forms of female circumcision do exist but are often problematic. Perhaps the most recent estimate is that reported in a 1997 joint World Health Organization (WHO)/United Nations Children's Fund (UNICEF)/United Nations Population

Fund (UNFPA) statement that maintains "that over 130 million girls and women in Africa have undergone some form of female genital mutilation" (WHO, 1997, p. 5). Moreover, it is further estimated that an additional 2 million (roughly 4 per minute) girls and women are at risk annually.

According to Abdalla (1982, p. 72), research suggests that female circumcision has at one time or another been practiced on every continent. It occurs in Asian countries and among Muslims in India, Pakistan, Malaysia, and Indonesia. Reportedly, it occurs among some indigenous groups in Latin America, including those within Mexico, Brazil, Colombia, and Peru. Cases have also been reported in the Middle Eastern countries of Qatar, Yemen, Israel, Bahrain, Oman, and the United Arab Emirates. It is also practiced among immigrant populations in such countries as Australia, the United States, the United Kingdom, France, Italy, Belgium, Norway, Sweden, and Finland (Dorkenoo, 1994, pp. viii–xi, 32). In the United States alone, over 7,000 women emigrate annually from countries that routinely practice female circumcision (Burstyn, 1995, p. 33). In all, Maher (1996) claims, it is practiced in over 40 countries.

The WHO maintains that most cases of female circumcision have occurred within 28 African countries (WHO, 2000). These countries are listed in table 2.1, which provides the percentage of the countries' populations that are female (%FEM), the total number of females (TOTFEM), the percentage of the female population aged 15 years and above (15↑), the percentage of females operated on (OPER%), the total number of females who have potentially undergone circumcision or are at risk (TOTPOT), the total number of females aged 15 years and above who have most assuredly been circumcised (TOT15↑), the total number of females who are 14 years old or younger who have either had the procedure or are at risk of having it performed (TOT14↓), the total number of females having potentially undergone the practice or are at risk utilizing Hosken's estimations (HOSKENTOT), the population percentage growth rate (POP%GRO), and the estimated additional number of females at risk annually (FEMRISK).[5]

Several problems surround the estimates of the total number of females on the African continent that have undergone some form of circumcision. Many of these are based on Hosken's (1982) estimates of the percentage of girls and women in select African countries who have been operated on. Kouba and Muasher (1985) also use these estimates, but they suggest several points of controversy: first, some of the estimates may be overinflated; second, it is virtually inconceivable that you would find that every female in some countries

Table 2.1 Selected Indicators of Female Circumcision, 2002

COUNTRY	%FEM	TOTFEM	15↑	OPER%	TOTPOT	TOT15↑	TOT14↓	HOSKENTOT	POP%GRO	FEMRISK
Benin	49.8	3,819,000	56.0	30	1,145,700	641,592	504,108	584,716	3.18	36,433
Burkina Faso	49.9	5,995,000	52.0	70	4,196,500	2,182,180	2,014,320	3,824,406	3.17	133,029
Cameroon	50.3	7,778,000	59.0	15	1,166,700	688,353	478,347	1,072,563	1.88	21,934
Central African Republic	51.4	1,997,000	58.0	10	199,700	115,826	83,874	331,395	1.33	2,656
Chad	50.6	4,459,000	54.0	60	2,675,400	1,444,716	1,230,684	683,532	3.42	91,499
Congo (Zaire)	50.5	26,605,000	53.0	5↓	1,330,250	705,033	625,217	1,180,016	2.79	37,114
Djibouti	50.0	325,000	58.0	98	318,500	184,730	133,770	206,867	2.09	6,657
Egypt	49.8	34,817,000	67.0	55	19,149,350	12,830,065	6,319,285	15,724,149	1.91	365,753
Eritrea	51.0	1,978,000	56.0	80	1,582,400	886,144	696,256	1,536,462	4.26	67,410
Ethiopia	50.3	36,225,000	55.0	85	30,791,250	16,935,188	13,856,062	25,689,331	2.44	751,307
Gambia	50.5	705,000	61.0	79	556,950	339,740	217,210	362,111	2.85	15,873
Ghana	49.4	10,263,000	62.0	30	3,078,900	1,908,918	1,169,982	1,784,259	2.14	65,888
Guinea	48.8	4,297,000	57.0	60	2,578,200	1,469,574	1,108,626	1,883,488	2.17	55,947
Guinea-Bissau	50.7	734,000	53.0	40	293,600	155,608	137,992	296,562	3.00	8,808
Ivory Coast	49.0	8,497,000	59.0	40	3,398,800	2,005,292	1,393,508	4,330,367	1.63	55,400
Kenya	50.1	16,044,000	60.0	50	8,022,000	4,813,200	3,208,800	8,443,201	2.20	176,484

Liberia	50.1	1,607,000	53.0	50	803,500	425,855	377,645	520,626	1.37	11,008
Mali	50.2	6,209,000	52.0	80	4,967,200	2,582,944	2,384,256	4,466,118	2.98	148,023
Mauritania	50.6	1,421,000	58.0	50	710,500	412,090	298,410	296,232	2.98	21,173
Niger	48.9	6,173,000	50.0	20	1,234,600	617,300	617,300	912,019	3.39	41,853
Nigeria	49.5	60,967,000	56.0	40	24,386,800	13,656,608	10,730,192	25,644,628	2.24	546,264
Senegal	50.8	5,519,000	58.0	20	1,103,800	640,204	463,596	2,332,071	2.39	26,381
Sierra Leone	50.7	2,482,000	56.0	90	2,233,800	1,250,928	982,872	2,216,416	4.07	90,916
Somalia	50.4	3,764,000	52.0	98	3,688,720	1,918,134	1,770,586	4,702,474	3.20	118,039
Sudan	49.7	17,001,000	62.0	89	15,130,890	9,381,152	5,749,738	13,995,797	1.93	292,026
Tanzania	50.3	18,229,000	50.0	10	911,450	455,725	455,725	1,476,506	1.95	17,773
Togo	50.6	2,878,000	56.0	30	287,800	161,168	126,632	464,527	2.72	7,828
Uganda	50.0	12,994,000	57.0	5 ↓	389,820	222,197	167,623	503,875	3.40	13,254
Average	50.1	10,849,357	56.4	49.4	4,869,039	2,822,517	2,046,522	4,480,883	2.61	115,240
Total		303,782,000			136,333,080	79,030,464	57,302,616	125,464,714		3,226,730

Sources: Population Division of the Department of Economic and Social Affairs of the United Nations Secretariat (2006), World Population Prospects: The 2004 Revision, New York, United Nations; Population Reference Bureau (2005), 2005 Women of Our World, Washington, DC, Population Reference Bureau.

(e.g., Djibouti and Somalia) has undergone circumcision; third, it is unlikely that all countries are equally divided (i.e., in terms of population) with regard to gender (p. 99). One could also add that the variety of the ages at which circumcision is performed in different cultures would suggest that not all females have already undergone the procedure. As mentioned earlier, the Falashas of Ethiopia circumcise at six days of age, but the Ibo of Nigeria wait until adolescence. Consequently, there needs to be a conceptual redefinition in terms of how we look at the magnitude of the problem.[6]

The data in table 2.1 for the percentage of females operated on comes from Dorkenoo (1994, pp. 88–89). The rest are from the United Nations and the Population Reference Bureau.[7] Some of the estimates have been revisited and, in some cases, considerably revised. For instance, Hosken's estimate for Senegal was 50 percent, whereas Dorkenoo, and the data here, gives the figure of 20 percent. Many of the figures remain the same. This is the case for Burkina Faso, Niger, Sierra Leone, Tanzania, Uganda, and Zaire. The data also reveal that the populations of countries are not evenly split by gender. On average, however, 50.1 percent of the populations are female. It is also worthwhile to note that the average percentage of females who are 14 and younger is 42.0 percent. There are an estimated 303,782,000 females in these countries with, according to Dorkenoo, an estimated 136,333,080 who either have undergone circumcision or are currently at risk. This number is a little more than the aforementioned 130 million that the WHO is currently advancing.

By incorporating Kouba and Muasher's criticisms, one can maintain that the 130 million figure involves a misconceptualization about how the total number should be constituted. It is not reasonable to assume that all segments of the population are just as likely to have had the procedure done. In a 1980 survey of 70 Somali women, Abdalla (1982) found that 100 percent of the girls had been circumcised by age 13 and that on average, most girls were circumcised when they were barely eight years old (pp. 86–90). In a study of 133 Sara women of Chad, however, Leonard (1996) found that the majority were first circumcised between the ages of 10 and 15 years with an average age of 12.3 years (p. 260). What is obvious is that the age at which one is circumcised varies on the basis of the ethnic group's custom. Toubia (1994) sums it nicely by stating that "girls are commonly circumcised between the ages of 4 and 10 years, but in some communities the procedure may be performed on infants, or it may be postponed until just before marriage or even after the birth of the first child" (p. 712).

Given these insights, the present data were broken down by female age, resulting in two groups: those who are 14 and younger and those who are 15 and older. Incorporating the assumption that those who are 15 and older have probably already been circumcised, the total percentage of women in this age group was multiplied by the total number of females who had potentially undergone the procedure or were at risk (TOTPOT), 79,030,464. TOT14↓, 57,302,616, represents the number of females aged 14 and under who, in all probability, had either been circumcised or were at risk of being circumcised. This is perhaps a more suitable way to frame the magnitude of the problem. It is perhaps preferable to state the problem in this manner than to assert, as the WHO definition does, that over 130 million females have undergone this procedure in Africa alone.[8]

Similarly, the number of females who are added to the latter category on an annual basis can be approximated by multiplying the population growth rate of each country by the total number of females who have potentially undergone the procedure or are at risk (TOTPOT). What results is an estimate of an additional 3,226,730 females who will have either undergone the practice or are at risk. This estimate is considerably higher than the 2 million figure advanced by the WHO. The most beleaguered countries (on a percentage basis) are Djibouti, Somalia, Sierra Leone, and the Sudan. Studies in the Sudan from 1979 to 2000 indicate a steady rate of prevalence at 89 to 90 percent (Magied & Makki, 2004, p. 30). Looking at absolute numbers, we can note that Ethiopia, Nigeria, and Egypt are the most affected.

SPECIFICS OF THE PRACTICE

Perhaps the most difficult task surrounding female circumcision is the attempt to define and categorize the many forms of this practice. Classification, however, is important in order to further distinguish and more fully understand the degree of devotion that local practitioners in various cultures have toward the practice. The WHO (2000) defines female genital mutilation (FGM—the Dr. Jekyll side of Mr. Hyde, culturally speaking) as comprising "all procedures involving partial or total removal of the external female genitalia or other injury to the female genital organs whether for cultural, religious or other non-therapeutic reasons." WHO then goes on to depict four types of FGM:

1. *Type I*—excision of the prepuce, with or without excision of part or all of the clitoris

2. *Type II*—excision of the clitoris with partial or total excision of the labia minora
3. *Type III*—excision of part or all of the external genitalia and stitching/narrowing of the vaginal opening (infibulation)
4. *Type IV*—various unclassified procedures:

    a. pricking, piercing or incising of the clitoris and/or labia
    b. stretching of the clitoris and/or labia
    c. cauterization by burning of the clitoris and surrounding tissue
    d. scraping of tissue surrounding the vaginal orifice (angurya cuts) or cutting of the vagina (gishiri cuts)
    e. introduction of corrosive substances or herbs into the vagina to cause bleeding or for the purpose of tightening or narrowing it
    f. any other procedure that falls under the definition given above.

While the WHO definition of FGM is broad enough to be acceptable to numerous medical practitioners and academic researchers, it does not tell the whole story regarding codification attempts. Perhaps the most notable effort at codification in the modern era is the work of Verzin (1976), Hosken (1982), and Kouba and Muasher (1985), who have offered the following fivefold classification scheme:

1. *Mild Sunna:* The pricking of the prepuce of the clitoris with a sharp instrument, such as a pin, which leaves little or no damage. *Sunna* means "tradition" in Arabic.
2. *Modified Sunna:* The partial or total excision of the body of the clitoris.
3. *Clitoridectomy/Excision:* The removal of part or all of the clitoris as well as part or all of the labia minora. The resulting scar tissues may be so extensive that they cover the vaginal opening.
4. *Infibulation/Pharaonic Circumcision:* Clitoridectomy and the excision of the labia minora as well as the inner walls of the labia majora. The raw edges of the vulva are then sewn together with catgut or held against each other by means of thorns. The suturing, or approximating of the raw edges of the labia majora, is done so that the opposite sides will heal together and form a wall over the vaginal opening. A small sliver of wood (such as bamboo) is inserted into the vagina to stop coalescence of the labia majora in front of the vaginal orifice and to allow for the passage of urine and menstrual blood.
5. *Introcision:* The enlargement of the vaginal orifice by tearing it downward manually or with a sharp instrument.

While this classification has been very insightful, it fails to take into consideration "advances" in procedural techniques. Kelly (1993) discusses the notion of modified infibulation, also referred to as intermediate infibulation. This procedure is being incorporated by many "Westernized" Sudanese as a less-severe practice that can be "tailored" more to the desires of the family. As Kelly states:

> It is not as severe as complete infibulation. The procedure consists of excising the complete clitoris gland with part of the *labia minora*, while preserving the *labia majora*. The prepuce is not excised in whole or in part. The vaginal *introitus* is narrowed by suturing part of the *labia majora* over the excised clitoris. The vaginal canal is open and accessible. . . . The milder form is called *sunna kashfa* (uncovered sunna). Only the top half of the clitoris is removed. (pp. 49–50)

Many researchers and academicians have tried to refine (i.e., simplify) this fivefold classification scheme by utilizing various fourfold combination schemes (Al-Khudairi, 1997; Dorkenoo & Elworthy, 1992; Hicks, 1996; MacCormick, 1993; Morris, 1996; Rushwan, 1995). Finally, several researchers and practitioners utilize a threefold classification scheme that, in effect, neglects introcision and combines mild and modified sunna (Althaus, 1997; Johnson & Rodgers, 1994; Knott, 1996; Kopelman, 1994; Mohamud, 1991; Woolard & Edwards, 1997).

One attempt has also been made to try to simplify the categorization scheme by introducing two types of clitoridectomies and two types of infibulations (Toubia, 1994). The reality of this attempt, however, is that it merely drops introcision from the aforementioned fivefold scheme, combines mild and modified sunna, and then groups together intermediate infibulation with the more severe form of infibulation (p. 712).

Outside of the obvious benefit to medical practitioners, the reality is that these categorization schemes only allow Western policymakers, academic researchers, and casual observers to think that they can neatly compartmentalize the many forms of female circumcision. The truth of the matter is that the practice of female circumcision is not to be neatly placed into tidy categories based on the cutting to be done. In actuality, the conditions under which cutting often takes place does not lend itself to the identification of neat categories into which every case can be placed (Hicks, 1996, p. 16; Parker, 1995). As Toubia (1994) states:

> In reality, the extent of cutting and stitching varies considerably, since the operator is usually a layperson with limited knowledge of anatomy

and surgical technique. With local or no anesthesia, the girl may move, and the extent of cutting cannot be accurately controlled. (p. 712)

CULTURAL RELEVANCE

Explanations[9] for the practice of female circumcision are numerous and quite diverse depending on the particular cultural grouping (i.e., ethnic group) that one encounters. What is common among most practicing cultures is that the explanation is multifaceted and draws on socially related factors. Therefore, one runs the risk of being "culturally reductionistic," in that some important factors may be left out of an analysis (Johnson & Rodgers, 1994, p. 75). With this recognition in mind, the factors to be addressed here are patriarchy, tradition, religion, myth, social cohesion, sexual considerations, and economic concerns. To speak of each of these factors separately poses a problem because many of these are interrelated. We will proceed, however, in this manner in order to facilitate clarity. An attempt will be made to pull these varied explanations together after introducing each in turn.

Patriarchy is a very prevalent thematic focus both for various ethnic groups as well as for many researchers who are trying to understand the incorporation of female circumcision in local cultures. Broadly defined, patriarchy refers to a situation whereby the power, control, and authority of the unit (family, tribe, etc.) are in the hands of the males. The patriarchy is also hierarchical among the males, with the oldest male typically being more powerful than the others. Numerous characteristics are typically associated with the practice of patriarchy, including inferior status for all women, arranged marriages for children, double standards with regard to sexual behavior, multiple marriages (i.e., polygamy) for males, and a belief that males are most wise.

Given this listing, one might already have surmised that the "deck is stacked against" females not only with respect to the practice of female circumcision, but with respect to other concerns as well. Exactly why the game plays out this way needs to be further elaborated upon. The patrilineal family is a large part of numerous ethnic groupings on the African continent. This means that the female in society has virtually no control over most aspects of her life. The reality is that her father maintains great control over most aspects of her life and will transfer his right only after his daughter has become married. The daughter's marriage does not entitle her to greater self-rule, but in effect only amounts to a transfer of rights from her father to her groom and his family.

> For the purpose of these practices, whether it is admitted or not, is to control female sexuality. Some indeed do not hesitate to say that the aim is to reduce women's hypersensuality. In any case the result remains the same: to make the young girl essentially a future reproductive and productive element. Hence, her life is taken over and mapped out for her from birth to death by a patriarchical society, which ensures that she is kept in her place at all stages of her development. (Thiam, 1983, p. 750)

In the final analysis, if female circumcision is viewed as a necessary practice, for no other reason than the economic consideration of bride wealth, then the subjugation of females is considered allowable within patriarchal societies. Female subjugation, in whatever form, may be viewed as a necessity in terms of maintaining the patriarchical and harmonious society ("What's Culture Got to Do with It?" 1993, p. 1952). MacCormick (1993) talks about how female subjugation is in the interest of patrilineal inheritance. Others also lend credence to how female circumcision may assist in the maintenance of patriarchical societies. Montagu (1995) suggests that "in egalitarian societies, such as hunter-gatherer societies, female circumcision does not occur, and even male circumcision is rare," and that "there may be some correlation between male dominance of a society and the practice of female genital circumcision" (p. 13).

Tradition and culture also play a strong role in the continuation of female circumcision in many ethnic groups (Momoh, 2004, p. 632). Tradition is a twofold consideration. First is the concern about how long-standing a given practice is and whether the society should maintain that practice. The decision to forgo a practice that has long roots in the history of a people is difficult. In a study of 200 female and 100 male students at the College of Technological Sciences in Omdruman, Sudan, 57.5 percent of females and 33 percent of males indicated that female genital mutilation is a function of culture and tradition (Magied & Makki, 2004, p. 38). Moreover, a survey of 522 southwestern Nigerian women found that 63 percent believe that culture and tradition is the key causal factor (Dare et al., 2004, pp. 281–283). Perhaps the greatest barrier to breaking with tradition is the fear of losing one's cultural identity (Kelly, 1993, p. 57). This is often referred to as *culture inhibition syndrome,* a situation where positive attitudes for change are disregarded (Magied & Makki, 2004, p. 29). Moreover, the need for status, honor, and social acceptance, an acceptance that is predicated on highly valued practices such as female circumcision, is generally enough to persuade one to continue with tradition. Ostracization is too heavy a price to pay for breaking from tradition. Morris (1996) mentions: "Mothers also assert that because they were circumcised is reason enough for their daughters to be circumcised" (p. 46).

Second is the concern that tradition is often caught up with the notion of "rites of passage" or "initiation" ceremonies (Moschovis, 2002, p. 1131; WHO, 2000). Both of these concepts convey a certain "status" to others within the culture. In most cases one's status is elevated after having gone through the requisite initiation to gain access (i.e., incorporation) into the new group. As such, it is very important to understand how female circumcision is but one means by which girls elevate their status as well as promote the ongoing solidarity of the ethnic group.

Those rites of passage and initiations that are accompanied by ceremonies are constructed as such in order to convey to the girl the expectations that society will have of her in womanhood. Dorkenoo and Elworthy (1992) speak of the ceremonies that occur in parts of the Sudan, Kenya, and Mali: "An elaborate ceremony surrounded, and in some cases still surrounds, the event—with special songs, dances and chants intended to teach the young girl her duties and desirable characteristics as a wife and mother" (p. 14). In addition to this, the girls are often "showered with presents and their families are honored" (Althaus, 1997, p. 132). As Kelly (1993) states, these ceremonies and celebrations may have relieved much of the anxiety that girls experienced before and during the procedure (p. 56).[10]

Overall, tradition is often cited as the most important consideration in deciding to continue the practice of female circumcision (Williams & Sobieszczyk, 1997, p. 974). Aside from what has been stated here, the ongoing promotion of group solidarity as well as the desire to make one's own ethnic group "distinct" from neighboring groups are stated reasons for the continuation of female circumcision (Mackie, 1996).

Religion can be a strong consideration in the decision whether or not to undertake female circumcision (Magied & Makki, 2004, p. 32; Momoh, 2004, 632). Although female circumcision predates Christianity and Islam, the latter is often invoked in an effort to persuade followers of the necessity of circumcision. The extreme focus on Islam is due in part to the recognition that while other religious groups (e.g., Catholics, Protestants, Copts, and Animists) also have adherents who practice female circumcision, the majority of those who practice it are in fact Muslim. A common expression among this group is that one cannot become religiously "pure" until one has been circumcised. Being "unclean" can result in a variety of value judgements being levied against the offender, who may also be "barred from entering certain worship areas" (Maher, 1996, p. 13). Moreover, it is quite possible that the mistaken belief that Allah will not hear the prayers of an uncircumcised woman leads many to undergo the procedure (Hosken, 1980, p. 311).

As mentioned earlier, outside of the Koran the *hadith* is what gives substantiation to those who maintain that Islam requires female circumcision. It is important to note, however, that neither the Koran nor the *hadith* makes mention of more severe forms of female circumcision (i.e., excision and infibulation). Nevertheless, Islam is still noted as a very influential consideration among Muslims who opt for infibulation (Hicks, 1993). This is particularly perplexing given that female circumcision is not practiced in the Islamic spiritual Mecca of Saudi Arabia. Nor is it practiced in the majority of lands where Islam is the dominant religion. Moreover, Winkel (1995) maintains that the *hadith* is at times troubling because of the occasional lack of prophetic proof:

> The hadith is not considered revelational proof because the chain is not completely secure in all its links from the prophet, Allah bless and give him peace, to the hadith scholars, and because, according to the vast majority of scholars, a hadith, to be part of the sunnah, must be correctly transmitted word for word. But what is interesting is that despite its weak nature, the hadith is transmitted and becomes part of the Islamic legal discourse. (p. 5)

Perhaps one of the more appalling reasons (from a Western per-spective) for the continuation of the practice of female circumcision is the myths and beliefs that a group holds. Myths, in whatever form, lead to great conviction on the part of the followers, while they are met with great resistance by those outside the culture in which myths are prominent. To outsiders, myths often provide occasion for great hilarity on the one hand and ridicule and scorn on the other. But to those who believe ardently in the power of myth, the associated beliefs of a culture are deemed respectable, worth practicing, and timeless.

What follows is an abbreviated listing, in no particular order of significance, of some of the more popular mythical beliefs about circumcision that are routinely invoked (i.e., adhered to) by vari-ous cultures. The first set of beliefs relate directly to the clitoris and its potentially negative characteristics. It is commonly held that the clitoris is "ugly, dirty, and an impediment to intercourse"—three conditions that necessitate its removal (Al-Khudairi, 1997; Kelly, 1993, p. 52). One respondent noted the "beautiful" results of the operation saying, "Whoosh! The lumps are gone. It is smooth and clean. The stitching is like the zig zag stitch, so beautiful" (Morris, 1996, p. 51). Another popular belief is that the clitoris is a dangerous organ that can kill the male partner during intercourse as well as a newborn during childbirth if either comes into contact with it (Al-Khudairi, 1997). This is a widespread belief among the Mossi of Burkina Faso and the Bambara of Mali (Kouba & Muasher, 1985, p. 103).

Another myth directly related to the clitoris is that just as the feminine aspect of males exists in the form of the prepuce of the penis, so too does the masculine aspect of females exist in the form of the prepuce of the clitoris (Kelly, 1993, p. 51). Out of necessity this loose fold of skin needs to be removed in order to promote fecundity. Without the procedure the male "soul" generates problems in the female, leaving the *wanzo*[11] of the individual intact. Female circumcision, therefore, much like male circumcision, is utilized to remove the evil force of *wanzo,* so that the female can become a more fully productive member of her society. Moreover, the practice serves to distinguish the gender of the newborn (Kouba & Muasher, 1985, p. 103; Moschovis, 2002, p. 1131).

One can recognize another set of related myths that deal with sexual promiscuity and the potential for diseases born out of it. At least one analysis positively attributes to female circumcision the capacity to inhibit the growth of sexually transmitted diseases (Al-Khudairi, 1997). One can only assume that this is due to the inability to have intercourse after infibulation. Perhaps a more noted myth is that female circumcision aids in the prevention of sexual promiscuity (Dare et al., 2004, p. 283; Magied & Makki, 2004, p. 32; Moschovis, 2002, p. 1131) and the stigma that it may bring the family (Kelly, 1993, p. 52).

Finally, there are myths that are related to some aspect of health and hygiene. One of the more prevalent myths is that female circumcision actually enhances fertility (Dare et al., 2004, p. 283; "What's Culture Got to Do with It?" 1993, pp. 1950–1951; WHO, 2000). The ability to produce a large family is a positive quality for many of the cultures that practice female circumcision. Those perceived to lack this ability are disgraced, for they are seen as incapable of starting the very family that is the defining entity for their own person. The Tagouana of the Ivory Coast represent one such culture that strongly believes that female circumcision is requisite for obtaining family (Kouba & Muasher, 1985, pp. 103–104).

Many cultures also believe that female circumcision promotes cleanliness (WHO, 2000) and prevents disease (Magied & Makki, 2004, p. 32). It is easy to see how this idea might appeal to Muslims, as there is a great amount of emphasis in the Koran on cleanliness, especially during menstruation (Irving, 1993, p. 18). Because many believe that the clitoris obstructs the flow of menstrual blood (Kouba & Muasher, 1985, p. 103), they subsequently fall victim to believing that female circumcision allows freer flow and greater cleanliness of the vagina (Mulholland, 1992, p. 6). Somewhat related to this myth is the belief that female circumcision eliminates the malodor associated with menstrual discharge (Mackie, 1996, p. 1005). Much like the above, however, this particular belief is medically suspect because of the process of infibulation and the net result with regard to the female's ability to discharge menstrual blood, and also her ability to pass urine.

> Urinary retention is a common health problem following circumcision, especially infibulation, due to the fear of burning and increased pain with urination. As the scar heals, it is possible that the entire vaginal orifice will be occluded. Urinary infection can occur due to urine retention, the use of nonsterile or nonclean supplies during the procedure, and application of compounds such as cow dung to the fresh wound to promote healing. (Johnson & Rodgers, 1994, p. 71)

Another myth related to health and hygiene, generally speaking, is that female circumcision enlarges the vagina, which has the positive result of making childbirth easier. The reality, however, is that it makes the process more difficult, as additional cuts must be made in the perineum during childbirth (Kouba & Muasher, 1985, p. 104). Moreover, Hosken (1982) suggests that it inhibits dilation, which obviously makes the birthing process more difficult.

Outside of tradition, religion, and myth, several other reasons for the continuation of female circumcision exist. On a daily basis, modernization claims among its victims those who continue to incorporate traditional practices in their cultures. Given that many traditional cultures are aware of this, great emphasis is placed on the status and identity of the group. Many cultures continue female circumcision in order to emphasize their distinctiveness. This distinctiveness gives rise to a certain status (Mackie, 1996, p. 1005). The ability to ensure distinctiveness and status is based on how well a group can maintain both social and political cohesion, for if solidarity with regard to the values, beliefs, and so forth of the group is not maintained, the culture will suffer a great demise.

> When a tradition such as female circumcision becomes so deeply ingrained in a society—accepted by virtually everyone, either passively

or actively—it can serve as a power that helps to bind the community together and provides a source of cultural identity that is often crucial in small rural communities. (Slack, 1988, p. 455)

Sexual considerations are often cited as supporting female circumcision. For many societies the assurance of sexual purity is tantamount, given its relatedness to economic considerations (e.g., bride wealth) and social status. In reality two definable areas involve sexual considerations. First is the idea that women need to be sexually pure before marriage. For better or for worse, numerous cultures place the onus of responsibility for curbing sexual desires on the female. The female is often thought of as the sexual aggressor and in need of having her sexual desires attenuated (Dorkenoo & Elworthy, 1992, p. 13), failing which, it is feared, she will become sexually promiscuous. If this happens, she may reach out to others outside of her marriage, thus bringing disgrace and dishonor not only to her husband but to the entire family. Moreover, the female may turn to masturbation or lesbianism (Vickers, 1993, pp. 67–77; Whitehorn et al., 2002, p. 163). To be able to restrain promiscuity while concurrently promoting the virtues of chastity, sexual virginity, and purity is a very inviting proposition that many feel female circumcision advances.

The second aspect is the notion that the male should derive a heightened degree of sexual pleasure during intercourse. After childbirth, the female is often reinfibulated. This recurrence serves many ends, including those related to curbing the sexual "aggression" of females. Reinfibulation is in the service of another myth that is recognized in various cultures. Some groups believe that sperm, after childbirth, can potentially contaminate the mother's breast milk and thus result in the baby's death (Morris, 1996, p. 47). Perhaps most important, however, is that reinfibulation is related to the need to provide the husband with greater sexual pleasure that stems from the tightness of the opening (Kopelman, 1994, p. 64; Mulholland, 1992, p. 6) as well as to ensure fidelity (Morris, 1996, p. 47; Whitehorn et al., 2002, p. 163). While many in local cultures advance this notion, there are those who suggest that it is unfounded because a comparison group for most men in these cultures does not exist (Mulholland, 1992, p. 6).

Economic considerations are also important in terms of why the practice of female circumcision continues. Perhaps the most noteworthy consideration here is "bride wealth." Every society that practices female circumcision also incorporates the concept of bride wealth. In short, bride wealth is the price that is to be paid by the prospective husband and his kin to the bride's family at marriage. Depending on the ethnic group, bride wealth comprises many diverse items, but most of all, material goods. In exchange for it the husband-to-be has control over the woman's services as well as the future children.

It is very important to many cultures that the bride's purity be very high, so that her family might receive a very high bride price (Abdalla, 1982). Circumcision is regarded as a modern-day chastity belt that ensures the purity (i.e., virginity) of the female. Conversely, those women who are not circumcised are unlikely to obtain a high (if any) bride price for their families and, indeed, are unlikely to be married. "You see, an uncircumcised woman can hardly find a man to marry her. It offers better marriage prospects" (Mulholland, 1992, p. 6). Female circumcision, in essence, is a very important consideration in arranging marriages and ensuring a high bride price. This is so important a consideration that families might routinely inspect their daughters.

> In Somalia, for example, a prospective husband's family may have the right to inspect the bride's body prior to the marriage, and mothers regularly check their infibulated daughters to ensure that they are still "closed." In this context, parents see both infibulation and early marriage as means of ensuring that their daughter remains "pure" and thus worthy of the bride price. (Althaus, 1997, pp. 131–132)

A second aspect related to economics is the extent to which those who conduct the operations rely on this practice for most of their earned income. It is quite conceivable that those who are the "operators" are quite reluctant to dismiss the practice as unhealthy, hurtful, and purposeless. To do so would be tantamount to crippling their ability to provide for their own families (Dorkenoo & Elworthy, 1992, p. 14; Vickers, 1993, p. 74). Moreover, the increased social status that accompanies the "operators" is also a consideration that serves to perpetuate the procedure (Kouba & Muasher, 1985, p. 107).

In sum, there are numerous interrelated considerations that serve to perpetuate the practice of female circumcision. It does not take much to identify that the purity, chastity, and virginity that is preached in the Koran is very much related to a father's expectation that his daughter will get him a high bride price. Moreover, it is necessary to curb sexual transgressions not only with respect to the aforementioned economic considerations, but with respect to maintaining a certain social status and honor for the family. It is quite simple to identify the need to maintain the identity of the group and culture with the continuation of initiation rites and ritual activities. Whether taken separately or together, cultures that practice female circumcision have many reasons that can often be invoked to justify its continuation today.

THE CLASH OF CULTURES

Thus the amount of perceived control in decision making varies according to the structure of social relations in the society in which we live. For us, as we look from our individualistic society through our own culturally constructed lens, the idea of female circumcision is unacceptable and to some even abhorrent. We cannot imagine why any women would choose or permit this practice. For the African women, at this time in the development of her own hierarchical culture where transgression against the norm is more visible and where adherence to the norm is expected and critical to integration into society, the decision is less individual than collective. She is nonetheless making a choice. (Johnson & Rodgers, 1994, p. 73)

Even to the novice in this field, the clash of cultures is readily apparent. It is more than simply a difference in values, beliefs, customs, and so on. At a minimum it involves looking at the individual versus the collective and assessing the impact that our "culturally constructed lens" has on our outlook toward others. In short, an assessment of the clash of cultures is no easy task.

The emphasis on the collective is vital to understanding female circumcision. Most ethnic groups that practice female circumcision also place a high premium on making decisions within a social context. In short, this often involves putting the interests of the community above those of the individual. This attribute permeates the whole of society. The problem, however, is that not every society around the world operates in this manner. Moreover, even in those societies that do make decisions within a social context, the practice of female circumcision may still be quite alien and offensive.

In many Western societies the emphasis is on individualism in decision making. The idea that the daughters of societies, although having some input, will be relegated to a lesser status when the decision regarding female circumcision is made, is repugnant to most in the West. After all it is a decision that because it is made within a "social context," has extraordinary implications for the individual. In sum, the perception of the collective having more status within society is quite alien to most in the West. "In an individualistic society, personal choice would likely bear more weight than pressure to conform to the dictates of the culture" (Johnson & Rodgers, 1994, p. 73).

Perhaps the most important issue related to the cultural clash over female circumcision deals with our "culturally constructed lens." Unfortunate for most of the world's population is the notion that these lenses hardly ever allow us all to see the same random event in an identical manner. There are a multitude of factors, such as individualism versus collectivism, that "shape" us into seeing events and issues differently. The key with respect to any of these issues is to look at the different sides and at the implications arising from each point of view.

From a Western perspective the practice of female circumcision is perhaps best construed as bizarre. Many question the practice on grounds that have less to do with culture and more to do with medical considerations and lofty issues related to human rights. Various points of view are made known by the language that is used to address the issue as well as the attitudes that are detectable while addressing the issue. For example, anyone who has ever spent a considerable period of time in another culture and has then come back and informed others about the "peculiarities" of that culture has surely encountered the range of responses from serious inquiry to laughter and ridicule of the culture in question. Parker (1995) provides an excellent example of this when speaking with colleagues upon her return to England:

> It was difficult not to resent the fact that very few people appreciated the importance of thinking about the issue of circumcision in terms other than physical mutilation and the denial of sexual pleasure. Their views became increasingly offensive and the confidence with which they espoused them was, it seemed to me, little short of racist. There were times when their views appeared to amount to the following: "Circumcision is a barbaric practice. It is carried out by simple and uncivilised people. If they were sophisticated and educated like 'us' in the West they would realise that there are new, different and better ways of behaving. The solution is simple. They should behave like 'us.' " (p. 513)

Obviously, this is quite an arrogant position to take. It does, however, tell one a good deal about the potential destructiveness that each of our culturally constructed lenses has. We would, as this quote suggests, rather destroy the "peculiarities" of another culture with regard to female circumcision so as to make the world appear more in sync with how we in the West think it ought to be. This becomes even more problematic when the degree of ethnocentrism and prejudice exhibited allows us to dismiss not only a specific practice such as female circumcision but also the entirety of the culture in which the practice is found (Gruenbaum, 1996, p. 456).

The language used in the literature on female circumcision is quite diverse. We have already looked at the use of "explanations" rather than "justifications" when dealing with the relevance of the practice to different cultures. It was later explained that "justifications" implies that the custom of female circumcision in the culture in question is being implicitly judged as evil or wrong. But perhaps the most important language component is how one refers to the practice in question. As mentioned in note 1, the current text uses the term "female circumcision" because it is believed to be more value-free than the term "female genital mutilation" and does not convey the sense that all of these procedures are performed in "modern" facilities, as the concept of "female genital operations" suggests.[12]

Emphasis on language is not to be taken lightly. The implications arising from a certain usage can be quite extreme. Knott (1996) makes this explicit: "To use the term 'mutilation' is, in my view, judgmental and will do little to achieve the WHO's aim of a global eradication of the practice" (p. 127). Althaus (1997) notes that activists and clinicians use the term "female circumcision" when working in local communities, but that policy documents have begun to use "female genital mutilation" (p. 130). Seemingly ironic, the latter has been the practice of the WHO, although they qualify their usage of the term by stating:

> In presenting this statement, the purpose is neither to criticize nor to condemn. Even though cultural practices may appear senseless or destructive from the standpoint of others, they have meaning and fulfill a function for those who practice them. However, culture is not static; it is in constant flux, adapting and reforming. People will change their behaviour when they understand the hazards and indignity of harmful practices and when they realize that it is possible to give up harmful practices without giving up meaningful aspects of their culture. (WHO, 1997, pp. 1–2)

The implications of both particular language usages and attitudes (e.g., ethnocentrism) evinced while discussing the issue are abundant. On the lesser side, one might be accused of a certain lack of understanding or perhaps be indicted for expressing a xenophobic attitude. On the extreme side, however, the West may be denounced for nothing less than cultural imperialism—that is, the desire to replace the beliefs and customs, in short, culture, of proponents of female circumcision with those of Westerners. This is perhaps the most stunning of indictments to those in the West who, as already seen in the summaries by Leonard and the WHO, are quite sure that they know what other people "need" as well as how they should behave.

This indictment of lack of understanding or denunciation of cultural imperialism is born out of the respect that many who engage in female circumcision still have for the practice. And there appears to be broad-based support for it. In Nigeria, Onadeko (1985) found that 66.9 percent of women favored the continuation of the practice. Hicks (1996) found that the percentage of women in the Sudan that favor the continuation of either *sunna* or infibulation ranges from 67 to 90 (p. 202). Similarly, Mohamud (1991) reports that 91 percent of urban Somali women support and will continue the practice with their daughters. Moreover, Morris (1996) found that respondents to a survey in Kenya were quite supportive of the practice (they preferred type 1) and suggested that it "was their tradition and that no one had the right to tell them to abandon it" (p. 49).

In sum, many in the cultures where female circumcision is practiced feel a certain degree of resentment toward outsiders, predominantly toward Westerners, who feel that they know what is the best path to pursue —that is, eradication of the practice. This view is often substantiated by those in the West who know nothing of the relevance of the practice to the culture—for instance, the importance of a girl entering the transitional phase of personal development, which includes the ritual of circumcision, before entering womanhood. Entering womanhood, of course, might also allow her a certain access to the patriarchy, if not at least equality in status to other women. This is to say nothing of the importance of the bride price to the status and economic well-being of the family. Moreover, as important as marriage and family are to fulfilling "womanhood," one cannot objectively deny the importance of the practice to the culture while being more than confident that the practice should be abolished. In the face of perceived cultural imperialism, there has always been a certain resistance to change.

IMPLICATIONS FOR FOREIGN RELATIONS

What is perhaps most distressing about the issue of female circumcision is that the majority of the countries where it is practiced daily are among the most impoverished countries of the world. This is readily apparent in the most recent statistics from such indicators as the United Nations Development Programme's (UNDP) Human Development Index (HDI), human development index rank (HDIRANK), gender-related development index (GDI), as well as data on adult literacy (ADLIT) and real growth domestic product per capita (GDPPC), which are provided in table 2.2.[13] The data in table 2.2 depict a situation of general deprivation that has had a profound

Table 2.2   HDI, GDI, ADGDI, ADLIT, and GDPPC in 28 African Countries, 2002

COUNTRY	HDI	HDIRANK	GDI	ADGDI	ADLIT	GDPPC
Benin	0.421	161	130	(163)	39.8	1,070
Burkina Faso	0.302	173	143	(176)	12.8	1,100
Cameroon	0.501	141	111	(144)	67.9	2,000
Central African						
Republic	0.361	169	138	(171)	48.6	1,170
Chad	0.379	167	135	(168)	45.8	1,020
Congo (Zaire)	0.365	168	136	(169)	62.7	650
Djibouti	0.454	154	—	—	65.5	1,990
Egypt	0.653	120	99	(132)	55.6	3,810
Eritrea	0.439	156	127	(160)	56.7	890
Ethiopia	0.359	170	137	(170)	41.5	780
Gambia	0.452	155	125	(158)	37.8	1,690
Ghana	0.568	131	104	(137)	73.8	2,130
Guinea	0.425	160	—	—	41.0	2,100
Guinea-Bissau	0.350	172	141	(174)	39.6	710
Ivory Coast	0.399	163	132	(165)	49.7	1,520
Kenya	0.488	148	114	(147)	84.3	1,020
Liberia	—	—	—	—	—	—
Mali	0.326	174	142	(175)	19.0	930
Mauritania	0.465	152	124	(157)	41.2	2,220
Niger	0.292	176	144	(177)	17.1	800
Nigeria	0.466	151	122	(155)	66.8	860
Senegal	0.437	157	128	(161)	39.3	1,580
Sierra Leone	0.273	177	—	—	36.0	520
Somalia	—	—	—	—	—	—
Sudan	0.505	139	115	(148)	59.9	1,820
Tanzania	0.407	162	131	(164)	77.1	580
Togo	0.495	143	119	(152)	59.6	1,480
Uganda	0.493	146	113	(146)	68.9	1,390
Average	0.426				50.3	1,378
World Average	0.729				82.6	7,804

Source: UNDP (2004), Human Development Report, 2004: Cultural Liberty in Today's Diverse World, New York, UNDP.
Note: "—" indicates missing data.

impact on literacy rates, wealth, the country's position vis-à-vis other countries, and the position of women within their own countries. The picture becomes bleaker when these data are compared with world "averages." Only Egypt approximates the world average in the areas of HDI and wealth (GDPPC). Moreover, only Kenya approximates the world average in adult literacy. In sum, there is considerable need for development in these areas of concern. Finally, the adjusted GDI

(ADGDI) illustrates that the HDI rank of these countries becomes even lower if the human development of women specifically is emphasized.

Continuing the practice of female circumcision has implications for the practicing ethnic groups and the countries of which they are a part. These implications are present not only in terms of the ethnic group's ability to continue the practice, but in terms of the country itself alienating the West and jeopardizing the much-needed financial assistance for development efforts. The latter, of course, is linked directly to the Western conception that the practice of female circumcision constitutes a human rights violation. While it should be said that development in these countries is not entirely dependent on international financial assistance, it should be noted that financial flows have been shown to have a positive impact on economic growth and general development.[14] Given the positive nature of the various forms of financial assistance to African countries, one cannot dismiss the importance of maintaining these valued linkages.

The problem, however, is that the practice of female circumcision, because it is construed by the West as a human rights abuse, has the potential to interfere with these valued financial sources. This problem is not taken lightly in the foreign policy statements of the United States or in the pronouncement of enforceable statutes by other, more developed countries. Many countries, for example, have shown their resolve on the issue by making the practice illegal within their national boundaries. At least ten countries in the West have criminalized the practice because of immigrant populations wishing to continue it in their new homes or on "holidays" to their homelands. Among several such countries are Australia (over the 1994–1997 period), Belgium (in 2000), Canada (in 1997), Denmark (in 2003), Great Britain (in 1985 and 2003), New Zealand (in 1995), Norway (in 1985), Spain (in 2003), Sweden (in 1982 and 1998), and the United States (in 1996). Specific penalties are imposed on any individual who takes part in what is defined as an area that encompasses female circumcision. Moreover, the practice has also been criminalized in France (Center for Reproductive Rights, 2005). The degree to which these countries feel strongly about the practice is evident in the 1993 decision of a French court to sentence a Gambian woman to "five years in prison after she paid $70.00 to have her two daughters circumcised" (Burstyn, 1995, p. 33).

The United States is a relatively recent convert to the movement to ban female circumcision both at home and abroad. Until 1993 the United States did not consider "female genital mutilation" to be a human rights abuse worth reporting in its "Country Reports of Human Rights Practices" (Mackie, 1996, p. 999). Since 1993, however, a detailed study of the countries where the practice continues has been made available annually (United States Department of State, 1995).[15] The United States has also begun working through the United States Agency for International Development (USAID) for the outright eradication of female circumcision. This commitment was "strengthened" during the fiscal years 1994 and 1995 by the infusion of $1.5 million into educational programs (USAID, 1996).

The United States has also shown its commitment to persuade other countries to comply with its efforts to eradicate female circumcision. Woolard and Edwards (1997) report that the Omnibus Consolidated Appropriations Act of 1996 included a provision "requiring US representatives to international financial institutions to oppose loans to governments in countries where the practice is common and no educational measures have been taken to prevent it" (p. 231). This plan specifically targets development funds that are, as already mentioned, badly needed by every one of the 28 African countries that practice female circumcision. The plan to do this, however, is quite intentional. As Senator Leahy stated:

> Some in the World Bank bureaucracy have always taken the position that if the United States suggests another country do something differently, the client countries will react against it. . . . In fact, it is through this kind of pressure that we've had changes necessary in a number of countries, ranging from privatization in the former Soviet Union to female education in developing countries. This requires diplomacy on the part of the international financial institution, but they have a lot of people paid a great deal of money to practice that diplomacy. (quoted by Dugger, 1996, p. A28)

A plan that is designed to force compliance, however, is not without potential problems. Eric Chinje, a World Bank official for Africa, maintains that if the provision "provides an instrument for fingerpointing, it will be counterproductive" (quoted by Dugger, 1996, p. A28). In either event it is additional pressure that the United States will place on the governments of these countries so that they move to effectively abolish female circumcision and in the process make themselves eligible for necessary development capital. It is this pressure that has already been utilized by the International Monetary Fund against Burkina Faso before it could receive a loan (Parker, 1995, p. 506). In sum, these countries face a large task if they are to be successful in obtaining additional development funds from countries and international financial institutions that are striving hard to eradicate female circumcision.

Beyond this there are several international organizations, conventions, and treaties that add to the pressure that these governments feel to eliminate the practice of female circumcision. Not to do so would mean that the country in question would suffer the wrath of the international community. Perhaps the most noteworthy of international institutions working for change are the WHO, the UNDP, and UNICEF. Their opinions have already been summarized in this chapter. Other organizations, such as the International Monetary Fund and the World Bank, have also been discussed within the parameters of how the United States wishes to exert pressure on these governments for change.

There are others as well, however, who continuously work for change. Perhaps the most prominent of these is the Inter-African Committee on Traditional Practices affecting the Health of Women and Children (IAC). Founded in 1984 and headquartered in Addis Ababa, the main objective of the IAC is to "initiate and carry out programmes for combating traditional practices that are harmful to the health of women and children" (IAC, 1996). The IAC is the most important of all regionally based organizations because of its joint collaboration with WHO and the fact that while it does not deal exclusively with female circumcision, the practice is one of its most important considerations today. It is also notable that the IAC is a recipient of World Bank funds used expressly in the effort to eradicate female circumcision. To this end, the IAC initiated the International Day of Zero Tolerance of FGM on February 6, 2003 (UNICEF, 2003).

There also exist several conventions and treaties that are designed to bring these countries into compliance with the Western norm that female circumcision constitutes a human rights violation and should be abolished. Perhaps the most notable convention has been the Fourth World Conference on Women that took place in Beijing during September 1995. In its declaration and platform for action, the participants made explicit mention of the ills of female circumcision and called for its elimination. Among other initiatives, the declaration states that governments should

> enact and enforce legislation against the perpetrators of practices and acts of violence against women, such as female genital mutilation, prenatal sex selection, infanticide and dowry-related violence and give vigorous support to the efforts of non-governmental and community organizations to eliminate such practices. (Fourth World Conference on Women, 1996, Art. 125, Sec. i)

More recent is the 2003 Cairo Declaration for the Elimination of FGM. Inter alia, the declaration detailed 17 spheres in which recommendations to national governments were made. Working within the framework of the Stop FGM Campaign of 2002, the declaration was signed by the First Ladies of several of the aforementioned 28 African countries. Noticeably absent from the signatories were Guinea-Bissau and Somalia, two countries that have not legislated against FGM (Cairo Declaration for the Elimination of FGM, 2003).

In addition to declarations that are issued by conferences, the United Nations periodically gets involved in prompting governments to recognize existing convention declarations, treaties, and earlier commitments. For example, in 1993 the General Assembly passed a resolution titled the Declaration on the Elimination of Violence against Women. This resolution served the notice that it was time that governments ratify, if not accede to, the 1979 Convention on the Elimination of All Forms of Discrimination against Women. In so doing the General Assembly detailed more specifically what it meant by "violence against women," suggesting that "female genital mutilation and other traditional practices harmful to women" fall within the definition (United Nations General Assembly, 1993). UNICEF (2003) recommended strongly that governments abide by their commitments at the United Nations' Special Session on Children and end the practice of FGM by 2010.

Treaties are also utilized to illustrate the norms of the West, with regard to human rights, to those countries that are thought to be in violation and consequently to be held in contempt by the West. Among the more popular that have relevance to the issue of female circumcision are the 1948 Universal Declaration of Human Rights; the 1966 International Covenant on Economic, Social, and Cultural Rights; the 1966 International Covenant on Civil and Political Rights; the 1967 Declaration on the Elimination of Discrimination against Women; the 1975 Declaration on the Protection of All Persons from Being Subjected to Torture and Other Cruel, Inhuman or Degrading Treatment or Punishment; the 1986 Declaration on the Right to Development; and the 1990 Convention on the Rights of the Child. Either implicitly or explicitly stated, all of the aforementioned are vital documents that serve to pressure governments into compliance with Western standards of human rights on such general topics as "violence" and on such specific ones as female circumcision.

POTENTIAL RESOLUTIONS

Any potential resolutions regarding the subject of female circumcision are tainted by whether or not one considers the practice to constitute a human rights abuse. Obviously, for those who focus on the concept of universal human rights, the only potential resolution revolves around the elimination of the practice. For those who believe in cultural relativism, however, elimination is not the goal. Rather, one might argue for the protection of current cultural practices, including female circumcision. While these extremes are clearly recognizable, there may well be some middle ground between them. Finding the middle ground, however, is inherently distasteful to those at both extremes of the issue.

Those who argue for the application of universal human rights mostly desire the elimination of female circumcision. Given that the practice is currently in existence, one might best label this argument as the revolutionary position. Although there are a variety of measures that may be taken to achieve this goal, emphasis is most often placed on legislating the problem away and educating the local ethnic groups about the ills associated with it. The attempt to legislate the custom away is not always a successful proposition. Although it is often done by governments to illustrate to the West that they are serious about eradicating female circumcision (or at least qualifying for development funds), it is evident that laws do not always bring target populations into compliance. This has been a considerable problem for many of the African countries currently practicing female circumcision.

Several of the aforementioned 28 African countries have not passed legislation to outlaw female circumcision. They include Cameroon, the Democratic Republic of the Congo, Eritrea, Gambia, Guinea-Bissau, Liberia, Mali, Mauritania, Nigeria, Sierra Leone, Somalia, and Uganda (Center for Reproductive Rights, 2005). While legislative efforts are indications to the West that the government in question takes seriously the ills associated with female circumcision, it is a poor assumption that the laws that are in place in several countries are actually having an impact. For example, while Egypt issued a presidential decree in 1958 and a subsequent ministerial decree in 1996 that outlawed the practice, it is not entirely clear that female circumcision is not highly regarded and still practiced without an effective legal deterrent. In fact, there has been quite a debate in recent years on whether the government has outlawed the practice. A recent court ruling overturned a recently imposed ban on the practice, but President Mubarak and several ministers in his cabinet continue to insist that the practice is not allowed (Jehl, 1997, p. A12).

The ability to legislate this concern away is quite problematic for other countries as well. In 1994 Ghana passed legislation specifically banning the practice of FGM, but there were only two convictions under this law in the following three years. Moreover, the National Committee against the Practice of Circumcision in Burkina Faso has noted that "circumcisers have been smart enough to substitute adolescents with little girls" in order to circumvent the law ("Mixed News on Female Genital Mutilation," 2004, p. 8). The problem might well be that most laws in this area do not discuss who it is that might report those who violate the law. Certainly, local practitioners are not going to do this. Moreover, girls who wish to enter into womanhood and enjoy all its associated entitlements are not going to do it. Moreover, it is quite possible that if one is convicted, the punishment for the crime will actually hurt the whole of the family unit more than the practice that is being outlawed (Kangberee, 1994). In sum, the effectiveness of legal attempts to dissuade cultures from continuing the practice has been questionable (Althaus, 1997, p. 133; Johnson & Rodgers, 1994, p. 76; Mohamud, 1991). The following sentiment offered by Kouba and Muasher (1985) is typical of those expressing the impractical nature of legislating the problem:

> In those countries where legislation levied against the practice does exist, the laws have had a negligible effect as a deterrent because they are not strictly enforced. If anything, the laws have made a practice already shrouded in secrecy even more so. In some cases, efforts to stop the practice have failed to the extent that the opposite of the effect intended has occurred. . . . The task of eliminating female circumcision in Africa will require more than stricter laws enacted against circumcision and/or greater enforcement of existing ones. Previous efforts in this direction have demonstrated that such measures are likely to be counter-productive. (pp. 107–108)

As an alternative to legislating female circumcision, many of those in favor of its elimination advocate educational programs that over time will have a positive effect on eradicating the practice. This is the approach that notable international organizations such as WHO, UNICEF, and the UNDP take. Although also advocating legislation, these organizations believe that community education programs are an effective way to bring a local cultural practice into line with a Western-derived notion of human rights (WHO, 1997, pp. 13–15). Scholars as well expect that educational programs, in the many forms that they take, are perhaps the most influential way to bring about change (Althaus, 1997, p. 132; Mackie, 1996, p. 1015; Williams & Sobieszczyk, 1997, p. 980). One example is a group in Kenya that replaces FGM that is performed for "coming of age" considerations with a "non-cutting ritual event" (Brothers, 2002, p. 1133).

On the other end of the continuum are the cultural relativists who maintain that the practice of female circumcision should be allowed in the interest of cultural identity and preservation. In particular, these are the voices of the men and women who are already part of the local ethnic groups that maintain the practice. Although typically not given much attention or consideration by those in the West, the proponents of the status quo with respect to female circumcision maintain that the intrusion by the West, under the guise of promoting universal human rights, is nothing more than cultural imperialism and an attempt to erase not only the practice of female circumcision but the culture as well. Winkel (1995) observes this with respect to the culture of Islam when he states:

> The agenda of international and national campaigns to eradicate female circumcision is widely perceived by Muslims as racist and ethnocentric. The entire thrust of "development," after all, includes paternalistic and racist notions of who stands in need of education and development, and why. So whether international or national, a campaign to eradicate female circumcision will carry with it a largely hidden agenda to change people's lives according to a particularly western model of development. . . . Muslims will quickly suspect that "female circumcision" is not what is really at stake; what is at stake is Islam itself, the presence of a Christian as a campaign leader suggesting yet another missionary assault on Islam. (p. 3)

In sum, one side of the argument believes that female circumcision is both a health and a human rights concern. Consequently, the West and the governments of the practicing countries need to incorporate policies that will serve to eradicate the practice seemingly without much consideration for the culture. The other extreme posits that what is really at issue is not female circumcision, but rather the continued existence of the entire culture. Moreover, it is readily apparent to adherents of this faction that the West is instigating the process of change. In the face of these two extremes, is there a middle ground to be found between the dictates of universal human rights and cultural relativism? While any position along this continuum can be criticized by either extreme, it is perhaps possible to identify several intermediate positions that have some potential for successfully resolving the dilemma.

Although by no means the definitive answer, the following prescriptions are not without some merit. First, governments of countries that currently have groups practicing female circumcision, including those in the West, should legalize its mildest form—what was referred to earlier as type 1 or *mild sunna*.[16] This move should be coupled with an educational campaign that provides information that is primarily concerned with the health consequences of the more severe types of female circumcision as well as informing local populations where they can turn to have a more sanitary condition in which to perform the procedure (Mohamud, 1991). This is very similar to the idea that physicians at the Harborview Medical Center in Seattle, Washington, were considering in 1996. The assumption was that a mild prick of the prepuce could satisfy the "needs" of many families and not be as injurious to the women as more severe forms of female circumcision. The doctors abandoned this idea, however, after then Representative Pat Schroeder wrote to the hospital suggesting that this would be a violation of the new federal law banning female circumcision (Dugger, 1996, p. A28).

One assumption behind this proposal is that a more literate population will be better informed about the harmful health effects of female circumcision, the structured patriarchical society that maintains the practice, and the necessity of either lessening the severity of the practice or eliminating it altogether. This assumption is warranted given that Williams and Sobieszczyk (1997, p. 979) found that women with greater education were more likely to not have their daughters circumcised and were generally more in favor of ending the practice. Moreover, Onadeko (1985) also found a positive relationship between education and support for ending the practice.

A second assumption related to this proposal is that it is unlikely that a practice as long-lived as female circumcision will fall by the wayside overnight. Moreover, the historical entrenchment of the practice in several ethnic groups suggests that adherents to the practice, while perhaps allowing it to continue in a different form, will nonetheless continue to support it for some time. There is great support for the assumption that it will be a long process that may take several generations (Althaus, 1997, pp. 132–133; Williams & Sobieszczyk, 1997, p. 980; WHO, 1997, p. 16). Several studies have indicated that women, while opting to continue the practice of female circumcision, desire a "less severe" form of it. Hicks (1996), for example, found that while most Sudanese women (82% of whom were infibulated) wanted to continue the practice, 46 percent favored the continuation of infibulation and 48 percent favored the less severe *sunna* form (p. 204). Magied & Makki (2004) found that while 21 percent of Sudanese women wanted their daughters to be circumcised, with

57 percent of them favoring clitoridectomy. Similarly, 42 percent of men said that they would circumcise their daughters, with 71 percent preferring clitoridectomy (pp. 34; 38–39). Finally, Dare et al. (2004) found that 19 percent of Nigerian women wanted their daughters to have the procedure, while another 40 percent were indifferent (p. 282).

A third prescription for change is to encourage international financial institutions to *increase* assistance to countries most affected by female circumcision. This increased funding would go to support programs that increase the status of women, generally speaking, in these cultures. This proposal is based on the assumption that most cultures that practice female circumcision are of a hierarchical and patriarchical structure. Facilitating the general development of women will allow for greater female participation in the decisions made by the society for its betterment.

Much commentary has hinted at the ills associated with cutting down funding and the advantages associated with increasing it. Dorkenoo and Elworthy (1992), for example, maintain that without access to education or other vital resources, "the rural and urban poor cling to traditions as a survival mechanism" (p. 17). Hicks (1996), moreover, found that infibulation was positively related to, inter alia, the relatively low position of women in society (pp. 139–148). Finally, Rosenthal (1996) recommends that the United States begin allocating 1 percent of its foreign aid budget (i.e., approximately $100 million) to governments and organizations that participate in field education (p. A31).

Although all of the above prescriptions can be attacked by both extremes, they represent a middle-of-the-road strategy to effectively deal with the extremes of universal human rights and cultural relativism. In the end, however, any attempt at invoking universal human rights to eradicate female circumcision is likely to be met with continual resistance. As a women's rights advocate in Sierra Leone stated:

> For me, you cannot bring a Western approach, lecturing people about their customs. . . . The more you decide you are going to take something like this on, the more you are going to face resistance. Instead, a dialogue has to be established, and women here have to understand that Sierra Leone is part of a global community and should not be left out." (French, 1997)

3

The Case of Female Infanticide

In the pre-Ramrajya state of India, in the culmination of kalyug, the evil cycle of eternal time, as kali . . . evil . . . became riper and riper, men took over his (god's) functions, they killed their brides for dowry, the greed and lasciviousness of a highly materialistic and consumeristic society . . . in tens of thousands. They murdered fetuses in thousands . . . after sex determination tests, amniocentesis, a needle into the womb drawing out the amniotic fluid and testing it in a laboratory. Then an abortion if it was a female fetus. . . . Also, in India, fathers and mothers used to give more food, more medical attention to sons rather than daughters because of their strong obsessive desire for sons, for protection in old age as well as for funeral-offerings. Old habits do not die. So, even in Ramrajya they give everything to the sons, and daughters are dying. That is why our great leader Ram was forced to take this decision—until the danger of extinction of the Ramrajya human race passes, all sons will be killed and it will be so for a long time . . . and we Vidavai Athais have to obey him. Otherwise we will be extinct.

Venkatachalam & Srinivasan (1993, pp. 8, 14)

History of the Practice

Female infanticide[1] is a practice that has been performed in numerous cultures throughout the world. Infanticide has, in its early history, included males as well as females. In keeping with the thematic focus of this book, however, the emphasis here is primarily on the killing of females.[2] Throughout its history the practice of female infanticide has encompassed a wide geographical spread and has consumed more countries than has the practice of female circumcision. In brief, the practice has occurred on virtually every continent at some point in history (Mays, 1993, p. 883; Williamson, 1978, p. 63).

Like female circumcision, female infanticide dates to antiquity and beyond. Hrdy (1993) suggests that it predates Homo sapiens, as primates also practice infanticide (p. 648). On the basis of archeological evidence from burial grounds, Williamson (1978) contends that it is conceivable that infanticide was "probably universal" (p. 67). Moreover, it has been suggested that preferential female infanticide was probably the primary strategy for population stabilization during the Pleistocene epoch (Birdsell, 1968, p. 239).

Various Chinese dynasties illustrate the lengthy history of female infanticide. As early as 2,000 B.C. in China, "girls were the main, if not exclusive victims of infanticide and tended to have a higher infant mortality rate in times of poverty and famine" (Elisabeth Croll, as quoted in Hom, 1992, p. 255). The practice continued during the Qin dynasty (221–207 B.C.) and both the western Han dynasty (202 B.C.–A.D. 24) and the eastern Han dynasty (A.D. 25–220) on through the Yuan dynasty (A.D. 1271–1368), even though it was illegal during this entire interval. The decriminalization of infanticide appears to have occurred sometime during the Qing dynasty (A.D. 1644–1911), as the Criminal Code contained no specific punishment for infanticide (Jimmerson, 1990). The practice continues in present-day China.

Evidence also exists indicating that female infanticide was common during the Greco-Roman period. In a dispatch from 1 B.C., dated June 17, Alis's husband wrote, "I ask and beg you to take good care of our baby son. . . . If you are delivered a child . . . if it is a boy keep it, if a girl discard it" (Lewis, 1985). Moreover, by using DNA analysis of skeletal remains, Faerman et al. (1997, pp. 212–213) discovered the existence of five one- to two-day-old females that were most likely the victims of infanticide in the fourth-century Roman Ashkelon (i.e., a city in southwest Palestine on the Mediterranean).

Infanticide during this period was continually illustrated by various Greek plays (both tragedies and comedies) that either depicted or referred to the practice. Euripides depicted it in the tragedy *Medea* when Medea murdered her sons. Moreover, Menander, in the comedy *The Arbitration,* spoke of leaving Pamphila's son exposed in the fields (Oates and O'Neill, 1938). It is important to note, as Weir (1984) makes clear, that "normalcy," as opposed to gender, was the primary consideration in most of these infanticide decisions (pp. 7–8).

As with the history of female circumcision, there is ultimately no conclusive resolution about where female infanticide originated. It is, however, a practice whose backdrop is woven through thousands of years. Unlike the practice of female circumcision, the rise of Christianity did appear to have an impact on the Roman legal system with respect to condoning infanticide. Throughout a large part of history, *patria potestas* (i.e., the idea that the father has the recognized right to punish his children) was commonplace. The November 16, 318, revision of the Roman law against parricide (i.e., the unlawful killing of one's mother or father) to include the killing of a son or daughter by the father was a result of the influence that Christianity exacted. Moreover, a distinction was made between *direct* and *indirect* infanticide when on February 7, 374, it was decided that *direct* infanticide (i.e., directly murdering the child as opposed to abandoning it) would no longer be condoned (Noonan, Jr., 1965, p. 86).

Along with Christianity, Islam specifically decried the practice of female infanticide. In the pre-Islamic setting, desert Arabs indulged in burying female infants alive (Kader, 1998). Several verses from the Koran address the infanticide that the pagan Arabs committed before the rise of Islam and also address the Islamic perspective on infanticide. The pagan practices of the Arabs are lamented in sura 6, which deals with livestock:

> My people, act according to your situation; I [too] am Acting! You will know who will have the Home as a result. The fact is that wrongdoers will not prosper. They grant God a share in what He has produced such as crops and livestock, and they say: "This is God's," according to their claim, and: "This is our associates'." Anything that is meant for their associates never reaches God, while what is God's reaches their associates [too]; how evil is whatever they decide! Even so, their associates have made killing their children seem attractive to many associators, to lead them on to ruin and to confuse their religion for them. If God so wishes, they would not do so; so leave them alone and whatever they are inventing. (Irving, 1991, 6:135–137)

The more specific emphasis on the pagan practice of *female* infanticide is noted in sura 16 and in the poetic sura 81:

> They assign a portion of what We have provided them with, to something they do not know (by God, you shall be questioned about whatever you have been inventing)! They (even) assign daughters to God. Glory be to Him! They themselves have what they desire. Yet whenever one of them receives word he has had a daughter, his face becomes black with gloom and he feels like choking. He hides from folk because of the bad news that he has just received. Will he hold on to her and feel disgraced, or bury her in the dust? (Irving, 1991, 16:56–59)

> When the sun has been extinguished,
> when the stars slip out of place, . . .
> when the buried girl is asked
> for what offence she has been killed, . . .
> each soul shall know what it has prepared!
> (Irving, 1991, 81:1–2, 8–9, 14)

Although Giladi (1990, pp. 185–186) notes that the Prophet Muhammad absolutely rejected the practice of infanticide, there is some indication that Islam might have viewed it as appropriate only as a last resort when both coitus interruptus and abortion had not proved to be successful measures (p. 191). Of obvious note here is the fact that the practice was neither condoned nor widespread in Islam, as it was in other religions in the Greco-Roman period.

The practice continued throughout the Middle Ages (A.D. 476–1453) over a large geographical expanse. Although a distinction was often made between *direct* and *indirect* infanticide, many different methods were maintained during this period, including murder, ritual sacrifice, drowning, burying, "overlaying," starvation, and exposure. Of curious inconsistency during this period, given the role of Christianity in exacting changes in Roman customs, is the contention that Christians were just as likely to commit infanticide, via exposure, as were pagans (Maier-Katkin & Ogle, 1997, p. 306).

Opposition to the idea that infanticide was widely practiced during the medieval period concentrates on the interpretation that Westerners have given to the concept *expositio*. Post (1988, p. 15) maintains that the real Western tradition was to provide an alternative to infanticide during this time. Post also communicates support for Boswell's (1984) alternative understanding that *expositio* means "offering" or "putting out" as opposed to "exposure." To adopt the former understanding is to suggest that infants were not subjected to exposure but were placed in the care of an alternative guardian. It is said that the church acted as an intermediary between those who would "offer" their unwanted children and those in society who would receive them. Moreover, Post (p. 15) intimates that monasteries were at times flooded beyond capacity with "abandoned" infants and provides de facto proof for the suggestion that this is the true Western tradition with respect to unwanted infants.

The system of "putting out" was common throughout much of Europe, including Renaissance Italy, where otherwise infanticidal mothers would relinquish their female infants to the *balia* (i.e., wet nurse) who would, under the pretense of caring for the child, kill it (Weir, 1984, p. 10). This system was especially useful for those who wished to appear in harmony with the doctrines of the church. Moreover, the system provided a greater likelihood that the birth mother and father would not be charged with any crime. As Piers (1978) maintains:

> It seems that everywhere infanticidal *mothers were punished by death. Wet nurses were not.* They played the role of the executioner, whose

deeds were difficult to prove and were silently condoned. An execution of a wet nurse is never mentioned in the pertinent literature. And the only mention of any punishment at all concerns a 1415 law that forbade *balie* to "relinquish their charges before they were thirty months old." The punishment inflicted on the guilty *balia* was a fine or a public whipping. Not, however, the death penalty. Society simply could not have afforded to kill her. (p. 51; emphasis in the original)

The continuation of such practices throughout Germany, France, Italy, and much of Europe necessitated action. The result was that several countries, such as England, attempted to legislate the problem away. The Stuart Bastardly Act of 1623 was an attempt to restrain the liberal attitude with regard to infanticide. However, the attempt to control the extent of the practice was largely unsuccessful, which led to its repeal in 1803 (Maier-Katkin & Ogle, 1997, p. 309). In its wake came the practice of "baby farming" in Victorian England (i.e., the nineteenth century), a practice that largely paralleled the behavior of the *balia* in Renaissance Italy. Rather than wet nurses, farmers would take the infants for pay and, usually with the consent of the birth couple, leave them to die in the fields (Kader, 1998).

Beyond the European continent, female infanticide has been practiced by diverse countries. Between 1880 and 1930, the Inuit (i.e., various Eskimo communities) of Canada and upper Alaska practiced the custom to varying degrees, depending on the level of available resources (Bower, 1994, p. 358). During the colonial period, almost one-third of the homicide cases in England and the United States were constituted by infanticide (Maier-Katkin & Ogle, 1997, p. 309). The inability to provide any clearer picture of the degree to which the practice occurs in the United States is difficult because infanticide cases are consumed under the heading of homicide.

The practice has also been recorded throughout Latin America. In 1873, Argentina implemented a law that prescribed imprisonment for three to six years if the infanticidal act occurred within three days of birth, and the legal penalty for homicide if it occurred after this time (Ruggiero, 1992, p. 354). It is legal to abandon one's child in Brazil, but imprisonment may result for direct infanticide (Scheper-Hughes, 1985). Moreover, infanticidal practices have been noted for the Ayoreo of Bolivia, the Yanomamö Indians of Venezuela, the Amahuaca of Peru, and the Mundurucù of Brazil.

The practice has also been carried out in eighteenth- and nineteenth-century Japan. The Japanese practice of "mabiki" was utilized as a way of "thinning" or spacing out births (Hrdy, 1993, p. 645;

Post, 1988, p. 14). If, on being asked, the father did not wish to keep the newborn, it would be promptly returned to its "maker" (Pitt & Bale, 1995, p. 376). Furthermore, the Japanese commit female infanticide during the "Fire Horse" year (*Hino-Uma*) because superstition holds that girls born during that year are cursed. The Fire Horse year occurs once every 60 years, the last being 1966, which resulted in a significantly higher female infant mortality rate (Kaku, 1975).

Female infanticide has been not only prevalent throughout both Western and non-Western history but also commonplace in the contemporary record (Chunkath & Athreya, 1997, p. WS21). Perhaps the most notable countries where the practice continues today are China and India. It is not entirely coincidental that the two most populated developing countries of the world have become the focus of female infanticide.

The history of the practice with respect to China was briefly mentioned. In the contemporary period, however, there has been much speculation that governmental adoption of the one-child policy in 1979 has led to a resurgence of the practice. Kristof (1991a) maintains, through a quick glimpse at sex ratios before the one-child policy and after, that it was not until the policy was incorporated that female infanticide significantly resurfaced in China (pp. A1, A8). Regardless of the policy's impact, there are many Chinese provinces that have been found to practice female infanticide. At a minimum, these include Fuyang, Henan, Zhejiang, Hubei, and Guangxi. Cities throughout China, such as Beijing, Guangzhou, Tianjin, and Chongqing, have also reported female infanticide (Hom, 1992).

India has also been a considerable focus of Western countries that are concerned with female infanticide. Venkatachalam and Srinivasan (1993) suggest that the practice has been in existence for hundreds of years, perhaps dating back to the Vedic period (p. 17). The practice has been reported throughout Indian states. Several states in north and central India, such as Bihar, Uttar Pradesh, Punjab, Haryana, Rajasthan, Gujarat, Maharashtra, and Madhya Pradesh, have been affected. While the sex ratio in India worsened from 945 to 927 girls per 1,000 boys over the 1991–2001 period, the situation is most dire in Gujarat, where the ratio is 878 per 1,000; Haryana, where it has dipped to 865; and Punjab, where it is 793 (Oomman & Ganatra, 2002, pp. 184–185. The trend in Punjab since 1981 is particularly noteworthy, as the ratio went from 908 to 793 (Snehi, 2003, pp. 4302–4303). Moreover, southern India has not been exempt, as Tamil Nadu has experienced the phenomenon, and it is feared that the practice is spreading into Karnataka (Kulkarni et al., 1996, pp. 525–526).

The scope of the practice of female infanticide today is considerably wide: it is currently present in numerous geographical settings encompassing almost every continent. Moreover, although the major religions express abhorrence for it, members of each have been known to practice it. Those who practice it tend to come disproportionately from the lower economic strata of society and have relatively little education. Moreover, the structure of the societies in which they live is typically patrilineal or patriarchal. Unlike female circumcision, female infanticide has not "spread" among immigrant populations but has largely remained in areas for which it has a long-standing history. The age at which it occurs is variable and ranges from the prenatal period on through birth, infancy, and childhood. To the alarm of many in the West, it continues today, both in public and in secrecy, and does not appear to be lessening in frequency.

There are no exact data about the number of females (i.e., fetuses, infants, and children) killed. Various estimates of the total number of females who are victims of all forms of infanticide do exist, but are often problematic and inconsistent owing to the method by which the estimates are derived. Bunch (1997) estimated that 60 million women are "missing" today because of female infanticide. Kristof (1991a, p. C1) suggests that there are at least 60 million "missing females" in Asia alone and perhaps more than 100 million "missing" worldwide. Dreze and Sen (1989, pp. 51–53) maintain that there were roughly 104.7 million "missing women" in the year 1986, including 44 million in China and 36.9 million in India.

The ability to produce an estimate of the total number of females that infanticide has affected, and will continue to affect, is marred by the lack of reliable data. There are obvious problems in trying to ascertain the truth when asking families if they have ever committed an act of female infanticide. If cultural differences do not get in the way, surely questions pertaining to morality, economics, tradition, legality, and so forth obstruct one's ability to come close to the "actual" number. In the final analysis, most researchers rely on reasonable "guestimates" that are based on sex ratios. Kristof (1991a) accurately states that the real problem is in determining "the sex ratio that would exist in a population if males and females were treated equally" (p. C12). This ratio can be compared with the actual male/female ratio of the population for a particular age group. The aforementioned difference in opinion about the number of "missing females" is derived almost exclusively from different estimates of the male/female sex ratio.[3]

To better understand the "guestimating" process, one must first grasp the difference between primary and secondary sex ratios. While the primary sex ratio refers to the proportion of males to females that are *conceived*, the secondary sex ratio refers to the proportion actually *born*. It is this secondary sex ratio that is often used in the equation to determine the number of "missing females." The inability to easily determine embryonic ratios makes the addition of this information into the equation virtually impossible. Consequently, the secondary ratio is almost exclusively relied upon for these estimates and is a more conservative measure of the total number affected than if one could also ascertain data on primary sex ratios.[4]

Coale (1991) factors in the male/female mortality ratio in order to arrive at a more accurate picture of the total number of missing females, but only with respect to the secondary sex ratio. At first glance, however, it would appear that this has the general effect of making even more "conservative" estimates of the total number of "missing females" than if one only relied upon the secondary sex ratio without the inclusion of the male/female mortality ratio.

Given that researchers are, for the most part, unable to acquire reliable data for the primary sex ratio, perhaps it is best to utilize only the total number of "missing females" obtained by incorporating the secondary sex ratio without further biasing the estimate downward by including the male/female mortality ratio. One could make a strong case that this number, owing to the inability to acquire numbers for the primary sex ratio, is "conservative" enough in its estimation of the total number missing. Even so, research suggests that this, too, may even be conservative, as the number of abortions (or prenatal sex selections) that are performed in countries that practice female infanticide is considerably higher for female than for male fetuses. Kristof (1991a, p. C12) and Anderson and Moore (1993) speak of a United Nations report indicating that out of 8,000 abortions recorded in Mumbai, only one involved a male fetus. Quoting two scholarly studies, Weiss (1996) communicates that an estimated 1 million female fetuses were aborted in India from 1981 to 1991 and 1.5 million in China between the mid-1980s and 1990.

One must also differentiate between the sex ratio for the general population and the sex ratio at birth. The sex ratio of the entire population considers all age groups in the calculation. For example, the female to male sex ratio (FMR/GENPOP) in table 3.1 refers to the ratio for the entire population, whereas the birth sex ratio (FMR/BIRTH) reported in table 3.3 refers to the secondary sex ratio, which is the ratio of females to males at birth. Table 3.1 contains the raw data on total (TOTPOP), female (FEMPOP), and male population (MALEPOP) and the consequent female to male sex ratio for the

Table 3.1 Total Population by Gender (in Thousands) and Female/Male Gender
Ratio in General Population (Females per 100 Males), 2002

ENTITY	TOTPOP	FEMPOP	MALEPOP	FMR/ GENPOP
WORLD	6,236,841	3,099,662	3,137,179	98.8
EUROPE	727,383	376,758	350,625	107.5
Northern Europe	94,651	48,536	46,115	105.2
Southern Europe	146,293	74,804	71,489	104.6
Western Europe	184,300	94,167	90,133	104.5
Eastern Europe	302,140	159,251	142,889	111.5
Russia	144,271	76,788	67,483	113.8
NORTHERN AMERICA	322,296	163,877	158,418	103.4
USA	290,856	148,002	142,853	103.6
LATIN AMERICA & CARIBBEAN	536,819	271,216	265,603	102.1
Caribbean	38,414	19,327	19,086	101.3
Central America	140,399	71,053	69,346	102.5
South America	358,007	180,836	177,171	102.1
AFRICA	834,365	419,373	414,992	101.1
Northern Africa	180,723	90,010	90,714	99.2
Sub-Saharan Africa	608,744	306,431	302,315	101.4
OCEANIA	31,891	15,883	16,009	99.2
ASIA	3,784,086	1,852,555	1,931,532	95.9
Western Asia	201,158	98,182	102,976	95.3
Eastern Asia	1,502,194	734,443	767,750	95.7
China	1,294,561	629,339	665,222	94.6
South-Eastern Asia	537,140	269,123	268,017	100.4
South-Central Asia	1,543,595	750,806	792,789	94.7
India	1,053,965	510,688	543,277	94.0

Source: Population Division of the Department of Economic and Social Affairs of the United Nations
Secretariat (2003), *World Population Prospects: The 2002 Revision,* New York, United Nations.
Note: Sub-Saharan Africa does not include northern Africa, Sudan, and South Africa. See Dreze
& Sen (1989, p. 52).

entire populations (FMR/GENPOP) of select regions and countries
of the world.

Table 3.1 indicates that the world average FMR is 98.8 females per 100
males. This is quite consistent with the 99.0 ratio reported for 1985 by
the United Nations Development Programme (1991) and the supposed
"normal" ratio of 98 to 106 females per 100 males (Banister, 2004).
Several regions surpass this average, including all of Latin America and
the Caribbean, Europe, North America, sub-Saharan Africa, southeastern

Asia, and Oceania. Those areas of the globe that fall below the world average (i.e., the "belt region" of female infanticide) include northern Africa, western Asia, south central Asia, and eastern Asia, and select sub-Saharan countries. Not by coincidence, this pattern of where a majority of females are missing has also been found to coincide with excessive female infant mortality (Banister, 2004).

After the decision to utilize the secondary sex ratio to determine the total number of missing women has been made, the question arises as to what that ratio should in fact be and to what countries the ratio should be applied. Owing to the lowered female infant mortality in most of the developed regions of the world, it would appear patently unfair to presuppose that the "normal" FMR ratio would approximate Europe's average of 107.5, the United States' average of 103.6, or North America's average of 103.4. Utilizing any of these FMR ratios would make for a considerably more "liberal" guesstimate of the total number of "missing women" in the "belt region" (Nussbaum, 1995b, p. 3). Conversely, using the world average would unduly bias the guestimates in a more conservative fashion, because the majority of the world population lives in the developing regions of the world, with the bulk of it in China and India. These two countries alone serve to significantly bias the estimates downward. In light of these biases, earlier analyses have seen fit to utilize the average obtained for the sub-Saharan African region (FMR = 101.4) given a host of demographic similarities (Dreze & Sen, 1989).

Utilizing an FMR of 101.4 as the "baseline" secondary sex ratio, one can now calculate the total number of missing women in the "belt region." Table 3.2 shows those countries in this region that have "excess males" and identifies, on the basis of the sub-Saharan African FMR baseline, the total number of missing females (TOTMISSFEM) in these countries.[5] In sum, the total number falls just over a staggering 110.6 million. One should remember, however, that the numbers for western Asia are certainly tainted somewhat by the inclusion of Bahrain, Kuwait, Oman, Qatar, Saudi Arabia, and the United Arab Emirates, each of which has other considerations at work that result in a considerably lower FMR/GENPOP in their populations than would typically be expected. Without their inclusion, however, the total number would still be over 106.5 million. The most beleaguered countries in absolute numbers are China (45,235,096) and India (40,202,498), which are constantly in the media spotlight when the issue is female infanticide.

The incorporation of the birth sex ratio will allow us to tentatively evaluate the number of females in these countries that might be added

Table 3.2   Total Population by Gender (in Thousands) and Total Missing Females, 2002

COUNTRY	FMR/ GENPOP	TOTPOP	FEMPOP	MALEPOP	TOT MISSFEM
NORTHERN AFRICA	99.2				
Algeria	98.0	31,371	15,526	15,846	538,764
Egypt	100.4	70,664	35,396	35,268	352,680
Libya	93.5	5,465	2,641	2,824	223,096
Morocco	99.7	30,144	15,050	15,093	256,581
Sudan	98.8	33,014	16,405	16,608	431,808
Tunisia	98.5	9,764	4,846	4,918	142,622
Western Sahara	92.4	302	145	157	14,130
SUB-SAHARAN AFRICA	101.4				
Comoros	98.9	750	373	377	9,425
Cote d'Ivoire	96.2	16,437	8,058	8,379	435,708
Guinea	98.7	8,388	4,167	4,221	113,967
Niger	98.2	11,539	5,716	5,822	186,304
Nigeria	98.6	121,406	60,285	61,121	1,711,388
WESTERN ASIA	95.3				
Bahrain	73.8	711	302	409	112,884
Iraq	97.1	24,594	12,116	12,478	536,554
Jordan	92.0	5,359	2,568	2,791	262,354
Kuwait	65.9	2,449	973	1,476	523,980
Occupied Palestinian Territory	96.7	3,445	1,693	1,752	82,344
Oman	73.6	2,777	1,177	1,600	444,800
Qatar	57.0	603	219	384	170,496
Saudi Arabia	86.2	23,623	10,934	12,688	1,928,576
Syria	98.5	17,470	8,667	8,803	255,287
Turkey	98.5	70,525	34,988	35,537	1,030,573
United Arab Emirates	53.5	2,945	1,027	1,918	918,722
Yemen	96.9	19,356	9,526	9,829	442,305
SOUTH-CENTRAL ASIA	94.7				
Afghanistan	93.8	22,937	11,104	11,833	899,308
Bangladesh	95.0	144,561	70,421	74,140	4,744,960
Bhutan	97.8	2,200	1,088	1,112	40,032
India	94.0	1,053,965	510,688	543,277	40,202,498
Iran	97.2	68,226	33,624	34,602	1,453,284
Nepal	95.8	24,689	12,081	12,608	706,048
Maldives	95.0	310	151	159	10,176
Pakistan	95.2	150,318	73,328	76,990	4,773,380
Sri Lanka	93.2	18,927	9,128	9,799	803,518

Continued

Table 3.2 *Continued*

COUNTRY	FMR/ GENPOP	TOTPOP	FEMPOP	MALEPOP	TOT MISSFEM
EASTERN ASIA	95.7				
China	94.6	1,294,561	629,339	665,222	45,235,096
Mongolia	99.7	2,568	1,282	1,286	21,862
South Korea	98.8	47,488	23,596	23,892	621,192
TOTAL		3,343,851	1,628,628	1,715,219	110,636,696

Source: Population Division of the Department of Economic and Social Affairs of the United Nations Secretariat (2003), *World Population Prospects:* The 2002 Revision, New York, United Nations.

annually to the total number of females affected. Table 3.3 reports total births (TOTBIRTHS), the FMR at birth (FMRBIRTH), total female births (TOTFEMBIRTHS), and the total number of females who are potentially affected on an annual basis (TOTFEMPOT). If the FMR baseline for sub-Saharan Africa is used, it is observed that the total number of females potentially affected is over 2.8 million.[6] Again, it is instructive to note that China (1,004,340) and India (894,851) add most significantly to the annual increase.

SPECIFICS OF THE PRACTICE

The history of infanticide reveals that the means used for child destruction have been limited only by human imagination and the available technology of particular times and places. Children have been killed through starvation, drowning, strangulation, burning, smothering (often by "accidental" overlaying in the parent's bed), poisoning, exposure, and a variety of lethal weapons. With the advances of medical technology and the establishment of NICUs over the years since the 1960s, new means of killing neonates—or at least hastening their dying—can be added to the list: lethal injections, overdoses of sedatives, and "accidental" coughs or sneezes over neonates highly susceptible to infection. (Weir, 1984, p. 5)

Although arriving at the estimates of the total number of females who are victims of infanticide is tedious, perhaps the more difficult task is the attempt to define and categorize the many forms of the practice. Classification is important in order to further understand the cultural diversity with regard to this practice, and also important to understand that the total numbers arrived at earlier probably understate the enormity of this cultural practice.

Table 3.3 Total Births, Female/Male Gender Ratio at Birth, Total Female and Total Missing Female Potential, 2002

COUNTRY	TOTBIRTHS	FMR/ BIRTH	TOTFEMBIRTHS	TOTFI
NORTHERN AFRICA		95.0		
Algeria	803,000	95.0	391,205	25,037
Egypt	2,017,000	95.0	982,641	62,889
Libya	143,000	95.0	69,667	4,459
Morocco	760,000	95.0	370,256	23,696
Sudan	1,216,000	95.0	592,410	37,914
Tunisia	191,000	93.0	92,040	7,731
Western Sahara	9,000	96.0	4,337	234
SUB-SAHARAN AFRICA		97.0		
Comoros	30,000	95.0	14,615	935
Cote d'Ivoire	651,000	97.0	320,557	14,105
Guinea	389,000	97.0	191,546	8,428
Niger	652,000	97.0	321,050	14,126
Nigeria	5,229,000	96.0	2,561,339	138,312
WESTERN ASIA		95.0		
Bahrain	16,000	95.0	7,795	499
Iraq	948,000	95.0	461,846	29,558
Jordan	175,000	95.0	85,256	5,456
Kuwait	54,000	97.0	26,590	1,170
Occupied Palestinian Territory	146,000	95.0	71,128	4,552
Oman	97,000	95.0	47,256	3,024
Qatar	12,000	95.0	5,846	374
Saudi Arabia	838,000	95.0	408,256	26,128
Syria	559,000	95.0	272,333	17,429
Turkey	1,643,000	95.0	800,436	51,228
United Arab Emirates	56,000	95.0	27,282	1,746
Yemen	924,000	95.0	450,154	28,810
SOUTH-CENTRAL ASIA		95.0		
Afghanistan	1,135,000	94.0	549,950	40,696
Bangladesh	4,800,000	95.0	2,338,461	149,662
Bhutan	85,000	95.0	41,410	2,650
India	28,700,000	95.0	13,982,046	894,851
Iran	1,510,000	95.0	735,641	47,081
Nepal	891,000	95.0	434,077	27,781
Maldives	12,000	96.0	5,878	317
Pakistan	5,829,000	95.0	2,839,768	181,745
Sri Lanka	326,000	95.0	158,820	10,164

Continued

Table 3.3 *Continued*

COUNTRY	TOTBIRTHS	FMR/ BIRTH	TOTFEMBIRTHS	TOTFEMPOT
EASTERN ASIA		90.0		
China	18,597,000	90.0	8,810,000	1,004,340
Mongolia	65,000	95.0	31,667	2,027
South Korea	609,000	93.0	293,468	24,651
TOTAL	80,117,000		38,797,027	2,893,805

Source: Population Division of the Department of Economic and Social Affairs of the United Nations Secretariat (2003), *World Population Prospects: The 2002 Revision,* New York, United Nations.

The definition of female infanticide is variable. Nineteenth-century Argentinean law specified that [female] infanticide was "the killing, through either negligence or violence, of a [female] child by its mother 'in order to hide her dishonor' " (Ruggiero, 1992, p. 354). Mays (1993) defines it as "the killing of unwanted babies, usually at or soon after birth" (p. 883). Hrdy (1993) defines it as "the killing of an infant or young child, technically 'pedicide,' by a conspecific" (p. 644). Weir (1984) maintains that for centuries, infanticide has meant "the intentional destruction of young children ranging in age from newborns to children just under the 'age of discretion.' " (p. 4). Hom (1992) used the term to refer to "the induced death (euthanasia) of infants by suffocation, drowning, abandonment, exposure, or other methods" (p. 255). Williamson (1978) defines it as "the deliberate killing of a child in its infancy, up to two years of age" (p. 62).

Among these definitions are some noteworthy considerations. For instance, most agree that infanticide involves the killing of infants, from newborns through a predetermined age, whether it be the "age of discretion" or otherwise. Perhaps it is instructive to note here that the root of the word *infant* is the Latin *infans,* meaning "unable to speak" (Reiman, 1996, p. 193). Many who practice infanticide do not consider a newborn to be fully human (and consequently fully accepted) until it takes on physical human characteristics such as speaking and walking or has been named (Williamson, 1978, p. 64). Incorporating this underlying meaning would necessitate a much shorter period of time for the killing to be performed. Several studies indicate that a shorter time period is preferable so as not to allow a greater bond to occur between mother and child (Smith & Kahila, 1992, p. 668) and greater suffering for the girl newborn, which starts almost immediately after birth (Venkatram, 1995, p. 16). Williamson (1978, p. 62) continues by stating that infanticide defined as taking place between birth and two years of age would be sufficient to cover the majority of cases.

A second point of consideration is the emphasis on whether the act of female infanticide is *direct* (i.e., violent) as opposed to *indirect* (i.e., negligence) in its orientation (Weir, 1984, pp. 9–10; 21). This is perhaps better interpreted as an *active* versus *passive* orientation. Although this interpretation will be touched upon later, it is important to recognize, as many who have tried to define the boundaries of female infanticide have recognized, that there are various means by which to accomplish the desired objective. Some of these methods, such as the suffocation of the newborn in the placenta, are quite direct or active, whereas other methods, such as leaving a newborn outdoors in cold weather, are more indirect or passive in their orientation. Both, however, accomplish the objective.

A third important consideration is that, when female infanticide is mentioned, it is typically the case that the mother or a midwife is the individual responsible for the killing of the female child (Weir, 1984, p. 17). This is in part due to the responsibility that women are said to have in cultures where giving birth to a female child brings disgrace upon one's self. In essence, it is the obligation of the female to dispose of the female child that she has delivered, because she has failed to provide a son for her husband (Venkatramani, 1986, p. 32). Females often accomplish this obligation in an indirect fashion. In a review of the literature, Pitt and Bale (1995, p. 379) found that when men are responsible for the death, they typically utilize a more active or direct method than do women.

Fourth, it is instructive to note that the female child is typically considered "unwanted." In most instances it is improper to equate "unwanted" with "unloved." This is a consideration that is very difficult for most in the West to fully understand. The key to understanding this, however, is to draw a distinction between the "here and now" and the longer-term life conditions of the female child. Resnick (1972) refers to the orientation of saving a female child from all the ills that she will encounter while growing up in a culture that assigns lesser value to the female gender as "altruistic filicide." Others maintain that this is less altruistic and more functional, so that the life chances of an already existing child will be enhanced (Williamson, 1978, p. 63). Moreover, Ruggiero (1992, p. 361) maintains that this "not hatred but love" orientation was presented in Argentinean courts as a successful defense against more harsh penalties. In essence, there was (is) no apparent contradiction between loving one's daughter and committing female infanticide (Giladi, 1990, p. 18).

As mentioned earlier, most researchers make distinctions on what "infanticide" entails. The problem with most attempts is that they are far from holistic in conveying the relatedness of terms. Perhaps the most useful way of overcoming this problem is to regard "infanticide" as a generic term that entails several related considerations, including neonaticide (i.e., death from 0 to 27 days), postneonaticide (i.e., death from 28 days to 1 year), and infanticide (i.e., death after 1 year). Filicide, moreover, refers specifically to the *parental killing* of an infant that is at least one day old.

Another area of concern that is very much related to female infanticide is the practice of prenatal sex selection or feticide (i.e., the destruction of a fetus). Although a politically charged topic throughout many countries in the West, feticide entails more than the issue of abortion. The two differ appreciably: abortion, in general, is concerned with the "right to life" of the fetus, whether male, female, or yet undetermined, whereas feticide is concerned with the systematic destruction of *female fetuses* because of social, economic, and cultural pressures. The latter practice, due precisely to the overwhelming emphasis on expunging female fetuses, is often referred to as "femicide" or "gendercide."

Having adequately defined the parameters of female infanticide, one can move on to the specific methods by which the practice is conducted. It is perhaps best to divide these methods into three identifiable categories. Beyond the "direct" techniques of suffocation and the use of weapons and toxic substances are the more "indirect" methods that fall under the general category of abandonment and exposure. The use of any one technique or its prevalence is culture specific, which makes widespread generalizations about the method of choice difficult. As mentioned earlier, however, it appears that suffocation techniques and strangulation are the preferred methods of choice.

The general category of suffocation techniques for female infanticide involves drowning (Williamson, 1978, p. 64), the pressing together of the nose and mouth (Venkatachalam & Srinivasan, 1993, p. 25), putting the face into the ground (Williamson, 1978, p. 64), snapping the spinal cord (Kulkarni et al., 1996, p. 526), placing a wet towel over the face (Buchanan, 1994; Jones, 2002; Kulkarni et al., 1996, p. 526), and "overlaying" (i.e., the practice of smothering a child while it is sleeping with its parents) (Maier-Katkin & Ogle, 1997, p. 306; Weir, 1984, p. 16). Moreover, it has also involved the burying alive of female infants. They have been killed by "potting" them in jars, pots of grain, or sand bags and waiting for them to suffocate (Kader, 1998; Sharma, 2003, 1553; Weir, 1984, p. 7); by

burying them in dunghills (Anderson & Moore
p. 7); or by burying them immediately after ¹
dug adjacent to the birthing spot (Giladi, 19
1978, p. 64).

Weapons and toxic substances are also
infanticide. Here, a weapon is broadly defineᴅ
employed in facilitating an infant's death—that is, alɪ.
object that is used to induce death (Kulkarni et al., 1996).
boiled water (or milk) is given along with uncooked grains oɪ
induce choking (Buchanan, 1994; Jones, 2002; Venkatachalam
Srinivasan, 1993, p. 27). Moreover, rose petals have also been used
for this purpose (Muthulakshmi, 1997, p. 25). Besides, newborns
have suffered from gauze pads dipped in alcohol being placed in their
mouths (Aird, 1990). A recent case involved the feeding of salt water
("Sentenced to Life for Female Infanticide," 2004), which quickly
corrodes a newborn's lips and infiltrates its lungs.

Of the methods that remain, a distinction is made as to whether
it is a doctor or a family member who typically commits the act of
infanticide. Often, doctors will administer, when the sex of the fetus
is known, an injection of formaldehyde or alcohol into the fontanel,
thus causing a quick death (Aird, 1990). A physician, again with the
knowledge of the sex of the fetus, may administer an injection to the
expecting mother so that she gives birth to a stillborn (Aird, 1990).
Finally, an obstetrician may crush the female child to death immediately after delivery by using forceps or another instrument (Aird,
1990).

Members of the family may also employ additional methods that
focus on the application of toxic substances. For example, one might
feed the newborn a mixture of tobacco paste and pesticides or fertilizers (Jones, 2002; Venkatachalam & Srinivasan, 1993, p. 27). If this
does not work, one might administer the paste or milk of the poison-
ous oleander or calotropis plant (Buchanan, 1994; Venkatachalam
& Srinivasan, 1993, p. 27). Of particular interest here is the fact
that many husbands will begin to grow the calotropis plant when
their spouse becomes pregnant, just in case a daughter is born
(Venkatramani, 1986, p. 33). Finally, one might allow the mother to
breast-feed the newborn after the mother's breasts have been smeared
with opium (Weir, 1984, p. 7).

Indirect methods are largely related to issues of abandonment
and exposure. Abandonment is defined to also include neglect of or
disregard for the infant. Included in this category are the practices
of allowing the female infant to starve (Jones, 2002; Weir, 1984,

oleeding her to death by not tying off the umbilical cord after
. (Giladi, 1990, p. 190; Ruggiero, 1992, p. 360), and exposing
to the elements (Weir, 1984, p. 7). Female infants have also been
ɔandoned at "baby farms," where the responsibility for their care is
assumed by the "farmer," who then ensures their death (Weir, 1984,
p. 16). Women have often left their newborns at the "water closet"
so that they get pushed into the sewage system (Ruggiero, 1992,
p. 358). Abandonment is also illustrated by the use of "dying rooms"
at Chinese orphanages. Ninety-five percent of orphans at one such
site were girls, while the other 5 percent were mentally or physically
disabled males (Jones, 2002).

Other methods have also been used to achieve the objective. Ritu-
alistic killings, which might include virtually any technique from stab-
bing to drowning to burning, are often undertaken (Muthulakshmi,
1997, pp. 6–7; Weir, 1984, p. 7). One might also list here the technological advances of ultrasound, or "scanning," as it is sometimes
referred to, and amniocentesis as other factors that lead to any of the
above-mentioned methods, along with feticide, being utilized to kill
an unwanted female infant or fetus (Buchanan, 1994; Venkatachalam
& Srinivasan, 1993, p. 25; Venkatram, 1995, p. 16).

Although to the West the use of any of these methods is, at best,
cruel and unusual punishment, the following passage gives some indication about what must be going through the minds of the parents
who undertake female infanticide.

> There was only one way out of a lifetime burden of bringing up two
> daughters. And Kuppusamy decided on what they had to do. That
> evening he trudged—somewhat unsteadily—into a nearby field, plucked
> a handful of oleander berries that are known for their lethal poison, and
> returned home. Chinnammal mashed them into a milky paste and fed
> her crying infant with the substance. The parents then shut the small
> door of their hut, sat outside, and waited for the poison to do its work.
> Within an hour the baby began to twitch and tremble fitfully. Slowly
> she started spouting blood through her mouth and nose. The parents
> heard her whining. A few more minutes and all was quiet. Chinnammal
> knew that everything was over. She quietly walked over to her mother's
> hut close by, dug up a little patch of ground inside, brought and buried
> the dead baby. (Venkatramani, 1986, p. 28)

Cᴜʟᴛᴜʀᴀʟ Rᴇʟᴇᴠᴀɴᴄᴇ

Explanations for the practice of female infanticide are numerous and
quite diverse, depending on the particular cultural group (i.e., ethnic

group) that one encounters. As in the practice of female circumcision, there are commonalities among cultures that practice female infanticide. More than anything else, the explanations encountered are multifaceted and draw on a host of social, economic, and culturally related concerns. Although one always runs the risk of being "culturally reductionistic" in terms of the explanations that are offered, the following inquiry revolves around the influence that patriarchy, patrilineal society, economics, myth, and population pressures have had on the decision whether or not to commit female infanticide. As these factors are often interrelated, an attempt will be made to pull them together after each has been introduced separately.

As in the practice of female circumcision, patriarchy and patrilineal societies are key concepts that are relevant to the study of female infanticide throughout northern Africa and west, central, and east Asian countries. To reiterate, patriarchy refers to control, power, and authority over the social unit being in the hands of the male. Numerous characteristics are typically associated with the practice of patriarchy, including inferior status for all women, arranged marriages for children, double standards with regard to sexual behavior, multiple marriages for males, and a belief that males are most wise. Patrilineal society, simply put, is a social situation where the family can be traced historically through the male line of descent.

Both patriarchal and patrilineal societies place an inordinate amount of significance on the birth of the male child because of his role throughout his life. The male is often viewed as able to work harder for the family, allow for the male lineage to continue, provide a "safety net" for his parents in their old age (Croll, 2002, p. 23), allow for increased wealth to accrue to the family via dowry, and subsequently inherit his father's wealth (Secondi, 2002). Moreover, Hindu scripture dictates that only a son can light the funeral pyre and hence take his parents to heaven (Girish, 2005, p. 11; Muthulakshmi, 1997, p. 52; Ren, 1995). Additionally, the Confucian value system in China continues to place a premium on males (Banister, 2004). The reasoning behind this male overemphasis is quite simplistic, but at times questionable to the West given the range of implications that derive from overemphasizing the strategic importance of the male. Ultimately, patriarchal societies are closely related to concepts of patrilineal descent as well as patrilineal inheritance and patrilocal residence. Perhaps most important to the patrilineal society is the notion that the male child will be able to carry on the family existence, in both name and socioeconomic or cultural position ("India's Disappearing Females," 2004, p. 8).

This is no less the case in most countries that have ethnic groups practicing female infanticide. The basis for this practice is almost always caught up in the need to carry on the family line and wealth. In countries where the female child is destined to take up residence with her husband's family (i.e., patrilocal residence or "marrying out"), the implication is that she is not as profitable and, indeed, is less honorable than the male child. The male is consequently held in higher favor, as he is able to acquire "wealth" for his family via the transfer of dowry, as well as to inherit from his father (i.e., patrilineal inheritance). The latter also allows for the maintenance of family status in systems that operate along a strict division of economic groupings (e.g., a caste system) (Girish, 2005, p. 11). Hrdy (1993) mentions an elite Indian clan that practiced this form of "status infanticide":

> Particularly in highly stratified societies, maintenance of social rank may require limiting the number of heirs. In one of the most extreme such cases, among various elite Rajput clans, such as the Jharejas in precolonial Northern India, almost all daughters born to the highest-ranking families were killed to avoid diverting family resources to provide for their dowries. A dearth of daughters at the top meant that wives had to be obtained from lower-status families, who competed among themselves to accumulate large dowries, or more nearly "groom prices," to marry their daughters into these elite "daughter-slaying" families. (p. 645)

The significance attached to the negatives associated with patrilocal residence and the fact that a female child will emerge to provide wealth for another family is evident in the following passage taken from an autobiographical account of the revolutionary China:

> Sun's wife was about twenty years old. She had been married to Sun when she was thirteen. She had given birth to three babies and now she was carrying her fourth, yet the couple had no children: All three babies had been girls. As soon as they were born, Sun had taken them away from his wife and left them in the brushwood on a mountainside. There they had died of hunger and cold, not knowing they had lived. Old ideas die hard. Girls were still considered "useless baggage." You raised them and just when they could be useful around the house they were married off and went to serve some other family. (Chen, 1980, p. 193)

The idea that the father will determine whether the female child is killed is reflective of the patriarchy of most societies that still incorporate the practice. Venkatramani (1986) summarizes this well when stating, "If a Kallar father doesn't force his wife to kill their second daughter, it usually means that the first daughter must have died a natural death" (p. 33). The key here is on the use of the word "force." It is most often the case that the male determines the fate of the female child irrespective of the wishes of his spouse (Lester, 1986, p. 59). This is imperative given the need to maintain the lineage or clan affiliation. It is also instructive to note the importance of birth order as second daughters in families suffer a mortality rate that is 53 percent higher than that of their older sisters (Croll, 2002, p. 27; Das Gupta, 1987).

In sum, the role of patriarchy and the influence of patrilineal society are immense among the ethnic groups that continue to practice female infanticide. Given the perception of this prevalence of male superiority, vis-à-vis females, in the aforementioned facets of society (e.g., inheritance), it would appear that female infanticide offers the patriarchy an efficient means by which to achieve its goals.

Perhaps just as important as patriarchy and patrilineal society is the role that economics plays in promoting female infanticide. Of primary importance here is the general concept of poverty and the specific concept of "dowry" (Croll, 2002, p. 29; Girish, 2005, p. 11). It is not surprising to find that most of the cultures that practice female infanticide are, economically, relatively impoverished. While it is difficult for most commoners in these societies to live in any other manner but hand to mouth, it is even more difficult when the customs of one's culture require that one spend inordinate amounts of income on celebrations that are related to the female child.[7]

These ceremonies vary in expense, are quite numerous, and are most often required for every daughter. Of course, the extent of the ceremonies also depends on the specific practice of the culture in question. Among many Indian cultures the various ceremonies include marriage, which is often very expensive, and the postmarriage invitation known as *maruveedu*. After these legitimizing ceremonies is a ceremony announcing the pregnancy—*valaikappu* and *marunthukkali*—and the subsequent birth of the girl child. After the required time passes, both the ear-boring and puberty ceremonies are held. Finally, the death ceremony culminates what is a pre-cradle-to-grave economic expense for the family of the female child (Muthulakshmi, 1997, p. 21).

Whereas bride wealth is a major economic consideration in female circumcision, many cultures that practice female infanticide incorporate "dowry" into their economic relations. Dowry is generally defined as the price that the bride's father is to pay the prospective husband and his kin group or family. Dowry is not an inexpensive ordeal and amounts to perhaps as much as 10–15 years of income

(Buchanan, 1994; Jones, 2002). For better or worse it is viewed as nothing more than an economic drain for the parents of the female child and an economic windfall for the bridegroom and his family. This "disproportionate loss" is spoken of by many who believe that "bringing up a girl is like watering the neighbour's plant" (Venkatachalam & Srinivasan, 1993, p. 31). Consequently, signs stating "Pay 500 rupees [now] and save 50,000 rupees later" reinforce the tendency for infanticide (Girish, 2005, p. 11).

Land ownership by the prospective bridegroom is also tied to size of the dowry. As greater ownership conveys a different status in society, an individual of "lesser" status would have a greater economic burden in securing a suitable dowry than a family of "greater" status (Venkatachalam & Srinivasan, 1993, p. 41).[8] Moreover, the following passage makes quite clear that the dowry is related to the perceived economic worth of the prospective groom:

> Even if you want to marry your daughter to a poor agricultural worker who does not even own a square inch of agricultural land and who has to lead a hand to mouth existence, you have to give Rs 2,000 cash to the bridegroom and make jewellery worth five sovereigns of gold for your daughter. If the potential bridegroom happens, by chance, to own some land, however meager the holding, the automatic demand is Rs 10,000 and 10 sovereigns of gold. If a Kallar family wants to celebrate a daughter's marriage in a fairly decent manner, the minimum cost will be something like Rs 30,000 to Rs 40,000, including all the cash and jewellery and marriage expenses. And if your would-be son-in-law has the high socio-economic status of an engineer, lawyer, doctor, or member of Parliament, you have to spend a lakh of rupees and in addition give a kilo of gold. (Venkatramani, 1986, p. 31)

Although made illegal in India, the practice of dowry continues to be a major economic factor that leads to female infanticide. In the middle to late 1990s, the dowry and overall wedding expenses incurred often surpassed 1 million rupees (i.e., US$35,000). This is quite prohibitive in a country where the average annual pay for a civil servant is around 100,000 rupees (i.e., US$3,500) (Chandra, 1996). The ability to offer a sufficient dowry is of the utmost importance. As Anderson and Moore (1993) state, "Her parents are considered caretakers whose main responsibility is to deliver a chaste daughter, along with a sizable dowry, to her husband's family." The inability to offer a sufficient dowry may well have many negative repercussions, including the possibility that the bride would not be allowed to remain with her husband (Venkatramani, 1986, p. 32). Moreover, the inability to provide the necessary dowry may result in a daughter being married to a person of a lower caste, a predicament that can cast only shame on the bride's father and family (Snehi, 2003, pp. 4302–4303). As the expenses of these ceremonies are compounded, the poverty becomes worse. In light of this knowledge, many families resort to female infanticide as a way to alleviate the economic burden that has accrued to the family by virtue of the female's birth. Consequently, female infanticide is especially considerable during periods of great economic "want" and poverty (Giladi, 1990, pp. 189–190; Mays, 1993, p. 887). Moreover, it is viewed as an effective way to avoid starvation (Williamson, 1978, p. 68) and to excuse oneself from the cost of milk in case the mother has died during childbirth. It is also seen as a way to avert the large drain of ceremonial wealth that the family of the female child knows is expected of it.

Beyond patriarchy and economics, female infanticide is committed for a variety of sociocultural considerations. Among the more popular of these concerns are those that arise from mythical beliefs and population pressures. The prevalence of myths in many cultures is consequential to the decision to hasten the death of the female newborn. The overwhelming power of myth is of critical importance to almost every existent culture and more so in cultures that incorporate this practice. In fact, the practice of committing female infanticide is most often caught up in the power that myth holds with regard to being rewarded later with a son. In essence, female infanticide often occurs because of an overwhelming mythical belief that killing a daughter now will generate a son in the *very next* birth (Anderson & Moore, 1993; Venkatramani, 1986, p. 30). As a consequence, many mothers would rather give their daughters up to the "god of death" than to have them live in an orphanage or a healthcare center (Buchanan, 1994).

The power of myth also provides comfort for many who practice female infanticide. Many, such as the Australian aborigines, believe that the death of a female child does not mean that the child has ceased to be. Rather, as Williamson (1978, p. 64) states, they believe that "the spirit of a dead infant goes to a store of spirit children to await birth, and thus the infant continues to live, although in a different form." This belief, it could be argued, is not only comforting to the parents but also arguably a more humane choice for the child. Rather than living a life characterized by cradle-to-grave discrimination and poverty, the child enters into a new surrounding in which it is perceived to be in a better condition.

Myth also surrounds the phenomenon of multiple-child births. The mythical belief here, however, does not deal directly with the ability of the mother to beget a son in her next pregnancy, but rather with the reasons for why the multiple-child birth occurred and why infanticide must be resorted to in this event. Many cultures believe that a multiple-child birth signifies that the mother had conceived via "intercourse with an evil spirit," or that she was not faithful to her husband, or that she resembled a litter-bearing animal. In any event, the multiple-child birth would be a basis for eliminating the female child (Williamson, 1978, p. 65).

Population pressures, although largely related to the economic status of a society, has also led to increased female infanticide. The effort to stabilize populations is not new to modern-day society (Birdsell, 1968, p. 229). Moreover, some medical doctors in contemporary India have made the argument that selective-sex abortion is a means of controlling the population growth of their country (Buchanan, 1994). The problem, as has been introduced earlier, however, is that prenatal sex selection involves more than an effort for population control: rather, it is a systematic effort to reduce the number of female fetuses.

The emphasis on population pressures also involves "birth spacing" concerns. In sum, birth spacing is essential in an impoverished culture where families simply cannot afford to raise one child after another. In cultures where the modern-day (Western?) birth control practices are less frequent, it would appear that infanticide is the next best way to promote birth spacing (Giladi, 1990, p. 191). Moreover, infanticide appeared to be a formidable force in family planning efforts.[9] The fact that the unlucky child that is not kept most often happens to be female is a matter of design in a highly patriarchal community.

In sum, there are several interrelated factors that contribute to the continuation of female infanticide in various cultures. It is imperative to note that while economic poverty may be the root cause of this phenomenon, the societal structure in which the poverty occurs only serves to exacerbate the practice. Residing in a highly patriarchal and patrilineal system only serves to elevate the importance of female infanticide in achieving the goals of the family with regard to dowry and general economic status. Moreover, the highly stratified nature of some societies (e.g., caste systems) in which the practice occurs also serves to place additional undue focus on the need to "regulate" the female child. It is to these ends that the phenomena of myths, population control, and spacing are utilized.

THE CLASH OF CULTURES

Infanticide is a practice present-day westerners regard as a cruel and inhuman custom, resorted to by only a few desperate and primitive people living in harsh environments. We tend to think of it as an exceptional practice, to be found only among such peoples as the Eskimos and Australian Aborigines, who are far removed in both culture and geographical distance from us and our civilized ancestors. The truth is quite different. Infanticide has been practiced on every continent and by people on every level of cultural complexity, from hunters and gatherers to high civilizations, including our own ancestors. Rather than being an exception, then, it has been the rule. (Williamson, 1978, p. 61)

The history of female infanticide reveals that it has been a practice commonplace not just to the "savage" beings of the non-Western world but also to those who are considered to have been among the most humane of populations. Throughout history, both modern and developing areas have incorporated this practice into their cultures. This is a fact, however, that the West is all too willing to forget. As a consequence, the West is often quick to dismiss the modern-day practices of other cultures as horrendous while quick to forget its own histories. As Hrdy (1993) states:

Moral issues raised by infanticide are complicated by ethnocentric values. For example, in many parts of the modern world, an impoverished mother faced with rearing a child she is unable to support would be punished for smothering her infant at birth . . . while infant handling practices that lead to death through starvation or "natural" causes are tolerated. . . . Populations of European descent who condemn the "savage" practice of eliminating an ill-timed infant at birth, often ignore their own recent histories of child abandonment. (p. 645)

This quick dismissal is due to advances in medical technologies. The main difference today is that technology has afforded those in the modern Western world, as well as those in the modern sectors of the developing world, to "sanitize" the practice of female infanticide by virtue of incorporating ultrasound scans, amniocentesis, and abortion rather than neonaticide, postneonaticide, and infanticide. This is confirmed by the finding that neonaticide is proportionally greater in rural areas as opposed to more modern sectors where technology to determine a fetus's gender is more readily available (Jason, Gilliland, & Tyler, 1983).

In reality, although it is difficult to obtain a full estimate of the numbers that it involves, feticide is a common practice throughout much of the world. Even areas that are approaching a "Western" conception of modernity, such as the Republics of Korea and Taiwan, suffer heavily from feticide (Weiss, 1996). The appearance of more civility in the destruction of the fetus is somehow perceived by many in the West to represent a more respectful and acceptable manner by which to commit female infanticide, albeit by another name. Moreover, there exists prima facie evidence for the argument that the rate of neonaticide in the United States was higher in the ten years prior to *Roe v. Wade* than in the ten years following the proabortion decision (Lester, 1992).

From a Western perspective, modernity involves, inter alia, a focus on economics. Almost by necessity, the perception that female infanticide is a "savage" practice is somehow rooted, in part, in the nature of one's economic position. Consequently, many in the West perceive the question of female infanticide to be related to the economic position of the culture in question. A wealthier culture, economically speaking, will not see the need to practice female infanticide. Notwithstanding the notion of "status infanticide," a relatively wealthier population will be able take advantage of the breakthroughs that technology provides those who can afford it or can choose to raise a female child secure in the knowledge that while it is an expensive endeavor, it is one that is affordable.

While many in the West may realize that female infanticide is related to one's economic position, this relationship does not "excuse" one from the duties of parenthood and the necessity of ensuring what are considered to be fundamental and universal human rights. This viewpoint is justified by the "doctrine of the sanctity of life," in which the West conceives of both the newborn and the adult as equally worthy of protection by society (Post, 1988, p. 14). The Western belief would then appear to be that economic status, in essence, cannot be used as a legitimizing force that serves to deprive female children of their basic human rights. Rather, economic status is most often attacked as a reason for why population control policies should be discussed and implemented. The problem with this logic, however, is that population control is a vital component of these cultures but, most of the time, only when it involves a second, third, or fourth female child.[10] Alternatively, the male child can only accentuate one's economic status and should not be included in any program of population control.

This is exactly where the "culturally constructed lens" of the West highlights the conflict with the cultural practice of female infanticide. While the notion of population control is admirable, especially given the populations of China and India, the structural bias toward females in an unsanitized manner, for what appear to the West to be purely economic reasons, is not. As a result of this viewpoint, the overall practice of female infanticide is abhorrent to the West even if it is functional in terms of population control and, to a lesser extent, is relieving some of the added economic stress that would otherwise be present for families with more than one daughter.

The implications that arise from this perspective are abundant. The most important of these, perhaps, is the lack of cultural understanding that non-Western cultures practicing female infanticide perceive Western countries to have. In essence, there is a feeling that the West, although probably somewhat cognizant of the role that poverty plays, does not fully appreciate the degree to which people are mired in poverty and the implications, both cultural and economic, that derive from this impoverished existence. For the practitioners of female infanticide, almost the entire cost-benefit calculation is one that is primarily based on one's economic condition (Weir, 1984, p. 17), with little emphasis placed on alternative factors.

The indictment against the West stems from this impoverished existence. If one does not realize the dire straits that people in the "belt region" of infanticide operate under and the choices that have to be made as a response to this condition of poverty, then one cannot fully realize—much less understand—that to commit female infanticide is not as much of a choice as it is a necessity. Moreover, it is the condition of poverty in which female infanticide flourishes. Muthulakshmi (1997) maintains that males symbolize money and that it is this money that allows one to avoid abject poverty. Communities practicing female infanticide know this, as 93.3 percent of respondents indicated agreement with the phrase "Male children bring money to the family" (pp. 53–55).

In light of the poverty consideration, a Western condemnation of the practice of female infanticide becomes as much an indication of the inability of the West to understand the economic plight of these people as it is a promotion of universal human rights. This lack of understanding only serves to underscore the belief that the West does not wish to cure the disease of poverty as much as it desires to treat the symptoms of that disease. It is to this topic (economic deprivation and the implications stemming from it) that we now turn.

Implications for Foreign Relations

As has been suggested, the issue of female infanticide is more complex than just stating that it is a fundamental human rights abuse committed by uncaring parents who do not understand that a female can be just as productive a member of society as her male counterpart. In fact the disease itself is caught up in an understanding of the depth of poverty that is commonplace throughout many of the countries that have cultures maintaining the practice. While this poverty is primarily economic, it is also important to look at the other forms that it takes. Table 3.4 provides data on the countries of the female infanticide "belt region" for such poverty-related concerns as the UNDP's HDI, GDI, ADLIT, and GDPPC.

The data in table 3.4 depict a situation of general deprivation (i.e., poverty) that has had a profound effect on literacy rates, wealth, the position of the country vis-à-vis other countries, and the position of women within their own country. The picture is increasingly bleak, depending on the region analyzed, when one compares these data with world "averages." The economic data reported in table 3.4 indicate that areas participating the most in female infanticide are also those that are, relatively, the most impoverished. All countries within the North African, sub-Saharan African, and south-central Asian regions fall below the world average for per capita gross domestic product ($7,804). This is also true for China and Mongolia even though the east Asian region exceeds the world average in GDPPC on average.[11] HDI values as well as adult literacy rates are routinely below world averages (0.729 for HDI; 82.6% for ADLIT). Finally, GDI figures are routinely lower than the world GDI average (0.693) and consistently lower than HDI values for every country, which indicates that the overall situation becomes increasingly bleak for all of these countries when one looks primarily at the human development of women specifically.

The obvious connection between the data in table 3.4 and the practice of female infanticide is that the more impoverished a country is, the more likely it is to practice female infanticide.[12] The four countries that account for over 85 percent of female infanticide—China, India, Bangladesh, and Pakistan—have an average GDPPC of only $558. Continuing the practice of female infanticide, however, is likely to promote a "catch 22" situation. Countries maintaining the practice need external financial support but are not likely to acquire much support because of their maintenance of the practice. As with the practice of female circumcision, many external entities do not wish to see their monies go to people who practice female infanticide.

Table 3.4 Selected Indicators of Female Infanticide, 2002

COUNTRY	HDI	HDIRANK	GDI	GDPPC	ADLIT
NORTHERN AFRICA	0.665		0.647	1,738	65.0
Algeria	0.704	108	0.688	1,785	68.9
Egypt	0.653	120	0.634	1,354	55.6
Libya	0.760*	72*	0.738*	3,512	81.7
Morocco	0.620	125	0.604	1,218	50.7
Sudan	0.505	139	0.485	412	59.9
Tunisia	0.745	92	0.734	2,149	73.2
Western Sahara	—	—	—	—	—
SUB-SAHARAN AFRICA	0.465		0.456	469	63.2
Comoros	0.530	136	0.510	437	56.2
Cote d'Ivoire	0.399	163	0.379	707	49.7
Guinea	0.425	160	—	415	41.0
Niger	0.292	176	0.278	190	17.1
Nigeria	0.466	151	0.458	328	66.8
WESTERN ASIA	0.758		0.746	7,723	81.9
Bahrain	0.843	40	0.832	11,007	88.5
Iraq	0.583*	126*	0.548*	3,197*	53.7
Jordan	0.750	90	0.734	1,799	90.9
Kuwait	0.838	44	0.827	15,193	82.9
Occupied Palestinian Territory	0.726	102	—	1,051	90.2
Oman	0.770	74	0.747	8,002	74.4
Qatar	0.819*	42*	0.807*	28,634	84.2
Saudi Arabia	0.768	77	0.739	8,612	77.9
Syria	0.710	106	0.689	1,224	82.9
Turkey	0.751	88	0.746	2,638	86.5
United Arab Emirates	0.810*	45*	0.793*	22,051	77.3
Yemen	0.482	149	0.436	537	49.0
SOUTH-CENTRAL ASIA	0.649		0.644	843	74.9
Afghanistan	—	—	—	—	—
Bangladesh	0.509	138	0.499	351	41.1
Bhutan	0.536	134	—	695	47.0
India	0.595	127	0.572	487	61.3
Iran	0.732	101	0.713	1,652	77.1
Nepal	0.504	140	0.484	230	44.0
Maldives	0.725*	89*	0.720*	2,182	97.2
Pakistan	0.497	142	0.471	408	41.5
Sri Lanka	0.740	96	0.738	873	92.1
EASTERN ASIA	.828		0.823	13,332	96.4
China	.745	94	0.741	989	90.9
Mongolia	.668	117	0.664	457	97.8
South Korea	.888	28	0.882	10,006	97.9

Source: UNDP (2004), Human Development Report, 2004: Cultural Liberty in Today's Diverse World, New York, UNDP.

Note: * denotes data for 1998 and "—" indicates missing data.

A written question addressed to the European Commission regarding the practice in Bihar and whether European Union funds were being used there indicates the concern that external financial sources have over the continuation of the practice ("Female Infanticide in the Bihar Region of India," 1996, p. 60).

Many countries have shown their resolve on this issue by making the practice of female infanticide—that is, all forms not including feticide—and related practices dealing with the use of certain technologies (e.g., ultrasound) illegal. The United Kingdom has been, perhaps, the most developed in this regard. The Stuart Bastardy Act of 1623 was a turning point in modern British history that served to recognize that the lack of any law in this general area was too permissive (Maier-Katkin & Ogle, 1997, p. 309). In more recent times the British Infanticide Act of 1938 has taken a middle road with regard to how the practice is viewed. While considered murder if undertaken after the child has reached 12 months of age, the crime is reduced to manslaughter due to an assumption of psychological impairment if committed in the first year (Maier-Katkin & Ogle, 1997, pp. 309–310). The recognition of a crime, but one of lesser severity than murder itself, is recognized generally throughout European countries.

The legal situation in the United States is considerably less developed than its European counterparts. Infanticide in the United States is considered to fall under the scope of homicide laws. That is to say that infanticide is considered murder, but not labeled infanticide. Moreover, legal enforcement of female infanticide is dependent on the state homicide statutes (Weir, 1984, p. 16). Some states, such as Pennsylvania, do recognize infanticide, and in at least one case has charged and convicted an obstetrician ("Doctor is Convicted," 1989, p. 118). In most cases, however, the legal situation regarding female infanticide is underdeveloped compared with European countries. This state of underdevelopment can be recognized in the 1994 case of Carolyn Beale, a British citizen who gave birth in New York City to what she believed to be a dead fetus, only to be charged with second-degree murder in New York rather than infanticide in the United Kingdom (Maier-Katkin & Ogle, 1997, pp. 305–306).

Although the legal situation is underdeveloped, the United States has repeatedly voiced concern over the countries where female infanticide is a normal, everyday occurrence. For example, on October 27, 1997, the U.S. Senate passed Concurrent Resolution 57 (1997) that expressed concerns that the body had over the state visit by

President Jiang Zemin of China. In its opening comments the resolution states:

> Whereas the Government of the People's Republic of China routinely, systematically, and massively engages in reprehensible, brutal, and coercive family planning practices, including forced abortion and forced sterilization, resulting in widespread infanticide, particularly of female infants . . . urges President Clinton . . . to demand that the People's Republic of China immediately . . . cease coercive population control practices, including forced abortion, forced sterilization, and infanticide. (Senate Concurrent Resolution 57, 1997)

This negative sentiment has been expressed in other proclamations as well, including the Chinese Human Rights Act of 1995 (House Resolution 1849, 1995), the Women's Human Rights Convention (House Resolution 38, 1993), and the "Years of the Child" proclamation of 1993 (House Joint Resolution 302, 1993). Moreover, the sentiment became exceptionally pronounced when a House bill required that the U.S. delegation to the Fourth World Conference on Women in Beijing should "oppose abortion and infanticide inflicted on account of the sex of the child" (House Resolution 2047, 1995).

Similarly to female circumcision, numerous conventions and treaties are designed to bring the countries that maintain the practice into compliance with the Western norm that female infanticide constitutes a human rights violation and should be abolished. As was mentioned in the discussion regarding female circumcision, the Fourth World Conference on Women weighed in heavily on female infanticide calling for countries to enact and enforce legislation that would abolish the practice (Fourth World Conference on Women, 1996, Art. 125, Sec. i).

The United Nations has also had its say in regard to female infanticide. In recommending that countries ratify the 1979 Convention on the Elimination of All Forms of Discrimination against Women, the General Assembly included "dowry-related violence" in its definition of violence against women (United Nations General Assembly, 1993).

Treaties are also used to illustrate the norms of the West, with regard to human rights, to those countries that are thought to be in violation and consequently held in contempt by the West. Among the more popular that have relevance to the topic of female infanticide are the 1948 Universal Declaration of Human Rights; the 1966 International Covenant on Economic, Social, and Cultural Rights; the 1966 International Covenant on Civil and Political Rights; the 1967 Declaration on the Elimination of Discrimination against Women; the 1975 Declaration on the Protection of All Persons from

Being Subjected to Torture and Other, Cruel Inhuman or Degrading Treatment or Punishment; the 1986 Declaration on the Right to Development; and the 1990 Convention on the Rights of the Child. Either implicitly or explicitly stated, all of the aforementioned are vital documents that serve to pressure governments into compliance with Western standards of human rights on such general topics as "violence" and on such specific topics as female infanticide.

POTENTIAL RESOLUTIONS

Any potential resolutions regarding the subject of female infanticide are tainted by whether or not one considers the practice to constitute a human rights abuse. Obviously, for those who focus on the concept of universal human rights, the only potential resolution revolves around the elimination of the practice. For those who believe in cultural relativism, however, elimination is not the goal. Rather, one might argue for the protection of current cultural practices, including female infanticide. While these extremes are clearly recognizable, there may well be some middle ground between them. Finding the middle ground, however, is inherently distasteful to both extremes of the issue.

Those who argue for the application of universal human rights mostly desire the elimination of female infanticide. Given that the practice is currently in existence, one might best label this as the revolutionary position. Although a variety of measures may be taken to achieve this goal, emphasis is most often placed on legislating the problem away and educating the local ethnic groups about the ills associated with female infanticide. The attempt to legislate the tradition away is not always a successful proposition. Although it is often done by governments to illustrate to the West that they are serious about eradicating female infanticide, it is evident that laws do not always bring target populations into compliance. This has been a considerable problem for many of the "belt region" countries currently practicing female infanticide.

Although feticide statistics are difficult to ascertain one can look at the policies of these countries with respect to abortion to determine their desire to terminate the practice of female infanticide. Among the "belt region" countries in table 3.4, only Tunisia, China, Mongolia, India, Bahrain, and Turkey permit abortion for "economic or social" reasons or because it was simply requested. Moreover, of the 193 countries for which data were ascertained, only one-third officially allowed abortion for either of these two reasons (UNDP, 1999).

The ability to simply legislate the cessation of female infanticide is not simple. While many countries have outlawed certain practices affiliated with female infanticide, the "loopholes" for circumvention remain many. Indian abortion law provides a great example of the potential for circumvention. Abortions were first legalized in India in 1971. Current Indian law maintains the legality of abortions through the twentieth week of pregnancy, but does not allow abortions for economic or social reasons or because it has simply been requested. By the mid-1980s, however, ultrasound technology was widely available (Weiss, 1996) and could be utilized to detect the gender of the fetus at 16 weeks (Venkatram, 1995).

Building on the recognition that ultrasound and amniocentesis now "complicated" the issue, the Indian Parliament passed legislation in August 1994 that expressly banned the abortion of healthy fetuses that amniocentesis or sonograms (i.e., ultrasounds) determined to be female. The legislation became law on January 1, 1996, after all Indian states passed the legislation by late, 1995 (Oomman & Ganatra, 2002). Many regarded this new law as a step in the right direction (Hughes, 1996) although it was, for the most part, not enforced (Sharma, 2003, p. 1553). While this law appears to be positive in the bid to lessen female infanticide, it is easily circumvented by the doctor "by merely stating the health and position of the fetus in the report, if they give one, while the baby's sex is conveyed verbally to the relatives" (Venkatram, 1995, p. 16).

Simply including "the verbal communication of the gender" in the law is also not an effective mechanism to deter feticide. For instance, China has gone "a step further" than the new law in India and made it illegal for doctors to inform parents of the sex of their child. The result has often been another circumvention of the law, but by other means. Kristof (1991b, p. C12) states that even official Chinese reports indicate that doctors do inform parents as to the gender of the fetus, but that it takes considerably more money now for the doctor to give in to the bribe.

What is quite obvious here is that one will not be able to simply legislate away what is perceived by the West to be a human rights abuse. Numerous accounts give support for this opinion. Venkatachalam and Srinivasan (1993, p. 49) indicate that while people know that the practice of "scanning and abortion" is illegal in Tamil Nadu, they will continue to do so anyway. The same can be said of the 1961 law in India prohibiting the practice of dowry. The fact is that dowry is an important economic aspect of many cultures that has an adverse effect on the female child in areas where it is practiced. The law, however, does not serve to effectively inhibit the practice. As Venkatramani (1986) declares, even families who have been "victimized" by the dowry system are unlikely to join campaigns to disallow the practice (pp. 30–31). In sum, the attempt to make illegal practices that are seen as necessary to the survival of the culture are at best ill-fated from the start. Williamson (1978) sums it up best when she states that no matter how hard the West tries to eradicate it, if those who are practicing female infanticide do not wish to eradicate it, it will not happen (p. 72).

As an alternative to criminalizing the practice of female infanticide, many adherents of elimination advocate educational programs that, over time, are said to have a positive effect on eradicating the practice. This is the approach that notable institutions such as the World Bank and UNICEF take. What is important to note about these programs, however, is that they do not target the practice of female infanticide *per se*. Rather the emphasis is on factors (e.g., literacy, health, and generalized poverty) that only serve to give rise to the practice of female infanticide. In essence, these are programs, albeit on a relatively small-scale, that attempt to strike at the root of the problem (i.e., the disease itself) rather than at the symptoms emanating from it.

The 2004 World Bank country brief for India indicates that the World Bank is not only cognizant of the supposed "causes" of female infanticide, but seeks to address the root causes in an instructive, but yet limited manner. The World Bank addresses the aforementioned factors giving rise to female infanticide when it states:

> While some gender indicators have improved, such as the declining gender gap in school enrollment and female life expectancy now exceeding that for men, the overall picture remains one of stark inequality. Bias against women and girls is reflected in the demographic ratio of 927 females per 1,000 males. Many of India's women are malnourished with anemia, which is present in 60 percent of the female population. (World Bank, 2004)

The problematic part of these programs is that large-scale elimination of poverty is not going to be accomplished without a large-scale economic program to facilitate greater change with respect to literacy, health, and poverty, in a lesser amount of time.

Conversely, some programs have had some success in producing declining cases. The Cradle Baby Centre in Dharmapuri, Tamil Nadu, government hospital has seen a decrease in abandoned babies from 207 in 2003 to 133 in 2004. Since 2002, the centre has received 498 babies, 94.9 percent of which have been female (Prasad, 2004).

Other studies, however, suggest that the numbers throughout Tamil Nadu have become worse (Ilangovan, 2005).

On the other end of the continuum are the cultural relativists who maintain that while the practice of female infanticide is a nauseating occurrence, it is still a "functional" part of a culture that is trying to deal effectively with the more timely concerns aforementioned (poverty, etc.). Seen in this light, the practice of female infanticide is a key component of the cultural milieu, a practice that has acquired a certain cultural acceptance with respect to how one deals with impoverishment. As a logical consequence of this relationship, one cannot simply eliminate the practice of female infanticide as it is inextricably entwined with poverty.[13] To do otherwise would be a grave infringement of a cultural practice that is found to be acceptable as well as practical in dealing with impoverishment.

An intrusion into the structured order, of which the practice of female infanticide is a part, is often seen as an invasion of one's sovereignty by the West. With respect to female infanticide, China certainly is supportive of the position taken by cultural relativists. As Hom (1992) states:

> The Chinese position, as reflected in official statements and in the legal discourse, views any effort to criticize its human rights practices as an interference with Chinese sovereignty and domestic affairs . . . it maintains that a "human rights system must be ratified and protected by each sovereign state through its domestic legislation." (p. 282)

In sum, one side of the argument believes that female infanticide is a human rights violation and is worthy of the effort to eliminate it. Consequently, both the governments of the "belt region" countries as well as the West need to comprise policies to this end. This is regardless of what is perhaps an unintended disruptive impact that such policies will undoubtedly have on the local culture. The other extreme posits that the real issue is that while these unintended "disruptions" may allow for a reduction in the rate of female infanticide, the entire process will cause irreparable harm to the culture. Moreover, it is readily apparent to cultural relativists that it is predominantly the West that is promoting this cultural change in the name of universal human rights. What is to be done?

The following prescriptions take into account the fact that female infanticide is not unrelated to pressing socio-economic concerns within a culture, but stems directly from them. Moreover, they are based on the understanding that no matter what the incentive, there is no short-term "cure" to what the West finds so distasteful.

Consequently, while any plan for change will undoubtedly incorporate short-term necessities, they are only in the service of the long-term goal. Finally, the continuation of female infanticide is not to be viewed as a necessarily bad thing in the short-term. Moreover, long-term cultural change that incorporates effective change with respect to poverty, health, and educational concerns is also not to be viewed as solely negative (i.e., an act of Western cultural imperialism).

Given the aforementioned concerns, the following is recommended. First, governments of countries in the "belt region" should take action not to make female infanticide illegal in the short-term. This action (or inaction in countries that do not currently have a specific law dealing with female infanticide) should be coupled with an educational campaign that provides information that is primarily concerned with the role of poverty, illiteracy, and dowry in society. The emphasis for change here should not involve a judgment as to the morality of cultures that practice female infanticide, but rather should be presented in terms of the unintended consequences that poverty has for illiterate populations that may or may not also practice dowry. The third part of the program involves a greater infusion of development capital (defined here as both economic and social development—that is, money for literacy campaigns that target females), by the West, that targets the more impoverished areas of the "belt region" as this is primarily where the bulk of female infanticide appears to occur.

If the goal of the West[14] is to reduce or eliminate the practice of female infanticide, then the first step is in the identification of just what areas need to be targeted. To make this practice illegal in the "belt region" will only serve to drive the practice "underground." In the event that the latter occurs, it will only have more damaging implications for maternal mortality in a region that already suffers disproportionately in this realm. Moreover, those who wish to eradicate the practice will be less able to identify where it is occurring with greater frequency and hence less able to implement programs for change. Pushing the practice underground has also had a profound impact on the cost:

> Oddly, legal interference has had a negative affect on the situation, leading an otherwise lawful practice in hygienic clinics to slip underground. When determination techniques were banned, health care workers—who now could face prosecution—raised the price for these sex determination tests dramatically. Procedures are now offered without written evidence so as to escape legal action. . . . "They don't

keep documentary evidence. They have heightened charges ten times. Earlier those who were charging, say, RS700, now are charging RS7,000." (Rajan, 1996)

Any educational campaign must target the younger ages, those who have a "positive approach to education" (Muthulakshmi, 1997, p. 38). Targeting the older populations will be, for the most part, money spent on deaf ears as it is the older population that is most resistant to change. The educational campaign must focus on increasing female enrollments, heightening literacy for females (and males), and providing opportunities for vocational learning. The separation of education from literacy might at first seem odd. The reality is, however, that much of the Indian population believes that literacy does not necessarily flow from education and that the latter is not necessarily a good thing for girls as opposed to boys (Muthulakshmi, 1997, pp. 43–52).

The infusion of education must also deal with the system of dowry that is still pervasive throughout a large part of India. Although many make the claim that dowry is a traditional practice not easily erased, not even by the existing legal prohibition, it is in reality a practice that is based more on economics than on tradition. It is essential that it be presented in this manner and that the relationship between impoverishment and heightened concern for male children be understood in terms that the former, outside of lineage concerns, is often accountable for the latter. Moreover, the drive toward elimination has been suggested by Indian women who also suggest that improving the vocational abilities of women may actually result in lessening the required dowry (Venkatachalam & Srinivasan, 1993, pp. 42–43).

A greater infusion of development capital, by the West, that targets the more impoverished areas of the "belt region," is a necessary complement to the emphasis on education and literacy. As aforementioned, development capital is used here to refer to capital that would "underwrite" both economic and social strategies to be implemented. Studies have shown that increases in household income are associated with a greater survival probability for females relative to males (Rose, 1999; Secondi, 2002). Several international institutions have taken responsibility for various aspects of the female infanticide issue. For example, UNICEF has continually worked to ensure that females are educated in locales that did not previously place great emphasis on female education. To this end UNICEF dollars have built schools closer to the homes of females, incorporated flexible class schedules, increased the numbers of female instructors, and provided childcare facilities

(UNICEF, 2004, pp. 1–6). Moreover, the UNDP has established a "Trust Fund in Support of Actions to Eliminate Violence against Women," although it has not secured a good deal of funding from donor countries (United Nations Development Fund for Women, 1998).

The World Bank has also funded India and other "belt region" countries. While these monies have been appreciated, they total a sum that is quite insufficient with the needs of local impoverished communities. While it is true that India has been the largest borrower of bank funds (over $59 billion cumulative through June 2003), it is also true that India remains one of the most impoverished countries of the world (along with many countries of the "belt region"). Currently, there is roughly $13 billion in "active" programs. One such program, which began in 1997 and is slated to end on June 30, 2005, is the Rural Women's Development and Empowerment Project. This was the first time that the World Bank instituted a "free-standing" women's development project in India ($19.5 million of the $53.5 million project cost was funded by the bank) that is designed to empower women in acquiring technical skills and so forth (World Bank, 2005).

These programs, and others similar to them, need to increase the level of funding that is currently maintained and target the three aforementioned vital areas. It is possible that this increased funding could be coupled with new relationships between these external funding sources and established internal entities that are already, albeit on a significantly smaller scale, working to empower females via greater literacy, education, and wealth. Among the possible partners, within India, are the Indian Council for Child Welfare, Tamil Nadu, ADITHI, *Sri Ramakrishna Tapovanam,* and government programs such as STOP (support to atrocities prevention) and STEP (support to employment promotion).

While they must be fitted to particular circumstances and may not even succeed, this is a three-prong attack that will not meet with the unconditional agreement of either the cultural relativists or those who are in support of the uniform application of universal human rights. The latter will certainly find the short-term removal of illegal barriers to the practice distasteful while the former will certainly recognize that what is being proffered certainly has a large degree of cultural change involved.

4

THE CASE OF PROSTITUTED
FEMALE CHILDREN

For millions of children prostitution remains a reality, a shadow side of
our culture. Cultures exist around the globe where children, like belong-
ings, are property to be bought and sold. When this is so, tens of millions
of children are reasonably and repeatedly raped, tortured and shamed
for the sexual gratification of adults. While in fact child prostitution may
be a shadow of humanity, the term "shadow," like other metaphors, can
disembody the suffering from the recipient. It allows a distancing and
spiritualization of the pain. It is but another in a long list of metaphors,
myths and justifications which continue to be advanced while serving to
keep this horror in place.

Joseph (1995, p. 7)

HISTORY OF THE PRACTICE

The prostituting of female children[1] has taken place in numerous cultures around the world. Although historically the practice
has included both male and female children, the emphasis here is
primarily on the prostituted female child.[2] Throughout its history
the practice of prostituting female children has encompassed a wide
geographical spread, consuming more countries than the practices of
both female circumcision and female infanticide together. The World
Congress against the Commercial Sexual Exploitation of Children
(WCACSEC, 1998a) maintains that although data are scarce the
overwhelming evidence suggests that "children are commercially
sexually exploited in every country of the world." In brief, the practice
has occurred on virtually every continent at some point in history and
for more numerous reasons than the number of countries in which it
continues today.

Considered to be the "oldest profession," prostitution in general
has enjoyed a lengthy history. Perhaps not too surprising, recorded
history provides evidence for the existence of prostitution among the

ancient Babylonian Empire, located over much of modern-day Iraq (the Babylonian capital of Babylonia was located approximately 40 miles south of Baghdad). The Babylonians were notorious for their pleasure-seeking ways and wholesale lust. Traditionally, Babylonian women were expected to prostitute themselves at least once in a temple before marriage. This "offering" of virginity was associated with an appreciation for fertility and was made to the fertility goddess, the great Mother Goddess. This form of "sacred prostitution," as it came to be known, was legitimized by King Hammurabi in the code named for him (McGuire, 1967, p. 881).

Sacred prostitution also manifested itself in the worship of various gods among the ancient people of Egypt, Syria, Phoenicia, Arabia, and Canaan. The traditional use of *hierodouloi* (i.e., temple prostitutes) was in the service of religious expression. In many of these cultures, temple prostitution entailed the prostitute offering her body to those who wished to become more "intimate" with the deity. Moreover, the payment for the "services rendered" was in reality an offering to the deity and not to be construed as remuneration for the prostitute or an offering to the temple per se. With respect to Babylonia the patrons were paying homage to Mylitta, otherwise known as the Goddess of Love (i.e., the Babylonian equivalent of the Roman Venus). At this juncture it is, perhaps, important to note that the majority of *hierodouloi* were female, although male practitioners are reported to have existed among the Canaanites (May, 1937, p. 553).

These practices, from at least the eighteenth century B.C., continued unabated for the most part and were further documented by the fifth-century Greek historian Herodotus. While obviously not lacking in intensity, the practice of temple prostitution was said to have taken on a distinct character from earlier centuries. In most cases, however, the emphasis in society still remained on prostituting the young female. As Sanger (1972) states.

> It was not considered wholly shameful for an Egyptian to make his living by the hire of his daughter's person, and a king is mentioned who resorted to this plan in order to discover a thief. Such was the astonishing appetite of the men, that young and beautiful women were never delivered to the embalmer until they had been dead some days, a miserable wretch having been detected in the act of defiling a recently-deceased virgin!
>
> In Chaldæa, too, religion at first connived at, and then commanded prostitution. . . . Once inside the place, no woman could leave it until she had paid her debt, and had deposited on the altar of the goddess the fee received from her lover. Some, who were plain, remained there

as long as three years; but, as the grounds were always filled with a troop of voluptuaries in search of pleasure, the young, the beautiful, the high-born seldom needed to remain over a few minutes. (p. 41)

While this pattern of prostituting young females was repeated in other cultures as well, several changes in the traditional practice transpired in these localities. For example, over time the Phoenicians began using the temple prostitutes for guests of the country. Moreover, with time the practice of the prostitute relinquishing the monies to the temple goddess also came to a halt (Sanger, 1972, p. 42).

Concurrent with much of this period of lust and pleasure seeking was the biblical condemnation of the practice of harlotry (i.e., prostitution). The practice is noted fairly early in the Bible as Judah, unbeknownst to him, slept with his daughter-in-law Tamar while on his way to Timnath (Genesis 38:1–30, King James Version). Moreover, the Lord spoke unto Moses instructing him, "Do not prostitute thy daughter, to cause her to be a whore; lest the land fall to whoredom, and the land become full of wickedness" (Leviticus 19:29). The sentiment throughout many of the pronouncements is one of negativity—that one should take care so as not to allow one's daughter to become a harlot. At least one writer, however, interprets the payment to the father of a "rape victim" during this time as tantamount to prostitution, whereby the father could keep his daughter and "hire" her out once more (Rush, 1980).

The lust for nubile children was no less present in ancient Greece than it was in ancient Babylonia. Greek society structured itself along very functional lines with respect to the role of women and female children in society. Sanger (1972, p. 46) identifies at least four classes of women prostitutes. The highest of classes, the *hetairæ,* were kept in lavish surroundings (Geis, 1993, p. 669). Their function was to provide the sexual intimacy that was not typically part of the relationship between a Greek man and his wife. In essence, these "companions" gave sexual favors while being kept in free union with their men (May, 1937, pp. 553–554). The following passage illuminates the exalted status of the *hetairæ:*

> They alone of their sex saw the plays of Alexander and Aristophanes; they alone had the *entrée* of the studio of Phidias and Apelles; they alone heard Socrates reason, and discussed politics with Pericles; they alone shared in the intellectual movement of Greece. No women but *hetairæ* drove through the streets with uncovered face and gorgeous apparel. None but they mingled in the assemblages of great men at the Pnyx or the Stoa. None but they could gather round them of an evening the

choicest spirits of the day, and elicit, in the freedom of unrestrained intercourse, wit and wisdom, flashing fancy and burning eloquence. What wonder that the *hetairæ* should have filled so prominent a part in Greek society! And how small a compensation to virtuous women to know that their rivals could not stand by the altar when sacrifice was offered; could not give birth to a citizen! (Sanger, 1972, pp. 54–55)

With regard to status, the *auletrides* (i.e., flute-playing dancers) were perhaps second only to the *hetairæ*. Like the *hetairæ*, the *auletrides* provided a key service to the men of Greek society. While the talents of these women were primarily reserved for the after-dinner enjoyment of the men, the manner in which they performed was, in contemporary terms, sexually immoral. Moreover, large sums of money were often exchanged for these lascivious performances (Sanger, 1972, p. 51). Finally, the Greeks often imported Asian slaves who were considered to be significantly more beautiful than Greek women. Sanger (1972) concisely portrays the sexuality of these performances when he recounts the visit of an Arcadian delegation to King Antigonus:

After the hunger of the venerable guests was appeased, Phrygian flute-players were introduced. They were draped in semi-transparent veils, arranged with much coquetry. At the given signal they began to play and dance, balancing themselves alternately on each foot, and gradually increasing the rapidity of their movements. As the performance went on, the dancers uncovered their heads, then their busts; lastly they threw the veils aside altogether, and stood before the wondering ambassadors with only a short tunic around the loins. In this state they danced so indecently that the aged Arcadians, excited beyond control, forgot where they were, and rushed upon them. The king laughed; the courtiers were shocked at such ill-breeding, but the dancers discharged the sacred duty of hospitality. (pp. 50–51)

The *dicteriades* were a third group of prostituted women in Greek society that were lower in status than either of the aforementioned groups. Named after the *dicteria* in which they worked, the *dicteriades* were little more than common prostitutes who were regulated by the local authorities. In brief, the dicteria were nothing more than state-sanctioned houses of ill repute that operated in close proximity to the ports of the city so that passersby to and from the city would readily fall prey to the assertive *dicteriades*. Moreover, it was expected that these passersby would indeed opt to enter the dicteria and be served

by so-called public servants. Sanger (1972) makes clear this relationship sanctioned by the state:

> Solon, while softening the rigors of the Draconian code, by law formally
> established houses of prostitution at Athens, and filled them with female
> slaves. They were called *Dicteria,* and the female tenants *Dicteriades.*
> Bought with the public money, and bound by law to satisfy the demands
> of all who visited them, they were in fact public servants, and their
> wretched gains were a legitimate source of revenue to the state. Prosti-
> tution became a state monopoly, and so profitable that, even in Solon's
> lifetime, a superb temple, dedicated to Venus the courtesan, was built
> out of the fund accruing from this source. (pp. 43–44)

The *concubines* were the final class of prostituted women in Greek
society. The *concubines* differed dramatically from the *hetairæ* in one
key respect. While the latter were freely born "companions," the former were more often than not slaves and prisoners of war (May, 1937,
p. 553). During the best of times, Greek society viewed *concubines* as
the lowest form of prostituted women, whose only duty was to ensure
the daily pleasure of their masters.

The role of prostitution during the pre-Christian Roman age is well
established. Although the Romans sought to elevate the perceived
status of its culture, vis-à-vis the Greeks, it is obvious that the role
of prostitutes *(meretrices)* was just as great, but perhaps less public,
in its orientation. This lower profile was perhaps the direct result of
the lessening of sacred prostitution in Roman society combined with
the increased use of female slaves (May, 1937, p. 554). As Murtagh
(1967) states, however, the Romans were in reality just as indulgent
of prostitution as were the Greeks:

> While the Greeks had few principles of sexual morality but a well-
> preserved sense of public decency, the Romans held much more
> exalted personal and family ideas but came to exhibit a general moral
> depravity of which prostitution was only one form. In this development
> prostitution remained shameful per se, for both parties. (p. 879)

The Romans, like the Greeks, had several classes of prostitutes,
some of which were legally recorded for any future reference regarding either moral or blood purity. Many unrecorded (i.e., unregistered)
classes resembled those in Greek society. For example, the Roman
delicatæ closely resembled the Greek *hetairæ,* in that they, too, were
close companions of Roman men. The Greek *auletrides* found their

counterpart in the Roman flute players, who were said to be more abundant in Rome than in Athens (Sanger, 1972, p. 69). Moreover, the Greek *dicteria* were very similar to the Roman *lupanaria*, where a bawd (i.e., madam) would oversee the rooms that would often be occupied by slave prostitutes or local females. The bawd would either oversee the women and the prices that they could command or simply rent the rooms to the prostitutes who would then serve as independent contractors. The former arrangement, conveys Sanger (1972), foretold the price structure that is so prevalent for child prostitution in today's society and the importance of obtaining a virgin:

> "He who deflours [*sic*] Tarsia shall pay half a pound, afterward she shall be at the public service for a gold piece." The half pound has been assumed by commentators to mean half a Roman pound of silver, and to have been worth $30.00; the gold piece, according to the best computation, was equivalent to $4.00 (p. 76)

> When a bawd had purchased a virgin as a slave, or when, as sometimes happened under the later emperors, a virgin was handed to him to be prostituted as a punishment for a crime, the door of his house was adorned with twigs of laurel; a lamp of unusual size was hung out at night, and a tablet exhibited somewhat similar to the one quoted above, stating that a virgin had been received, and enumerating her charms with cruel grossness. When a purchaser had been found and a bargain struck, the unfortunate girl, often a mere child, was surrendered to his brutality, and the wretch issued from the cell afterward, to be himself crowned with laurel by the slaves of the establishment. (p. 77)

During the Christian era the Romans tried to infuse into society a modicum of change with regard to the practice of prostitution. These attempts, though meager, were in part a consequence of a new attitude toward the prostitute as well as the procurers of prostitutes. Both the Greeks and the Romans had viewed prostitution as, perhaps, an added societal attraction that, while sometimes construed as hurtful to society, might have actually played a positive role. This viewpoint was illustrated perfectly by the Roman satirist Juvenal in his satirical exhortation to the youth about to enter a house of prostitution that he was doing well and that his visit would undoubtedly spare both maidens and matrons alike. While the prostitutes were to be differentiated from more honorable women in society, they were, in effect, providing a valuable service to society.

Christianity also tried but was unable to bring about significant changes with regard to prostitution. Whereas the Greeks had allowed prostitution to flourish for the good of the overall community, Christianity tried to be more forgiving of the prostitute and less forgiving of the procurers of prostitution. Attempts at reform were numerous, as rescue missions emerged to guide the victimized prostitutes to a more virtuous life. While these attempts were honorable, and to a certain degree encouraging for change, they were in large part a micromanagement attempt to control the problem at hand. Moreover, as Murtagh (1967) submits, "prostitution was tolerated as a necessary evil throughout the middle ages" (p. 879).

The continued tolerance of the practice throughout the Christian era of the Roman Empire (i.e., through A.D. 395) was fueled by the wishes of society. Sanger (1972, p. 81) states that when Augustus (emperor from 27 B.C. to A.D. 14) destroyed the temple of Mutinus,[3] the people built other temples to replace it and presumably its function. Moreover, the laws of Julian (emperor from A.D. 361 to 363) were designed to further disparage the status of prostitutes in society. Stringent restrictions, such as the inability to marry men who had preserved Roman blood, were laid upon prostitutes and their descendants.

Strange as it may seem, the continued toleration of prostitution during this juncture was also in part due to voices in early Christian literature. The acclaimed bishop of Hippo and African thinker St. Augustine professed that while prostitution was not characteristic of "good love," its presence in society might be a necessary evil. If one is to assume that lust will continue to be part of the human nature, as St. Augustine apparently did, then it is possible to maintain that prostitution might be a lesser criminal activity and outlet than more serious crimes, such as rape, that would in all likelihood occur but for the presence of prostitution (Geis, 1993, p. 669). In finishing a work that St. Thomas Aquinas had not completed at his death, Ptolemy of Lucca quotes St. Augustine: "A whore acts in the world as the bilge in a ship or the sewer in a palace: Remove the sewer, and you will fill the palace with a stench. Take away whores from the world, and you will fill it with sodomy" (Ptolemy of Lucca, 1997, p. 286). This sentiment prevailed among many Christian theologians and philosophers during the Middle Ages.

Another factor prevalent during the Middle Ages that served to perpetuate the practice of prostituting females was economics. From the time of temple prostitution onward, economics has been of prime importance in understanding the degree to which prostitution flourished. At its heart, the prostituting of females has always served two masters: lust and greed. Indeed, both of these factors are necessary conditions for the practice to persist. The fact that economic remuneration was involved made it even more difficult for both spiritual and temporal leaders to dissuade members of society from partaking in this vice. Moreover, spiritual leaders of the day who were chastising those involved were, in reality, speaking out of both sides of their mouths. The stark reality was that the church continued to profit heavily throughout the Middle Ages from this practice.

Given the two-sided nature of the church during this period, it is easy to understand how the so-called reform movements fell upon deaf ears. As some cities began to originate brothels for revenue, the trend to oppose most reform movements became even more steadfast. Governments benefited greatly from these brothels as profits amassed, and they were also able to tax the females working as prostitutes. In brief, prostitution continued to exist during this time because of the economic exploitation by government officials that occurred concurrently with the sexual exploitation of female innocence. Reform movements that did occur during the period concentrated on removing the incentives to prostituting females (i.e., removing the tax on both brothels and prostitutes) and finding an appropriate manner by which to spiritually enfranchise these exploited members of society. These movements, however, were often initiated not so much for the good of the female prostitutes as for the increased economic benefit of another segment of society. As May (1937) states:

> In the Germanic cities, as in some of the French provincial towns, brothels constituted a sort of public service and even figured in the hospitality tendered to important guests. Brothels under municipal protection were found in the thirteenth century in Augsburg, Vienna and Hamburg. The occasional "reform movements" in the Middle Ages were limited in time and place and rested not upon social policy or sustained attitude but upon local feuds and jealousies over the profits accruing from prostitution. (p. 554)

In summary, the Middle Ages can be largely characterized as a period during which the prostituting of females continued for the most part unabated because of the less than adamant voice of the church. Even in situations where the church was instrumental in bringing about a few positive changes, the changes can best be characterized as sporadic, vacuous, and indecisive. It would appear that the need to profit, protect public order, and protect the integrity of the family was the underlying consideration that led to the continuation of female prostitution during the period (May, 1937, pp. 554–555).

The attitude toward prostitution did not change significantly until the fear of sexually transmitted diseases became more prevalent throughout the European continent at the close of the fifteenth, and throughout the sixteenth, century. The impact of disease, in terms of the number of people gravely affected, began to convince some of the need to reassess their stance toward the prostituting of women and young girls. May (1937, p. 555) reports that during the first decade of its virulent existence, approximately one-third of the European population died from the effects of syphilis.

Armed with the knowledge of the harmful effects of disease, the church began to profess greater support for a higher morality with regard to prostitution. The sixteenth-century Protestant Reformation and the Counterreformation within the Catholic Church appeared committed to overcome the vices accepted by the church during the Middle Ages in favor of policies that would now "protect" society from the scourge of death via female prostitution. Throughout this period there were callings for the closing of brothels all over Europe. When moral argument was insufficient to bring about change, many cities resorted to issuing decrees to ban brothels. This was indeed the case in England, where separate laws and decrees were issued to close brothels in Ulm (1531), Basel (1534), and London (1546). Moreover, Paris and Nuremberg followed suit in 1560 and 1562, respectively (May, 1937, p. 555).

Although there were forceful attempts to limit the ill effects of lust and greed, most of the laws and decrees did not produce sufficient results as syphilis and other sexually transmitted diseases continued to persist throughout the Reformation. Consequently, countries began taking aim at treating the symptoms rather than attacking the roots of the disease. Paris, along with other major European cities, now began to register and periodically provide medical examinations in order to curb the growth of disease. The net outcome of this plan was that many prostitutes who were "unregistered" (i.e., not readily identifiable) surfaced and were treated when medically necessary. In sum, at this point in time sanitary control was of heightened importance while attempts at suppression of the profession were curtailed for lack of success. The success of programs such as these, however, was certainly suspect:

> In 1864, however, Great Britain enacted the Contagious Diseases Prevention Act, which provided among other things for the compulsory medical examination of prostitutes in certain military and naval districts in order that the presence of venereal disease might be detected. At first considered an ordinary measure for the well being of the armed forces,

the real significance of this regulation was not realized until 1869, when an amendment provided for the more frequent examination of prostitutes and extended the system to London. Had the act applied to both sexes and had it been a community wide attempt to fight disease, some degree of success might have followed. (May, 1937, p. 555)

The prostituting of female children in the modern age is considerably wider in scope than the aforementioned historical overview would suggest. In the contemporary world it is uncontroversial to state that the prostituting of females in general is happening in a majority of nations. Moreover, this practice is concentrated in Asia as well as in Central and South America (Muntarbhorn, 1997, p. 9). More controversial is the degree to which countries are questionable in allowing female children to be prostituted. Although sometimes hidden, the practice is currently present in numerous geographical settings encompassing most every continent. To the alarm of many in the West, the practice of prostituting female children continues today, both in public and in secrecy, and does not appear to be lessening in frequency.

Research investigating the frequency of prostituted female children is controversial in its reporting of numbers for several reasons. The first problem relates to the nature of estimates. Almost all of the research incorporates estimates regarding the total number of female children that are affected. As is the nature of estimates, however, there is considerable disagreement on which estimations constitute a more accurate reflection of the reality. What is a given, however, is that these estimations can only be characterized as extremely "soft" because of several constraints involved in gathering information on this phenomenon. Inter alia, the illegal and covert nature of this activity constrains the ability to produce a more valid estimate (Nyland, 1995, p. 547; WCACSEC, 1998a). Regardless of these concerns, however, even the most conservative estimates clearly illuminate the extent to which this practice occurs (Hodgson, 1994, p. 513). Perhaps Hornblower (1993) sums up this situation best by stating that "such figures are at best guesses and at worst only the tip of the iceberg" (p. 46).

A second problem relates to the distinction made with regard to gender. It is a given that both male and female children are dramatically affected by this age-old phenomenon (Joseph, 1995, p. 9). What is of some controversy, however, is arriving at a suitable ratio that more so reflects the extent to which females are disproportionately affected by this practice. This is further complicated by the fact that this ratio is itself variable, depending on the country brought into question. For example, Burrhus-Clay (1998) maintains that prostituted male children are more common in Sri Lanka and throughout North Africa. Moreover, Muntarbhorn (1997, p. 9) maintains that there has been an increase in the number of prostituted male children of late. Of considerable importance, however, is the notion that prostituted children are predominantly female in almost every country where children are prostituted (Levine, 1993, p. 481; WCACSEC, 1998a). This is especially true in countries like Thailand where the percentage of prostituted male children is virtually negligible.

Given these considerations, one can now move toward delineating the extent of the numbers. Both O'Grady (1992, p. 137) and the WCACSEC (1998a) suggest that 1,000,000 children enter the sex market yearly. Moreover, a Norwegian government report to the United Nations Working Group on Slavery also suggested that 1,000,000 children are lured, sold, or forced into prostitution yearly (Baker, 1995, p. 11). UNICEF concurs that 1,000,000 is the approximate yearly number (UNICEF, 2005c). The total number of prostituted female children worldwide is estimated, according to the United Nation's Human Rights Commission (UNHRC), to be in the neighborhood of 10,000,000 (Burrhus-Clay, 1998). Hornblower (1993), moreover, contends that 30,000,000 women have been sold into prostitution in the world since the mid-1970s. One can see from these numbers that a conservative assumption that prostituted children affect gender equally would result in a grave number of female children being prostituted on a regular basis. An assumption of 90 percent female, on the other hand, is perhaps a more accurate reflection of the gender breakdown and conveys a sense of extreme urgency to those in the West that view this practice as a fundamental violation of human rights.

The investigation of regions and select countries only adds to understanding the breadth of the phenomenon. Within Asia, UNICEF estimates that there are 100,000 prostituted children in Thailand alone (Tasker, 1995, p. 28). The Centre for the Protection of Children's Rights estimates the number of prostituted children at between 80,000 and 800,000 (WCACSEC, 1998e). Moreover, a UNESCO study indicated that as many as 2,000,000 Thai women are engaged in prostitution, of which 800,000 are children or adolescents (Simons, 1993, p. 3A). On the conservative side, the Thai police, in 1992, estimated that there were between 50,000 and 80,000 prostituted children under the age of 15. Moreover, they estimated that only 10 percent of sex workers were male (Leheny, 1995, p. 373). Finally, the Thai Ministry of Public Health has estimated that there are a mere 15,000 prostituted children in the entire country (WCACSEC, 1998d).

India reveals staggering numbers as well. A 1991 survey by *India Today* placed the number of prostituted children at 400,000–500,000 (WCACSEC, 1998e). Nyland (1995, p. 547) indicates that at least one human rights organization estimated that there were 400,000 prostituted children in India. On the conservative side, however, a 1993 survey conducted by the Central Welfare Board in India estimated that there were between 20,000 and 30,000 prostituted children in Calcutta, Bombay, Hyderabad, Bangalore, Madras, and Delhi. Moreover, temple prostitution is said to account for 5,000 female children yearly (WCACSEC, 1998d).

Data for China are extremely scarce and are derived almost entirely from anecdotal experiences. On the conservative side of the coin, the *People's Daily* reported in 1994 that more than 10,000 women and children are taken from Sichuan province alone (WCACSEC, 1998d). O'Grady (1994, p. 135) maintains that this phenomenon affects between 200,000 and 500,000 children. Taiwan is also said to have a good number of prostituted children. O'Grady (1994, p. 135) reports a 1987 university study that places the estimate at 100,000, while Lee (1993, p. 3) cites a 1992 government survey that estimates the number to be between 40,349 and 57,495.

In other parts of Asia the problem is not considered to be as great. For example, WCACSEC (1998d) estimates that there are between 60,000 and 100,000 prostituted children in the Philippines, mostly "street children." Joseph (1995, p. 11) claims that there are more than 100,000 prostituted females in Manila alone, many of them being children. More specifically, Burrhus-Clay (1998) contends that there are at least 40,000 prostituted females under the age of 14 in Manila. O'Grady (1994, p. 135) quotes a 1991 report from the Filipino Department of Social Welfare and Development that reports 50,000 prostituted children countrywide. Nyland (1995, p. 547) offers an estimate of 60,000 prostituted female children, with the qualification that sex with a child under the age of 12 is defined as rape and is consequently illegal.

The situation in Sri Lanka also warrants attention even though the majority of prostituted children in both the Philippines and Sri Lanka are male, such as the *pompons* of Filipino guesthouses (Baker, 1995, p. 12). Although the prostituting of children is a relatively recent phenomenon, Protecting Environment and Children Everywhere

(PEACE) estimates the number of prostituted female children to be at least 10,000 (WCACSEC, 1998d).

The problem is said to be less severe in some other Buddhist countries. A 1992 survey in Vietnam, for example, identified 60,000 prostituted women, of which 12,000 are under the age of 18 (WCACSEC, 1998d). The WCACSEC (1998c), moreover, identifies a study revealing that one-third of the 60,000 sex workers in Cambodia are female children between the ages of 12 and 17. The incidence is also on the rise in Laos.

Although the numbers of prostituted female children in Bangladesh, Myanmar, and Nepal are considerably small, these countries contribute heavily to the brothels in both Thailand and India. It is estimated, for example, that 200,000 women, including children as young as nine years old, have been "trafficked" from Bangladesh to India and Middle Eastern countries in the last 10 years. Moreover, nearly 200,000 Nepali females under the age of 16 have been prostituted and trafficked into India. Finally, an estimated 10,000 girls are trafficked from Myanmar to Thailand yearly (Asia Watch, 1993).

Although the Asian region is typically invoked when addressing the phenomenon of prostituted female children, the Central and South American region is no less affected. Next to Thailand, Brazil is said to have the largest number of prostituted children (Burrhus-Clay, 1998). While Nyland (1995, p. 547) reports a human rights group estimate of 250,000, Voss (1999, p. 5) states that the number exceeds 500,000 and that it includes some who are as young as six years old. Lee-Wright (1990), however, suggests that the number is closer to 700,000 for children aged between 9 and 17. Moreover, Hornblower (1993) states that nearly 25,000 girls have been prostituted in Amazonian mining camps.

Outside Brazil the prostituted female children are not estimated to be as numerous. A 1994 study by the Bogota Chamber of Commerce found that there are 5,000–7,000 prostituted children in the capital (WCACSEC, 1998e). Moreover, the finding that the prostituting of 8- to 13-year-olds has increased by 500 percent from 1986 to 1993 has led some commentators to suggest that the practice is running rampant (Simons, 1993, p. 3A). A survey of Dominicans found that 25,000 children are prostituted, 63 percent of whom are females (WCACSEC, 1998d). Finally, although numbers are not readily available, the prostituting of female children is a daily happening in several countries, including Argentina, Costa Rica, Cuba, El Salvador, Guatemala, Honduras, Mexico, Nicaragua, Panama, and Paraguay.[4]

The African region is also not exempt from the practice. Kenya, for example, is said to have between 10,000 and 30,000 prostituted children ("Kenya Struggles with Child Prostitution," 2003), while the practice is also on the rise in Ethiopia ("Child Prostitution on the Rise, Report Says," 2003; Teklu, 2004). Togo continues to be listed as a country where police corruption serves to further the prostitution of children ("Togo: Child Prostitution Goes Unchecked in Togo," 2004). Moreover, Voss (1999) reports that it is on the rise in Senegal, Ghana, Libya, Sudan, Burkino Faso, and the Ivory Coast (p. 5).

SPECIFICS OF THE PRACTICE

> At 10, you are a woman. At 20, you are an old woman. At 30, you are dead.
>
> Fashionable Saying in Bangkok's Red-Light District

While the practice of prostituting female children may at first appear to be fully understandable from the viewpoint of what occurs, a variety of its "forms" can be identified. Before elaborating the specifics of the practice, however, one should decipher what is meant by "prostituted female children" and several related concepts. The 1989 Convention on the Rights of the Child maintains that a *child* is "every human being below the age of eighteen years unless, under the law applicable to the child, majority is attained earlier" (UNESCO, 2004). This is a qualified definition, however, as Nyland (1995, p. 547) correctly points out that the legal age varies among countries. Indeed, the age of consent for many countries of the world is 16 (Kristof, 1996, p. A1) or ranges between 13 and 17 (Muntarbhorn, 1996, p. 10). The United Nations Special Rapporteur on the Sale of Children defines *child prostitution* as "the sexual exploitation of a child for remuneration in cash or in kind usually, but not always, organised by an intermediary (parent, family member, procurer, teacher, etc.)" (Muntarbhorn, 1996, p. 9).

Having briefly explored a few concepts related to the prostituting of female children, one can now proceed onward with the specifics of the practice. This section will be divided into two parts: how female children are enlisted in the trade and how their bodies, for lack of an alternative way to state it, are "portrayed and merchandised." Many female children are sold into prostitution. This does not always mean, however, that they are necessarily cognizant of the transaction, as their mental aptitude at the time of the transaction may not be very well developed. Moreover, female children who have not been sold outright into prostitution are either lured or forced into it (Baker, 1995, p. 11).While the methods of introduction differ considerably, the key commonality of these methods is that they are all generally effective means by which to enlist the female child into prostitution. Selling female children into prostitution is not new. Rather, this human indignity has occurred over a considerable expanse of time both within and between numerous countries. In Nepal, for example, thousands of adolescents are sold and taken to Mumbai for brothel prostitution (Hornblower, 1993, p. 45). What is of great concern, however, is the extent to which female children are sold into prostitution, often by their own parents, without any awareness of the transaction. Moreover, O'Grady (1992, p. 99) suggests that some parts of Thailand have become nearly denuded of children. The following excerpt from an interview is characteristic of female children who have no idea that they are being sold into sexual bondage:

> Her story is typical. Daughter of a poor farmer in a hamlet three days' walk from Katmandu, Manju was 12 when her mother died. Unable to cope with three children, her father handed her over a few months later to two strangers: she thought she was going to Bombay to work as a housemaid. When the two men sold her to a pimp for $1,000, "there was nothing I could do. . . . I was trapped." (Hornblower, 1993, p. 51)

These types of transactions are typically referred to as being sold into "debt bondage." This is due to the fact that even if the deflowering price is enough or more than enough to cover the expense incurred to acquire the female child, the overseer of this transaction will continue to maintain that the child has not paid off her initial debt, let alone the costs incurred (e.g., clothing, food, shelter) since beginning at the brothel (Budhos, 1997, p. 16).

Those who are not sold and forced into prostitution are typically lured into it by the promises of good jobs (e.g., laundresses, maids, waitresses, cooks), good money, and a great opportunity to help out the family back home. For many, regardless of age, these are ample incentives to place their trust in the individual(s) making the promises. Unfortunately, the reality of sexual exploitation and human degradation comes all too soon, while the positives that were promised go largely unrealized.

CULTURAL RELEVANCE

Explanations for the practice of prostituting female children are numerous and quite diverse, depending on the particular cultural (i.e., ethnic) group that one encounters. What is common among most practicing cultures is that the explanation is multifaceted and draws on socially related factors. Therefore, one runs the risk of being "culturally reductionistic," in that some important factors may inadvertently be left out of the analysis (Johnson & Rodgers, 1994, p. 75). With this recognition in mind the factors to be addressed here are patriarchy, culture and tradition, religion, myth, political indifference, and economic concerns. To speak to each of these concerns separately poses a problem, as many of these "causes" are interrelated. We will proceed, however, in this manner in order to facilitate clarity. An attempt will be made to pull these varied explanations together after introducing each in turn.

In many parts of the world, patriarchy is still a dominant force that serves to subjugate the inherent rights of female populations. Unfortunately, patriarchy is prominent and has continued to thrive into the twenty-first century. As was noted with respect to female circumcision, patriarchy refers to a situation whereby the power, control, and authority of the unit (e.g., family, tribe) are in the hands of the males. Moreover, the power of males themselves is hierarchically structured according to age. The practice of patriarchy provides many examples of how the interest of females is subordinate to their male counterparts, including, but not limited to, inferior status, double standards throughout all aspects of the male-female relationship, and general gender discrimination. Finally, within the context of prostituted female children, it is not enough to note that patriarchy involves male dominance over females. Moreover, as Lee (1993, pp. 9–11) contends, a form of "double patriarchy" exists that includes not only the traditional male-female dichotomy but also the dominance of the adult over the female child.

The female child in numerous societies today suffers disproportionately to her male counterpart, in that the attitude toward her and her associated status is quite low. For many societies this is a direct consequence of long-held opinions about gender. This low status is often stated to be a *precipitating* factor of prostituting female children (WCACSEC, 1998a). Moreover, girls are generally more vulnerable to sexual exploitation in the family (e.g., incest, abuse, neglect), which may lead to a greater likelihood of being sold or forced into prostitution. In Latin America as well as throughout Asia, many female children simply choose to continue a "sexually exploitative life on the streets" rather than suffer from male incest and other forms of violent sexual abuse in their families (Beyer, 1996).

Another plausible explanation revolving around patriarchy is the notion, as was elaborated on when discussing female infanticide, that female children are not valued as highly as their male counterparts. Consequently, the female is not apt to receive a good education as well as her fair share of necessary resources for personal growth and development. An unfortunate outgrowth of this situation is that the female child has considerably fewer choices afforded to her than does the male child. In a family that is already economically impoverished, there may be no other *realistic* option than to *merchandise* the lower-status daughters into prostitution (Burrhus-Clay, 1998).

Along with strong cultural predispositions, tradition plays a key role in many countries that continue to prostitute female children. Tradition is extremely important throughout numerous Asian countries whose family structure continues to be hierarchical in nature and in power relationships. For example, the Thai family structure is such that older family members exercise control (i.e., ownership) over the "rights" of younger family members (Levan, 1994, p. 875). As a result the elders of a family may dictate the direction that the female children will take with regard to this facet of their sexuality.

This hierarchically based decision is prevalent throughout many regions of the globe. In Thailand, in particular, this structure is played out daily. Women in Thai society have a duty to manage the finances of the family, although they work with the knowledge that the eldest male has the ultimate decision-making authority. Throughout the history of Thailand, women have sought to manage shortfalls in family finances by selling food. The shortcoming of the traditional method of rural subsistence agricultural farming has, over time, necessitated the prostituting of female children (Muecke, 1992). In essence, the prostituted female child in Thai culture today is merely viewed as upholding her obligation to the family with respect to finances.

Women have also suffered from a dualistic notion of morality that in many societies runs strictly according to gender. For example, Thai society has a dual conception about the defining criteria for males and females. While the status of the male is almost exclusively determined by his public interactions with others, the status of the female is almost exclusively defined in terms of her sexuality. She is often either viewed in terms of the pleasure that she can give to her husband and family or in terms of how she can generate productive labor via her sexuality. In essence, she is viewed as one of two figures: the *mother/caregiver* or the *concubine/prostitute*. Consequently, this dualism leads, especially in times of economic necessity, to the prostituting of female children in order to ensure an adequate income for the family unit (Levan, 1994, pp. 875–876).

This dualism is sometimes more clearly seen as a double standard with regard to the defining sexual morality that pervades society. While the promiscuity of men is an essential element of the cultural mystique of many countries, the objectification of women, in terms of personifying them as subservient to the wishes of males, is no less dominant throughout these cultures. The following excerpt, taken from a discussion regarding the relatedness of Thai prostitution and development issues, states this concisely:

> Culturally Thai society still very much flatters men for their promiscuity and polygamy. . . . While a woman is seriously condemned for allowing more than one man to gain access to her body, a man is, ironically, praised for being able to, on whatever basis—love, money or even force—have sexual relations with as many women as he wishes. (Sitthirak, 1995)

The emphasis on Thailand and the Asian region is not to negate the important similarities that exist in other parts of the world where the prostituting of female children occurs. Although the basis for the distinction is somewhat different, the role that machismo has in promoting the prostituting of female children is no less dramatic than in Asia. An unfortunate consequence of machismo is the fact that violence permeates the family unit as the call for prostituting female children becomes greater. As Beyer (1996) states:

> According to the cultural mores of these often rigidly patriarchal societ-ies, not only are men seen as superior, but there is an understood agree-ment within the society that men have ravenous, uncontrollable libidos and that these libidos are a sign of their strength and their power. It is therefore comprehensible, expected, and accepted by most Latin American societies that men will need more sex than women, and shall have more sex than their marital relations permit. . . . On the other hand, women, under the theory of *machismo,* are deemed to be by nature passive and much more rooted in family and domestic life. Their sexual urges, needs, and desires are considered to be satisfied by their domestic life, both in terms of their marital sexual relations with their husbands and in the satisfactions gained by the rearing of their children and the running of their homes. Consequently, it is not expected, con-doned or ascribed to women in this type of society, that they have the same need, right and desire to go outside of the home for sex. (p. 33)

Related to traditional beliefs in the Asian region is the impact that Buddhism has had on the continual prostituting of female children. As a religious practice, Buddhism dates back to the time of the Indian philosopher Gautama Buddha (563–483 B.C.).[5] Stemming from the original formulation of Buddhism are two main schools of thought. From its humble beginnings in Bodh Gaya, India, Buddhism has spread via the *Theravada* (i.e., southern) school throughout several central and east Asian countries, including Sri Lanka, Myanmar, Thailand, Cambodia, and Laos. The northern school of Buddhism, *Mahayana,* spread throughout Tibet, Nepal, China, Japan, Korea, and Vietnam. In all, adherents to Buddhism throughout Asia exceed 500,000,000. The main difference between the northern and southern schools is not with the core teachings of the Buddha's Dharma, but rests primarily with the "expression of and implementation of the Buddha's teachings" (Buddhanet, 1998).

While Buddhism appears on face to encourage all members of society to accumulate merit, many believe the reality is that there is a certain misogynistic strand throughout the religion that serves to denigrate and subordinate women vis-à-vis men. This is suggested in the following quote taken from Sitthirak (1995):

> Traditional Thai culture, partly rooted in the Buddhist concept of the accumulation of merit and the Law of Karma, encourages Thai women, particularly those living in rural areas, to view men as their superiors. Women see themselves as disadvantaged and less worthy. They need money as a means of showing gratitude to their parents for bearing and raising them, as a way of taking care of their younger siblings and giving them a wider range of opportunities, including education.

Merit making in the service of achieving good karma is very important not only in Thailand but in the other Buddhist cultures as well. Those members of society who are economically advantaged have a good deal of status and consequently merit. While Buddhist monks have the greatest "repository" of merit, those who have been prostituted, or have chosen to prostitute themselves, have the greatest number of demerits and lowest amount of merit. It is possible, however, for the prostituted individual to accumulate merit that can be transferred to more sentient beings. The relationship between prostitution, wealth, and merit is further detailed by Muecke (1992):

> A person can change her/his karma by purposefully making merit. The most common ways to make merit are to give gifts to monks and temples, and to sponsor an ordination of a monk. . . . Degree of economic wealth is popularly taken as a direct indicator of karmic status, with the royal family and Buddhist monks being those with the greatest store of merit. Popular belief holds that men are karmically

superior to women. According to this schema, prostitutes rank low on merit because they are women and come from poor families. (p. 893)

What is not entirely clear, however, is how the prostituting of female children can be linked to the accumulation of *parinama* (i.e., merit). Mensendiek (1997, pp. 165–166) suggests that this linkage is quite easily understood when considering the status of the female vis-à-vis the male and the degree to which the female feels the duty to illustrate gratitude to her parents for the nurturance that they have provided her. Moreover, the prostituted female child can accumulate merit by several means. These include such acts as sending the funds that are earned in the process of being prostituted home to one's parents, sponsoring the ordination of a monk, or even donating funds to a temple. All of these actions serve to enhance one's storehouse of merit even while the act of being prostituted, whether of one's own volition or not, would certainly add to one's accumulation of demerits. In essence, Buddhism results in a "dual prostituting" of the female child. Not only does it indirectly encourage families to prostitute their female children, but it also serves to repress the ability of the child to accumulate a great storehouse of merit, which, according to the dictates of the religion, is how one obtains good karma. On the positive side, however, this type of action serves to enhance the economic status of many impoverished rural households throughout the countries of both the northern and southern schools. A good example of this perceived economic benefit is offered in the following passage from Sitthirak (1995):

> All but four retained strong links with their families, supplying remittances which contributed substantially to meeting the basic needs of their families for housing, water and education, but little productive investment in rural areas. For example, there is the story of Taew, a girl from the village of Don Barg in the Northeast, who was persuaded to sell her virginity at one of the massage parlours. The client paid 8,000 baht (US $320), of which she got only 2,000 baht (US $80). She sent the money home right away to build a well for drinking water. (p. 64)

The continuation of prostituting female children is also a result of a profusion of myths that are, on face at least, all somewhat related to sex and general well-being. These myths operate in at least three distinct realms: personal longevity, economic prosperity, and medical curatives. It is important to note that the prevalence of the myth, regardless of the variety, is disproportionately attributed to the Asian cultures.

First, many cultures believe that coitus with a virgin will bring back one's youth (Kristof, 1996) and may also increase longevity. Indeed, a Chinese myth suggests that this activity can delay death by an additional 10 years (Berkman, 1996, pp. 397–400; Simons, 1994, p. 33). A second prevalent myth regards sex with a virgin as a positive happening that will accentuate one's business and power (WCACSEC, 1998b). A third myth suggests that sexual intercourse with children can cure a variety of ailments, including venereal disease (Berkman, 1995, p. 399; Joseph, 1995, p. 15) as well as HIV-AIDS (Klain, 1999, p. 37).

The point related to the last myth is perhaps the most widely addressed in the literature because of the great misconceptions that produce it and the far-ranging implications that are derived from it. Conventional wisdom, although misguided to say the least, suggests that having sex with a child will actually decrease the risk of contracting HIV-AIDS (Berkman, 1995; Klain, 1999, p. 37). The prevalence of this misconception is illustrated by the large number of people who participate in "sex tourism" and, consequently, are willing to pay a greater fee to have sex with a child, and even more if that child is a bona fide virgin. This quest for younger and younger female children is often referred to as the "spiral factor" (Levan, 1994, p. 871; Muntarbhorn, 1997, p. 8).

The reality is that the fear of HIV-AIDS should be greater among those who have sex with a child. Moreover, there is ample documentation regarding the physical immaturity of the anal and vaginal cavities that lends support to this notion[6]: the linings of these cavities are more easily torn, and the resulting fissures produce both sores and bleeding. The latter, in particular, speeds the spread of the virus, as it can enter directly into the bloodstream. The opportunity for lethal infection is only worsened by the fact that much of the clientele refuses to use contraceptives (Hodgson, 1994, p. 520).

Political indifference is also responsible for the onset as well as the maintenance of the prostituting of female children. As the earlier historical glimpse illustrates, many societies remained indifferent to the existence of this practice. Political indifference in contemporary societies takes on several forms. Perhaps the most notable is the passive allowance of the practice of sex tourism to occur in one's country. The linkage of sex tourism and prostituted female children is often seen in terms of the former being an outgrowth of the latter. At least one investigation views the creation of a market for sex tourism as the cause for the prostituting of female children (Hodgson, 1994, p. 517). Regardless of the exact causal relationship, it is fair to say that the two are highly correlated.

Related to political indifference is the idea that well-organized criminal and pedophile groups reap great personal benefits from prostituting female children. Organized crime emanating from several developed countries, including the United States and Australia, is responsible for the continuation of this practice throughout much of the Asian region. Moreover, the Japanese *Yakuza* are also involved in the practice (Hornblower, 1993, p. 49). Hodgson (1994) lends insight on how the organized crime groups enlist female children:

> At the grassroots level, girls are often committed by their parents to a procurement agent who visits their villages on behalf of the syndicates to identify prospective prostitutes for the city brothels. The form of exchange is usually a loan of money and the girl must work for the brothel until the loan and interest are repaid. The reality is that there is little real prospect of full repayment and the child becomes a virtual prisoner in the exchange. Many of the parents are deceived and do not become aware of the nature of the work until it is too late. (p. 519)

Because of the lack of any effective anticrime effort on this front, organized groups, taking advantage of the political indifference, continue to benefit at the cost of millions of children.

Organized pedophile groups exist throughout the world. Members of these groups travel to faraway destinations for the primary purpose of having illicit sex with a female child. Cognizant that their behavior would be punished in a much more stern manner if they were to operate in their home countries, many see the opportunity to have sex with a female child in a developing country as, politically and legally, less risky (Nyland, 1995, p. 549). To this end, clandestine pedophile groups organize to identify those countries that either have no laws governing this aspect of sexual behavior or do not rigorously enforce the statutes that do exist (Muntarbhorn, 1997, p. 8).

A second area of political indifference is related to law enforcement, or the lack thereof. Unfortunate as it may be, the police units of several countries are more than willing to accept bribes in exchange for complicity in the flesh trade and prostitution. Tasker (1995, p. 28) identifies the extent of this problem in Thailand when he suggests that police, countrywide, "are heavily criticized for reaping handouts from owners of brothels and turning a blind eye to the flesh trade." The turning of a blind eye, however, is an all-too-common experience throughout many of the countries in which the prostituting of female children occurs. This is often the case even in countries where statutes prohibiting the practice exist. Teklu (2004) reports, for example, that the prostituting of children is on the rise in Ethiopia even though

Ethiopian law is extremely clear on the issue. Berkman (1996) succinctly captures the relatedness of law enforcement, as well as other factors such as economics, to the prostituting of female children in the following passage:

> Despite these official attempts to curb the child sex trade, the problem remains prevalent. This is due largely to lack of enforcement on the part of police and government officials. The lack of enforcement is attributable in part to corruption within the police forces. Additionally, countries affected by the sex tourism trade are, for the most part, very poor, and socio-economic realities lead the governments to concern themselves more with the money that such tourism brings in than with the effect it might have on the children. (pp. 403–404)

Perhaps the most noted causal agent in the literature deals directly with the economic situation surrounding prostituted female children. Although the literature in this area is quite broad, it does suggest several key areas of concern (i.e., areas that may be construed as causes of this phenomenon). Inter alia, the topics to be addressed forthwith are the increase in consumerism, the lack of educational opportunities and consequent job opportunities, and poverty.

Before reviewing the areas of concern, it is necessary to put the causal agents into a more structured framework. Perhaps the best way to do this is to invoke the principle of commercialization. For lack of a better way to characterize the phenomenon, prostituted female children constitute a product. The marketing of any product involves supply and demand considerations (Muntarbhorn, 1997, p. 8). Up to this point this review has only examined causal factors that are related to the demand side of the commercialization coin (e.g., criminal networks, pedophile groups, corruption or indifference of authorities, the fear of HIV-AIDS and the promotion of the "spiral effect," traditional myths that place a premium on having sex with virgins). Conversely, emphasis on the aforementioned economic considerations constitutes a focus that is almost exclusively related to the supply side of the coin.

Having made the contention that the economic situation of families is a key consideration in determining the supply of female children to be prostituted, I will develop each of the aforementioned concerns in turn. Perhaps one of the more key areas that are often left untouched by analyses of this phenomenon is the degree to which the increasing consumerism of the developing world has led to an increase in families prostituting their female children. Consumerism, as it is used presently, refers to a family's desire to have those materialistic items that it deems appropriate to its existence. Although consumerism can also be investigated in terms of pedophiles creating a market, this is a demand consideration and one that has been briefly discussed earlier.

Consumerism in the developing world where the prostituting of female children has been most rampant is fueled by increased communications linkages. Regardless of the level of "economic development," one is apt to see the most advanced technological instruments in areas that are not perceived to be, developmentally, backward. The problem of consumerism as it relates to prostituted female children, however, is that not all societies are able to afford the consumption of what many might perceive to be luxuries. It is this latter circumstance that often leads families into making a choice between the virginity of young daughters and the existence of a television set (Simons, 1994, p. 35) or a karaoke system (Kristof, 1996, p. I8). Hodgson (1994, p. 517) suggests that while most families sell their female children into prostitution because of abject poverty, "an estimated 32% of transactions are motivated by the desire to pursue consumerism and materialism." Perhaps the WCACSEC (1998b) sums up the role of increasing consumerism best when it states the following:

> Consumerism is a major factor in the increasing incidence of commercial sexual exploitation of children. The push to own, buy, rent, have—fuelled by advertising, TV and video images, magazines and entertainment media—encourages those who do not value their children and respect their rights to quite simply trade them for something they want more. In some parts of the world children themselves, faced with the competition of peers and the desire to "keep up," sell their bodies for the money to buy consumer items they cannot otherwise afford. They are exploited by circumstance, by a society which constantly tells them that possessions are more important than dignity.

A second consideration that is largely tied to the economic situation of a family is the lack of educational opportunities that many female children experience (Teklu, 2004). While the reality is that cultural tradition has a good deal to do with the level of the female child's education, a relationship also exists present between economic status, level of education, and the prostituting of female children. Hodgson (1994, p. 517) suggest that "poverty results in illiteracy, under-education, a lack of marketable skills and employment opportunities and ultimately a lack of real and effective choices." The UNDP (2004, pp. 176–179) indicates that the 2002 average literacy rate for males and females within the south-central Asian region is 71.1 percent and 53.3 percent, respectively. The degree to which one's level of education is considered to be part of the cause behind prostitution is illustrated in a study of 50 Bangkok masseuses (i.e., prostitutes) who had come to Bangkok from a rural setting and were later prostituted. Of these females, 40 percent had absolutely no education while another 52 percent had benefited from less than four years of elementary school (Sitthirak, 1995).

The lack of educational opportunities is also closely related to the lack of job opportunities in the rural sectors of many of the afore-mentioned countries where prostituted female children exist. With a rather low level of education, even the jobs that are available in rural sectors are not readily accessible. The real problem becomes one of creating jobs that can utilize functional labor (i.e., functionally literate personnel) and creating better educational opportunities for the female population. As Baker (1995, p. 13) states, however, it is difficult "to create viable income-earning alternatives in poor villages that can compete with the earning power of prostitution." Levan (1994, pp. 872–874) concurs that the lack of job opportunities, for whatever reason, is a causal agent that encourages the continuation of the prostituting of female children.

This set of related factors also involves poverty. Poverty is often, rightly or wrongly, considered the root of the evil known as the prostituting of female children. Many researchers identify poverty as the root cause of the problem (Hodgson, 1994, p. 516; Levan, 1994, p. 872; Teklu, 2004). As Baker (1995) states, "endemic rural poverty continues to provide an enormous pool of children waiting to be exploited to meet the increasing demand" (pp. 12–13). Still others respond that poverty is not, in and of itself, an adequate justification or sufficient cause for the practice. As the former Special Rappor-teur of the Commission on Human Rights on the sale of children, child prostitution and child pornography, Vitit Muntarbhorn (1997) contends, "Poverty alone cannot be blamed for driving children into exploitative situations" (p. 8). Alternatively, poverty should be seen as one of several related factors, many of which have already been discussed here, that create a climate that invites this type of behavior. One might, as such, view it as a necessary, but not sufficient, cause for the prostituting of female children. The Draft Declaration and Agenda for Action of the 1996 WCACSEC conference in Stockholm, Sweden, stated this point of view:

> Poverty cannot be used as a justification for the commercial sexual exploi-tation of children, even though it contributes to an environment which may lead to such exploitation. A range of other complex contributing

factors include economic disparities, inequitable socio-economic structures, dysfunctioning families, lack of education, growing consumerism,
urban-rural migration, gender discrimination, irresponsible male sexual
behavior, harmful traditional practices, armed conflicts and trafficking of
children. (World Congress Against the Commercial Sexual Exploitation
of Children, 1996, ¶ 6)

Regardless of the exact role that it plays, it cannot be argued that
poverty, especially rural poverty, does not exist throughout many of
the countries where the majority of prostituted female children reside.
For example, the 1984–2002 rural poverty in Vietnam was 57.2
percent, while the urban rate was less than half of the rural rate (25.9%).
It is the same in Brazil, where 32.6 percent and 13.1 percent of
the rural and urban population, respectively, is impoverished. This negative picture becomes considerably more desolate when one looks at
the distribution of income in these regions. The wealthiest 20 percent
of Brazil consumed 64.4 percent of the income during 1983–2001,
while the lowest 20 percent consumed 2.0 percent. Similarly, the
numbers for Thailand during the same period were 50.0 percent and
6.1 percent, respectively. These patterns recur throughout many countries in South American and East Asian regions (Bread for the World,
2004, p. 131).[7]

Poverty is related to the level of education (i.e., literacy) as well
as consequent job opportunities. Most often, highly poverty-stricken
areas have a high rate of illiteracy as well as "a discernable lack of
marketable skills," which makes it considerably easier for procurement
agents to enlist female children into prostitution (Burrhus-Clay, 1998).
In essence, rural-urban migration is prompted, throughout many
poverty-stricken developing countries, by the need for families to
survive (Nyland, 1995, p. 548). Although sometimes misled by procurement agents about the type of work that their daughters would be
engaged in, many families choose to sell the "labor" of their daughters
with full knowledge that they will be prostituted, thus allowing the
buyer to recoup the initial purchase price and profit lucratively.

Pulling all of these causal agents, both supply and demand factors,
together is quite a task. It is perhaps best done by recounting the
experience of the child in the following passages:

> Tan is a fourteen year-old Thai girl. She is from the North-East of
> Thailand but like many girls of her age lives and works in Bangkok. Tan
> works as a dancer in a bar in Pat Pong which is a centre of the sex tourist
> industry in Bangkok. Tan has to dance half-naked on the bar. She also has
> to have sex with tourist men if they select her. Tan was sold to an agent

when she was only ten. For two years she cleared ashtrays and glasses in the bar until she was finally sold to a tourist who purchased her virginity. Since then Tan has had sex with many tourists and locals every night. She hates what she has to do as she has been beaten and abused often. But she cannot escape this life as it is her duty to honour her parent's debt and she has been threatened with violence if she tries to leave. Tan sends most of her money to her parents to take care of her brothers, sisters and grandparents—she believes it is her destiny. (Hodgson, 1994, p. 513)

Why have these girls become prostitutes? What would your choices be if you were born into a landless peasant family in a remote village in the poorest region of Thailand? . . . How can you possibly stay in your village where by going to Bangkok, you can work in a factory and earn as much as 25 times more than what you could at home. If you go into the sex trade, a couple of years of work would enable you to build a house for your family . . . which very few people in the countryside could ever hope to achieve on the earnings of a lifetime. (Sitthirak, 1995)

THE CLASH OF CULTURES

Special measures of protection and assistance should be taken on behalf of all children and young persons without any discrimination for reasons of parentage or other conditions. Children and young persons should be protected from economic and social exploitation. Their employment in work harmful to their morals or health or dangerous to life or likely to hamper their normal development should be punishable by law. (Article10, Paragraph 3 of the International Covenant on Economic, Social, and Cultural Rights, 1966)

An initial evaluation of the cultural differences that give rise to the prostituting of female children in some cultures, but less so in others, is problematic. On face, what one has in prostituted female children is a phenomenon that appears to be entrenched in almost every culture of the world. Regardless of whether these nations are developed or developing, rich or poor, democratic or nondemocratic, they all share a certain sense of responsibility for allowing the continuation of this phenomenon worldwide. The only factors that serve to distinguish these countries from one another are such things as the scope of the problem, the causal factors giving rise to the practice, the reasons for why it is allowed to flourish, and finally, the various means by which female children are "brought into" it (Flores, 1996, p. 41). In essence, it is difficult for any one country or culture to indict another when the reality is that most countries only differ in terms of the degree to which the practice occurs as opposed to whether it is said to exist at all.

The above quotation, taken from the International Covenant on Economic, Social, and Cultural Rights that was adopted by the United Nations General Assembly in 1966, gives us the ability to assess the clash of cultures that surrounds the issue of prostituted female children. At the heart of this "clash" is one's perception and understanding of the role of females today in societies throughout the world. Moreover, one's interpretation of what does and does not constitute a human right and whether there are acceptable "justifications" enabling countries to breach these ideas is also very important.

Regardless of the fact that many countries of the world have signed several international agreements dealing with the rights of women and female children, the reality today is that most of these signatories cannot say that the practice of prostituting female children does not occur within the confines of their own territories. In essence, a signature on paper does not mean that the signatory country is on a "higher moral ground" than those that have not acceded or ratified the agreement. What it does suggest, however, is that there is another dimension related to the primary consideration at hand (i.e., prostituted female children) that allows some countries, primarily rich, democratic, and developed ones, to suggest that they are strides apart from other countries in the world whose societies also suffer from a somewhat common plague. It is hereby suggested that this other dimension is the perception of the role of females throughout societies today.

While it is true that those in the West cannot wholly condemn the cultures that also suffer from the practice of prostituting female children, it has been possible for the West to stay clear of the practice specifically, but condemn the degree to which women's rights, generally, have not been trumpeted in other countries (i.e., cultures). With this distinction in mind, the West has been all too boisterous about its leadership in changing the status quo with respect to women's rights being equated with human rights. In brief, the clash of cultures is redirected so that the controversy is no longer over the practice of prostituting female children specifically, but rather focuses on the respect that a culture has for women and their role in society. Presented in these terms, it becomes quite easy for the West to "indict" various other cultures for their lack of commitment to challenging the status quo even though the reality is that the same practice that incites the West to make these condemnations occurs within the West as well.

Given this distinction, the West can point to several concrete developments with respect to advancing women's rights—developments that are not necessarily present or as widespread in the countries that continue to suffer disproportionately from the prostituting of female children. For example, the West can point to educational enrollments, literacy rates, infant mortality, health care, labor statistics (primarily wage rates and employment), and so forth, all broken down by gender, in order to suggest that the plight of women in the West is far less diminutive than in other cultures. The implication of these "suggestions" is that because the position of women is much better in the West than in other countries (that just happen to suffer the most from the prostituting of female children), these countries obviously regard the rights of women, and their role in society, to be dramatically different than how they are regarded in the West. While not a logical conclusion, it is nonetheless an avenue that the West has all too often traveled. This stance is often applied to specific situations, such as the prostituting of female children, to illustrate that the West has greater regard for the rights and role of women and female children than do other countries even though the practice continues in the West. Obviously, the difference in penalties evinced in the following passage would indicate the relative level of respect for women's rights that those in the West have vis-à-vis those in non-Western cultures.

> Few things bring out more anger in people than the idea of adults having sex with children. In April 1993, a man who kidnapped a young girl for sex in California was sentenced to 106 years in prison. In Florida, the crime of pedophilia can carry the death penalty. In Asia, however, crimes that would earn a 100-year sentence in the United States can be forgiven for a fine of a few hundred dollars. (Baker, 1995, p. 12)

One's interpretation as to what constitutes a human right and whether there are acceptable "justifications" enabling countries to breach these ideas is as important a part of identifying how cultures clash over this phenomenon as is the perception that one has of the female's role in today's societies throughout the world. Indeed, these two considerations are closely tied throughout any discussion regarding prostituted female children.

Several international documents, most of which have a Western "flavor," have been instrumental in identifying what it is that constitutes a human right for females. Indeed, when Ex-First Lady Hillary Rodham Clinton stated in Beijing in 1995 that "human rights are women's rights and women's rights are human rights," she was expressing an attitude with which many in the West wish to be associated. The key sentiment, of course, was that universal and fundamental human rights should be upheld for the world citizenry regardless of gender (and several other considerations that include one's cultural predisposition). More to the point, the West has identified, although not in specific detail, the human rights that ensure the dignity of the individual in society. Moreover, any violation of these general ideas, such as the right to an education, is viewed as a direct transgression against human rights in general and women's rights and the rights of female children specifically.

Violations of these women's rights can only be met with criticism from the West. Although such criticism may be tantamount to self-criticism, the West continues to indict those countries and cultures that are even more lax than it in upholding the rights of females. In conjunction with this indictment is the overwhelming notion that causal factors leading to the prostituting of female children, such as poverty and cultural myths, cannot be justifications for the continuation of the practice. Alternatively, these elements can only be regarded as "inroads" to cultural change.

IMPLICATIONS FOR FOREIGN RELATIONS

Given that the West generally disapproves of prostituting female children, the countries for which this is a measurable problem may well feel the wrath of Western policy making with regard to strategic areas of concern such as foreign aid packages. This is a vital consideration, as the majority of countries where the prostituting of female children occurs are located in the, economically speaking, developing spheres of the globe. Moreover, similar to female circumcision, the prostituting of female children occurs in large part in some of the most impoverished countries of the world.

Countries that continue to allow the practice of prostituting female children run the risk of further alienating Western countries and affiliated organizations. To continue to alienate these Western entities is tantamount to resigning oneself to the fact that Western "development" aid will not be forthcoming. Aid programs are, after all, often linked to compliance with Western norms of behavior. In this case, although the prostituting of female children occurs in Western societies as well as in non-Western developing countries, the implicit norm of behavior is that this practice constitutes a human rights violation. Consequently, governments need to illustrate that they are repulsed by the practice and to work toward elimination.

The overarching problem, however, is that the practice of prostituting female children occurs, in large part, because of poverty. Moreover, for many countries prostitution has served to accentuate the tourism sector of developing countries to the extent that tourism has become a critical component of government revenues that cannot easily be dismissed. In sum, allowing the practice to continue may allow tourism dollars to continue flowing, but will not win the economic favor of the West. To launch an all-out barrage on the practice, however, may have the net result of fewer tourism receipts, but a greater affiliation with Western aid donors. Clearly, the latter direction is the preferable path from the Western point of view. Although tourism dollars may shrink, development aid may help subsidize development of the agricultural, manufacturing, or services sector of the economy while giving lesser incentive for the practice of prostituting female children to continue.

To this end, many Western countries have shown their resolve by making the practice illegal within their own borders. Muntarbhorn (1997, p. 9) suggests that almost every country of the world has passed legislation "against exploitation of child victims of prostitution." The reality is that many countries do not have statutes dealing with child prostitution per se, but typically have a statute in the criminal code that deals with prostitution in general. Prior to the passage of the Prosecutorial Remedies and Other Tools to End the Exploitation of Children Today (PROTECT) Act of 2003, the United States dealt with child prostitution in this manner. As the United Nations Special Rapporteur on the sale of children, child prostitution, and child pornography, Ofelia Calcetas-Santos (1996), states:

> The act of child prostitution, like adult prostitution, is not usually singled out as a criminal offence in most States. . . . Child prostitution is usually dealt with under legislation designed to cope with prostitution generally, and attacks the instigator of the prostitution or those living off the earnings from prostitution. Offenders may also face the related criminal charges of rape, indecent assault and sexual exploitation of minors. The penalties for such crimes are usually aggravated if the child is of a very young age. (¶ 103–104)

Beyond national statutes criminalizing child prostitution or giving protection to the rights of children in society, many Western countries have recognized the extent to which their nationals create demand for sex tourism in developing countries and have subsequently passed legislation targeting sex tourism. The United States (2003), United Kingdom (2003), Canada (1996), Australia (1994), and Ireland (1996) are among the countries that have laws specifically targeting child sex tourism. Others, such as Portugal, Spain, Norway, Sweden, Finland, Iceland, Japan, Germany, France, Luxembourg, and the Netherlands, have established extraterritorial laws that pertain to child abuse (End Child Prostitution in Asian Tourism, 2005).[8] The degree to which these countries feel strongly about the practice is made evident by the prosecution of the 69-year-old Swedish national Bengt Bolin in 1995. Bolin was convicted for having sex with a minor at the Thai resort of Pattaya (Berkman, 1996, p. 409).[9]

Although a relatively recent convert to the movement to eradicate the prostituting of female children, the United States has continually voiced its view that the practice is a violation of human rights and should be eliminated. Mrs. Clinton, at the Fourth World Conference on Women in Beijing in 1995, maintained that "it is a violation of human rights when women and girls are sold into slavery or prostitution for human greed" (Otero, 1996, p. ii). This stated commitment complimented well the 1994 introduction of the Child Sex Abuse Prevention Act, sponsored by Representative Joseph Kennedy II. The Violent Crime Control and Law Enforcement Act of 1994 provided for fines and a potential 10-year prison sentence (20 years if it is the second offence) if a citizen or permanent resident of the United States traveled abroad for purposes of engaging in any sexual act with a person under 18 years of age.

The United States has also showed its support for the elimination of this practice by influencing both the International Monetary Fund (IMF) and World Bank (IBRD) to assist the impoverished countries that suffer disproportionately from this practice. This comes from the reductionist belief that the cause of this practice is inextricably tied to economic impoverishment. Some others, such as Representative Joseph Kennedy II, have gone so far as to suggest that the United States should pressure the IMF and IBRD to cut off development funding altogether if changes are not made. Kennedy II (1996) stated:

> We should also be creative in examining new ways to bring pressure on governments that tolerate the sexual abuse of children. We should explore these opportunities at the World Bank and the International Monetary Fund. If appeals to decency and morality fail, let us make attacks on these countries' pocketbooks in order to get their attention. (p. 5)

This commitment was furthered with the passage of the aforementioned PROTECT Act of 2003. This law provides for prosecution within the United States, fines, and up to 30 years of imprisonment. In June 2003, Michael Clark Lewis became the first person to be indicted under the PROTECT Act for his travels to Cambodia for the purpose of having illicit sex with children ("Enactment of PROTECT Act against Sex Tourism," 2004).

Moreover, several international organizations, conventions, and treaties add to the pressure that these governments feel to eliminate the prostituting of female children. Not to do so would mean that the country would suffer morally and, perhaps, economically from the wrath of the international community. Perhaps the most note-worthy of international institutions that also have a role to play in eliminating the prostituting of female children, beyond the IMF and the IBRD, are the International Labour Organization (ILO), the WHO, UNICEF, and the International Criminal Police Organization (INTERPOL).

There are others as well, however, who are lesser known yet continue to work for change via a plethora of techniques. End Child Prostitution, Child Pornography and Trafficking of Children for Sexual Purposes (ECPAT) is a Bangkok-based organization that has broadened its focus to include all regions of the globe. ECPAT, like the World Tourism Organization (WTO), seeks to prevent, uncover, isolate, and eradicate the exploitation of all children that occurs in sex tourism. Along with these organizations are a host of grassroots organizations that are scattered throughout the countries where the practice of prostituting female children is said to be the worst. These institutions, like the PREDA foundation (People's Recovery, Empowerment and Development Assistance) in the Philippines and the Daughters of Education project in Thailand, typically are concerned with efforts toward elimination but sometimes deal with bringing those who are already involved in the practice out and assisting them in the adjustment. They all have at their base, however, the goal of pressuring governments and their citizens to stop the practice.

There also exist several conventions and treaties that are designed to bring countries into compliance with the Western norm that the prostituting of female children constitutes a human rights viola-tion and should be abolished. Perhaps the most notable conven-tion has been the United Nations Convention on the Rights of the Child. Adopted by the United Nations in 1989 and subsequently entered into force in 1990, this is "the first legally binding inter-national agreement that protects children from sexual exploitation" (Berkman, 1996, p. 405). This convention was, in large part, born out of the failure of the 1924 Geneva Declaration of the Rights of the Child, the 1959 United Nations Declarations on the Rights of the Child, and the 1949 Convention for the Suppression of the Traffic in Persons and of the Exploitation of the Prostitution of Others to adequately regulate the practice of prostituting children. Although guarantees can never be issued, article 34 of the 1989 convention calls for State parties to take "all appropriate national, bilateral and multilateral measures to prevent . . . (a) The inducement or coercion of a child to engage in any unlawful sexual activity . . . (b) The exploitative use of children in prostitution or other unlawful sexual practices" (UNESCO, 2004).[10] One should note that while this convention represents an effort on the part of the West to pressure countries into compliance with regard to a prescribed human rights concern, as of 2005 the United States was the only Western industrialized country that had not ratified the convention or become a party to it.[11] Somewhat surprising, however, has been the stance of the United States (signed and ratified) with respect to the Optional Protocol on the sale of Children, Child Prostitution, and Child Pornography (United Nations Children's Fund, 2005c), which entered into force on January 18, 2002.

In addition to these convention declarations, the United Nations periodically gets involved in prompting governments to recognize existing convention declarations and treaties. For example, on December 18, 1990, the General Assembly decided to convene a world conference on human rights in 1993. The result was the Vienna Conference from June 14 to June 25, 1993. This conference served to give notice that the General Assembly thought it was time for universal ratification of the 1990 World Declaration on the Survival, Protection and Development of Children and Plan of Action that was adopted at the 1990 World Summit for Children.

Treaties are also used to illustrate the norms of the West, with regard to human rights, to the countries that are thought to be in violation and consequently to be held in contempt by the West. Among the more well-known that have relevance to the prostituting of female children are the 1948 Universal Declaration of Human Rights; the 1966 International Covenant on Economic, Social, and Cultural Rights; the 1966 International Covenant on Civil and Political Rights; the 1992 Programme of Action of the United Nations Commission on Human Rights for the Prevention of the Sale of Children, Child Prostitution and Child Pornography; the 1995 Beijing Declaration and Platform for Action of the Fourth World Conference on Women; and the 1996 Programme of Action of the United Nations Commission on Human Rights for the Prevention of the Traffic in Persons and the Exploitation of the Prostitution of Others. Either implicitly or explicitly stated, all of the aforementioned are vital documents that serve to pressure governments into compliance with Western standards of human rights on such general topics as "violence" and on more specific topics such as the prostituting of female children.

POTENTIAL RESOLUTIONS

Development strategies aimed at poverty alleviation are essential in confronting child prostitution since poverty is one of the main causes of the phenomenon. In those countries most affected by the child prostitution problem, there is still a lack of social subsidy for families. The satisfaction of the basic needs of children, parents and the local community, in conjunction with educational measures, will empower them to make informed choices and so protect them from the cycle of poverty and exploitation. (Hodgson, 1994, pp. 536–537)

Almost any potential resolution regarding the practice of prostituting female children will be tainted by whether or not one considers the practice to constitute a human rights violation. Western adherents to the concept of universal human rights will certainly maintain that the only conceivable resolution is to achieve total elimination of the practice. Cultural relativists, although cognizant that the atrocities committed on female children are abominable, are not so quick to dismiss all aspects of this cultural behavior. Reasons exist that not only serve to explain the behavior but also suggest a certain degree of legitimacy. In essence, one might argue that the prostituting of female children serves a function in some societies. While neither of the extreme positions on this issue is reconcilable with the demands of the opposition, there is perhaps a middle ground that would allow for both sides to achieve a compromise position. Although the latter position may not entirely suit either the adherents to universal human rights or the cultural relativists, the following is a first step, albeit in a somewhat revised form, in trying to eliminate the practice of prostituting female children while not impairing the ability of a culture to exist.

Those who argue for the application of universal human rights mostly desire the total elimination of the prostituting of female children. Because this practice is currently alive and has spread throughout most of the countries of the world, one might best label this as the revolutionary position. Although the revolutionaries have an arsenal of techniques at their disposal for achieving the goal of total elimination, they frequently attempt to legislate against the practice and use the IMF and the IBRD as "leverage," or to further develop the country in question.

The attempt to legislate the problem away is not always succesful. Legislation is, often, to express support for the cause as well as to illustrate to the West that the country in question takes the issue seriously and is attempting to effectively deal with it. In reality, however, the target populations of legislative attempts to eliminate the practice are largely noncompliant. While legislative efforts are indeed indications to the West that the government in question takes seriously the ills associated with the prostituting of female children, it is a poor assumption that the laws that are in place in several countries are actually having an impact.

The ability to legislate the problem away is not necessarily a function of whether appropriate statutes exist. Berkman (1996, p. 403) maintains that legislation exists in almost every country where the prostituting of female children is a problem. What is more problematic is the associated concerns such as law enforcement (Berkman, 1996, p. 404), adequate resources, domestic and international cooperation, and the lax penalties for violation. In sum:

> Although some countries have virtually no laws protecting children against sexual exploitation, it is usually a matter of having adequate laws on the books but extremely lax enforcement. A law is essentially useless if there are no real consequences for violators. For instance, in Port Alegre, Brazil there is a municipal law that stipulates that an establishment that employs child prostitutes will be closed down for 30 days after its first offense. The ramifications for the owner of such an establishment are almost inconsequential. If the penalty for breaking the law is minor, many will choose to continue offending and accept a small reprimand or inconvenience. . . . At other times ambitious legal reform is passed yet no resources are allocated for its implementation. (Burrhus-Clay, 1998)

Although many countries in the Asian region, such as the Philippines (1992), Sri Lanka (1995), and Taiwan, Cambodia, and Thailand (1996) have either amended existing laws or passed new legislation as the practice of prostituting female children continues to run rampant. The Thai case is especially telling of how new laws do not necessarily deal adequately with the concern at hand. According to the government, the 1996 Prostitution Prevention and Suppression Act allows for the punishment of customers, procurers, brothel owners, and parents. While most would agree that the prostituted female child should not be revictimized by being prosecuted or by having those involved in the crime receiving lesser sentences, the 1996 act only served to, in actuality, "water down" some of the sentences and work against the best interests of the child. For example, the Thai Criminal Code already calls for prison sentences of 4 to 20 years if convicted of having sex with a minor under 15. The new act, however, provides only two- to six-year sentences and a fine of 40,000 to 120,000 baht if convicted of having sex with a minor under 15 (Tourism Authority of Thailand, 2005). Critics suggest that the new legislation would only serve to drive the illicit activity further underground. Moreover, they claim that the existing law is strong enough—that what is really needed is effective enforcement, which has yet to be accomplished (Gill, 1995).

Complimenting efforts to legislate the problem away have been efforts to utilize the IMF or the IBRD to try to further the economic development of the country in question. The problem with this strategy has been that a particular set of circumstances tended to reinforce the development and maintenance of the prostituted female children. Thailand provides an example of how the IMF and the IBRD encouraged the development of tourism as a means of generating foreign currency even while knowledgeable of its linkage to child prostitution. Petras and Wongchaisuwan (1993) suggest that a 1975 World Bank report

> highlighted the growth potential of tourism as part of its "export strategy" with full knowledge of its links to child prostitution. A National Plan of Tourist Development commissioned by the Thai government in 1975 was explicitly designed to support the sex industry in the name of tourism. As a result, the sex industry turned to new markets: the growth of tourism with the "sex package." Its "success" resulted in a rapidly rising demand for new prostitutes which led to large-scale recruitment of child prostitutes. . . . The World Bank's support for the open economy and export-oriented development results in financial support of tourism. Western support has meshed well with the military elite and local promoters who control the recruitment to and enforced exploitation of child prostitution. (pp. 440–441)

Moreover, tourism has become an even more attractive industry in Thailand as it assists Thai development efforts and what has become known as the "Thai Miracle," responsible for the "single largest source of foreign exchange in Thailand" (Mensendiek, .1997, p. 171). The 1975 National Plan coupled with 1980 being declared the "Year of Tourism" was largely responsible for the economic upturn. But much like the 1975 National Plan, the 1980 Year of Tourism led to increased reliance on prostituting female children. This was seen in Deputy Prime Minister Rojanasathien's instruction to provincial governors in 1980 to

> consider the natural scenery in your provinces, together with some forms of entertainment that some of you might consider disgusting

and shameful because they are forms of sexual entertainment that attract tourists. Such forms of entertainment should not be prohibited if only because you are morally fastidious. Yet explicit obscenities that may lead to damaging moral consequences should be avoided, within a reasonable limit. We must do this because we have to consider the jobs that will be created for the people. (Sitthirak, 1995)

In sum, efforts to legislate the problem away as well as the IMF and the IBRD attempts to further economic development via tourism have met with questionable results. Moreover, it would appear that the primary means chosen by the West to try to eliminate the perceived human rights violation due to the prostituting of female children were inadvertently serving to strengthen the practice.

At the other end of the continuum are the cultural relativists who, even though the practice of prostituting female children is often perceived to be less culturally based than either female circumcision or female infanticide, contend that the practice is rooted in the cultural conundrum that is poverty. Consequently, the cultural relativists do not entirely agree with Western efforts to eliminate the practice. Moreover, it is a condition that for many countries now helps to define their sociocultural environment. In essence, the status quo maintains that Western intrusion into this arena, under the guise of promoting the notion of universal human rights, is nothing more than cultural imperialism.

Although not necessarily the definitive answer, the following prescriptions on how to manage these two sides of the issue are not without some merit. Because they represent a "middle ground," however, they will undoubtedly come under attack from each of the dogmatic extremes. These prescriptions should also be prefaced with the knowledge that any potential satisfactory resolution to the practice of prostituting female children must start by addressing both the supply and demand factors mentioned earlier. While this is an admirable goal, an implicit assumption at this juncture is the notion that one will never be able to fully eliminate all of the supply and demand factors that aid the continuance of this practice.

First, governments of countries that currently have a substantial portion of their citizenry practicing the prostituting of female children, including those in the West, should work to criminalize all child prostitution where it is not already criminalized while concurrently decriminalizing adult prostitution.[12] Adult prostitution specifically, and the sex industry in general, contributes greatly to the economy. The ILO, in noting that this sector contributed anywhere from 2 to 14 percent of the gross domestic product of some southeastern Asian countries, noted that taxation of an officially recognized sector would be beneficial to growth. The ILO continued its emphasis, however, on eliminating the practice of prostituting children (Kaban, 1998).

Second, this move should be coupled with an educational campaign that provides information that is primarily concerned with the negative aspects, such as the "spiral effect," of female child prostitution as well as with debunking the myth that female child prostitution provides greater protection from the risk of HIV-AIDS and other sexually transmitted diseases (O'Grady, 1994, p. 116). These steps might well be productive in decreasing the importance of some factors that contribute to prostituting female children, such as the fear of HIV-AIDS, as well as the demands of sex tourists, pedophiles, and military personnel.

Third, the criminalization of child prostitution must be supported by increased funding to ensure compliance by several "targeted groups" in society. Perhaps most important is the need to uncover the crime syndicates that are responsible for the recruitment and transportation of female children. Above this, however, is the need to decrease the degree to which corrupt government officials, including police personnel, can, by their willful inaction, allow the practice to continue. Moreover, those who are responsible for the international promotion of prostituting female children, including but not limited to those involved in sex trafficking, need to be targeted. Recently, one such child prostitution ring, organized by Nigerians, was broken up in South Africa (Taye Obateru, 2004). Targeting these three demand factors will surely be quite costly, but it is necessary if one is to make an inroad into decreasing the prevalence of this practice. Obviously, it is expecting too much, especially in countries where the prostituting of female children both directly and indirectly enhances the balance of trade, for governments to find the funds. Rather, international governmental organizations, such as appropriate organs of the United Nations, will have to boost their commitment for these endeavors. This commitment might take the form of the "carrot" approach, whereby adequate funds are made available so as to provide incentive for police to perform their jobs (Levan, 1994, p. 909).

Additional supply factors will also need to be addressed concurrently with these recommendations if lessening the practice of prostituting female children is to succeed. Generally, poverty is in large part responsible for the ongoing supply of youthful flesh. Broadly defined, poverty takes into account more factors than simply the immediate financial situation of families. In general, it requires that additional emphasis be placed on the availability of both education and jobs. A concerted effort to target these three related concerns, especially in rural areas, is a necessity if these supply factors for the continuance of prostituting female children are to be lessened. Education systems need to be established that will focus not only on gender equality in admission but on outreach programs that will serve to help educate families on the important contribution, outside of prostitution, that females can make (O'Grady, 1994, pp. 114–115).

Additional emphasis must be placed on both literacy and functional literacy because of the current limited availability of jobs, especially in the rural communities of the developing countries. Increases in assistance to support programs that improve the status of women in patriarchical societies would also prove beneficial in terms of overcoming long-standing cultural beliefs regarding the role of females in society. Concurrent with the greater inclusion of females in the education system is the need for governmental measures promoting a greater infusion of capital into the manufacturing sector of the national economy. Emphasis needs to be placed on attracting foreign capital not only in the form of grants, aid, and loans, but in the form of foreign direct investment as well. The role of international financial institutions, such as the IMF, the IBRD, and multinational corporations, should be viewed with cautious optimism, depending on the ability of these institutions to generate economic growth and related benefits.

Law enforcement is also critical with regard to supply factors. There is a great need not only for statutes that penalize the parents or immediate conspirators for their role in promoting the prostituting of female children, but also for rigorous enforcement of these statutes (Levan, 1994, pp. 892–893). One of the most noticeable problems associated with criminalization in this area is the inability to overcome what has been for many countries a lengthy cultural tradition in terms of how the female child is to be regarded. Although the aforementioned emphasis on education can help reconstitute one's perception about the worth of the female child, it is not practical to think that this change would necessarily result in an immediate transformation of attitudes.

These considerations all need to be seen in light of several assumptions that have been made regarding the ability of any program to help alleviate the prominence of the practice of prostituting female children. The first assumption is that the transformation that is necessary, without destroying entire cultures, will take considerable time to exact. Obviously, any process of cultural change, regardless of how limited or extreme the change is, takes time to accomplish. The aforementioned historical overview pays tribute to the fact that extremely long-lived traditions are present and that change can only be expected to be gradual. Indeed, gradualism (i.e., patience) is required if these alterations are to meet with any success. Immediate displacement of well-established norms of behavior only serves to provoke immediate disregard for the behavior that serves as a replacement.

A second assumption rests on the understanding that capital, in the many forms that it presents itself, is perhaps the most important concern that has not only served to help establish the cultural practice of prostituting female children but also served to maintain it. While it has been maintained that poverty is not the sole cause of the practice of prostituting female children, it is an unmistakably clear component of the process. Consequently, any attempt to dissuade one from continuing this sociocultural custom will prove futile if sufficient capital has not been created and utilized appropriately in such areas as job creation and education.

In sum, one must approach change in the status quo by addressing both demand and supply factors that contribute to the continuation of the practice of prostituting female children. Moreover, one cannot expect change to occur in a short period of time. One can, however, expect that no substantive change will occur without the capital that fuels many of the program recommendations for lessening the extent of the practice throughout the world. Finally, the above recommendations are certainly favoring the revolutionary position, as described earlier . It is true, however, that both the extremes of universal human rights and cultural relativism will view these recommendations with hesitancy.

5

THE CASE OF FEMALE CHILD LABOR

The UN's International Labour Organization estimates that as many as 200 million children go to work rather than to school. They are in developing nations throughout the world, making everything from clothing and shoes to handbags and carpets. These children are the dark side of the new global economy, an international underclass working 12 or more hours a day, six or seven days a week. In the carpet factories of India, they are often separated from their families for years at a time. In the leather-handbag plants of Thailand, children report being forced to ingest amphetamines just to keep up their strength. In the charcoal industry of Brazil, tens of thousands of children work in a soot-drenched hell producing ingredients for steel alloys used in the manufacture of American cars.

Schapiro (1996, p. 205)

Irrespective of what they do and what they think about what they do, the mere fact of their being children sets children ideologically apart as a category of people excluded from the production of value. The dissociation of childhood from the performance of valued work has been increasingly considered a yardstick of modernity. International agencies and highly industrialized countries now turn this yardstick into a tool to condemn as backward and undemocratic those countries with a high incidence of child labor.

Nieuwenhuys (1996, p. 246)

HISTORY OF THE PRACTICE

Child labor[1] is a long-standing practice that continues in numerous cultures around the world. Although historically the practice has included both male and female children, the emphasis here is primarily on female child labor. Throughout its history the practice of employing female children has encompassed a wide geographical spread and has, arguably, consumed as many countries as the practices of female circumcision, infanticide, and prostitution together.

The history of female child labor dates at least to antiquity. In large part, the existence of female child labor at that time was associated with the institution of slavery.[2] In both Greek and Roman society, children were often, for various reasons, proffered to others in the form of slaves.[3] The slave owner would then use them in various capacities. Enslavement took on many forms but at the very least included such involuntary methods as the sale of one's own offspring, the kidnapping and subsequent sale of the victims, and the "claiming" of infants left "exposed" by their parents (Harris, 1999, pp. 72–74). Still others entered into slavery via a "debt repayment scheme," whereby the debtors would submit to servitude or place their children into "debt bondage." Additionally, penal enslavement, mostly in Roman society, often occurred upon a legal conviction. Prisoners of war were often purchased at "disposal auctions" (Madden, 1996). Moreover, Pomeroy (1975) states that "when towns were conquered or raided, male prisoners were either ransomed by their relatives or put to death by the victors, but women[4] and children were enslaved" (p. 26).

Relinquishing female children into involuntary servitude was perhaps a foregone conclusion based on impoverishment and the worth that Roman society placed on female children. Unquestionably, those with greater resources were more able to provide for their families than were those with lesser means. The elite in Roman and Greek society rarely surrendered their children, male or female, to a status of involuntary servitude. Conversely, the relative impoverishment of the majority dictated that a good number of children would have to "volunteer" their labor in support of the family farm, business, and so forth (Aldrete, 2004, p. 51). In impoverished families whose size was thought to be exceptional, it was not uncommon to sell a daughter into slavery. Consequently, "free" female child labor arose principally from the economically disadvantaged strata of society.

As a consequence of their gender, "free" female children, throughout the whole of classical antiquity (i.e., 7th-century B.C. to A.D. 476), were disadvantaged in education. Cole (1981) maintains, for example, that literacy was not universal during this time and that "in all places women are less likely to be literate than men" (p. 219). Education was largely a function of perceived benefit with respect to status. Outside wealthy, high-status families, there was no tangible benefit from educating daughters. Moreover, while the daughter's role in upper-class families during the classical Roman era was relatively celebrated, the daughter's position was almost always defined in relation to the son's. This was perhaps most evident in language, as the feminine form (i.e., *filia*) of the Latin noun for "son" (i.e., *filius*) was used (Hallett, 1984, p. 82) to refer to a daughter. Education was treated similarly among the ancient Egyptians. The education of the female child was the responsibility of the mother and typically would cease by age four. After this the female child would be taught the skills associated with becoming not only a wife but a mother (Aldrete, 2004, p. 56). One would be remiss if one does not mention, however, that this patterned behavior became less apparent toward late antiquity.

In classical Greek and Roman society, both males and females worked in rural settings. Although sons were preferred for more visible work, working on the domestic front is said to have been valued as working in textiles and carrying water had higher status for women. Moreover, Greek women were urged to be diligent domestically because working outside the home would be tantamount to prostituting one's self, an action that society would certainly view with contempt (Keuls, 1985, p. 231). Likewise, "roman fathers were expected to feel equal pride in their children of both sexes" (Hallett, 1984, p. 82). Having said this, however, does not negate the fact that this applied primarily to the skills of daughters in the private sphere and the skills of sons in the public realm.

As Athens, by the fifth century B.C., illustrated, the work that "free" female children would learn in the home and come to perform was a consequence of migration to the cities. It was during this time that the work of female children became considerably less visible and, as Pomeroy (1975) maintains, "less valued" (p. 71). In essence, females became largely relegated to the domestic workplace to perform such tasks as acquiring water, spinning and weaving textiles, and grinding corn. In large part they most closely resembled modern day "child domestic workers." Moreover, women were also responsible for bathing and anointing the men. Pomeroy (1975) mentions the following passage in support of this proposition: "Polycaste, Nestor's virginal young daughter, bathed Telemachus and massaged him with olive oil" (p. 30).

From later antiquity throughout most of the Middle Ages, attitudes toward the role of children were such that children's inherent worth continued to be dismissed. The needs of children were continually forgone in favor of those of the family unit. To some extent this paralleled the perception about the worth of the female child during classical antiquity. After all, the key reason for the existence of the female child during this period was to produce offspring and bring daughters up in a manner that would facilitate the work in her father's home prior to transferring this loyalty to her future husband. As Jaiswal (2000) states, "in Western antiquity and till the thirteenth century, adult attitudes toward children were generally dominated by an ideology that had little empathy for the needs of children. This ideology looked upon the child as a nuisance and an unwanted burden" (pp. 23–24). It is instructive to note the opposing argument, however, that the perception of children entered a transitional phase, which was ushered in with the rise of Christianity, whereby the role of children in defending the empire was considered increasingly important (Wiedemann, 1989). At best, this "transition" might have been characterized only by a shift in how the soul of the child was viewed.

The enforcement, or lack thereof, of certain laws in place during late antiquity speaks to the continued lack of respect for the physical and emotional needs of children. While prohibitions against the sale of one's children into slavery existed in the early days of classical antiquity, toward late antiquity they were in large part ignored. In A.D. 391, Emperor Valentinian II provided for the sale of free children because of "family need." Soon thereafter, Valentinian III encouraged the practice because of the ills of widespread famine (Nathan, 2000, pp. 136–137). In essence, the rights of the children were once again relegated to lesser importance when circumstance necessitated. While other practices were also indicted, such as trafficking in girls and female debt bondage, the reality of the day was that very often the demand for labor, due to the lack of slave labor, dictated the continuation of the practice.

A change that did begin during the Middle Ages was the sphere in which female child laborers were seen. Over time, the lesser-valued private life of the female child transitioned into working in public. Haines-Eitzen (1998) overviews three separate examples, for instance, of how female children were trained for more "public" life roles as scribes. Similarly, Shahar (1983) also notes the extent to which female children began taking on public roles in the English workforce:

> The great majority of village girls married, and the girls who did not marry in rural areas were usually from the poorest sections of the population. It was they who emigrated from their villages to work as serving girls in towns or hired agricultural workers in other villages, and they who were the most likely to engage in extramarital relations and bear bastards. (p. 229)

It is important to note that agricultural work, however, was more readily available for boys than for girls and mostly during summer (Cunningham, 1990, p. 134). Even so, it was during this period that female children more openly worked alongside both women and boys. In fact, as Nicholas (1995) maintains, the norm during the

Middle Ages was "to employ children for long hours at low wages" (p. 1103). While they would typically work on the family farm, it was not uncommon for them to labor for more prosperous farmers or even in the homes of the manor lords (Shahar, 1983, pp. 231, 239).

In his review of Spanish Castilian society, Dillard (1984) also informs us about the greater incidence of "domiciled domestics" as well as "parented girls" who were characteristically unmarried and worked as domestics or in taverns to earn money to send home to their parents (p. 160). Moreover, parented girls as young as eight years are noted, during the fifteenth century, in both York and Tuscany (Nicholas, 1995, p. 1105). Medieval guilds, during this period, were still somewhat accepting of women because some women occupied "official" positions in the guild while girls were apprenticed as laundresses, seamstresses, textile workers, and so forth (Honeyman & Goodman, 1991, pp. 610–612).

Throughout the early modern age, children continued to be found in major manufacturing and mining sectors of the economy, but this practice would soon be in decline in Europe. Cunningham (1991) notes that apprenticeship was in decline during the eighteenth century and that during the late eighteenth and nineteenth centuries children were mainly visible in the cotton industries (p. 115). The seventeenth and eighteenth centuries also saw greater restrictions on females in the workplace as guilds set out to redefine male work as productive work and female work as domestic, unproductive work (Honeyman and Goodman, 1991, pp. 612–614).

In nineteenth-century Europe the debate over female participation in the formal economy raged on and one of the proposed responses, so as to protect the adult male role in the formal economy, was to introduce legislation that would restrict child labor in both manufacturing and mining enterprises (Cunningham, 1990, pp. 621–622). The great irony here is that child labor was addressed only in order to maintain the patriarchal society of the day. The emphasis on eradicating child labor was not as much a concern over the well-being of children as it was over the need to maintain or provide jobs for adult males. Nardinelli (1990) gives an alternative explanation when he states that society realized that the opportunity cost of child labor, which involved forgoing productive education, was costlier to society over the long term (p. 61). Increasing incomes during the industrial revolution, along with improving mortality statistics, spurred the transitional emphasis on the education and health concerns of children. This dynamic would repeat itself in the United States during the twentieth century.

It is important to reinforce the transition of female child labor, in what would become the developed countries, from the private to public sphere during the Middle Ages and back to the private sphere by the late nineteenth century. While apparent progress was being made in the relatively more developed countries of the day, other realms would soon come into greater focus as the world began addressing the human condition and dignity of female child laborers in the developing countries.

The practice of incorporating female child labor into the economies of the modern age appears to be quite significant. While the practice of female child labor has somewhat ebbed and flowed throughout history, the modern age has witnessed a resurgence of the phenomenon. Greater understanding about the practice of female child labor in the modern period is facilitated by definitional clarity of the concepts involved. While the emphasis of this chapter is on female child labor, this concept only touches the surface of the problem. In general terms, the idea of "economically active children" provides a conceptual "catchall umbrella" that consumes a variety of related terms. The ILO (2002c) defines economic activity as

> all market production (paid work) and certain types of non-market production (unpaid work), including production of goods for own use. Therefore, whether paid or unpaid, the activity or occupation could be in the formal or informal sector and in urban or rural areas. For example, children engaged in unpaid activities in a market-oriented establishment operated by a relative living in the same household are considered as working in an economic activity. Also, children working as maids or domestic workers in someone else's household are considered as economically active. However, children engaged in domestic chores within their own households are not considered as economically active. (pp. 29–30)

Societies, throughout time, have often argued that some economic activity performed by children is positive (Banerjee, 1995, p. 403) inasmuch as it is developmental (i.e., involving "purpose, plan and freedom," as Fuller, 1937, states). Conversely, economic activity that is considered to have harmful, negative effects on children is referred to as labor. In the early twentieth century, debates over economic activity by children were characterized by this "work vs. labor" dichotomy. Recent authors, however, have suggested the abandonment of this conceptualization by opting instead for a more intrusive "dispassionate analysis of the character of the work undertaken by particular children in particular settings" (Hobbs, McKechnie & Lavalette, 1999, pp. 56–57). The reality is that both types of analysis have come into play as the ILO (2002c) continues to seek a distinction between "acceptable forms of work by children (which may be regarded as positive) on the one hand, and child labour that needs to be eliminated on the other" (p. 31).

For purposes of this chapter, "child" is defined in accordance with Article I of the 1989 United Nations Convention on the Rights of the Child. Consequently, "child"[5] means "every human being below the age of eighteen years unless, under the law applicable to the child, majority is attained earlier" (UNICEF, 2005a). While most agree that "child labor" is a negative conceptualization of economic activity performed by children, there exist more numerous categories (i.e., settings) in which child labor occurs.

According to Article 7 of the 1973 ILO Minimum Age Convention (No.138), "non-hazardous work" most often refers to "light work" that is not injurious to the development and health of the child from age 13, does not consume more than 14 hours per week, and does not interfere with school attendance or vocational training.[6] Conversely, the ILO (2002c) considers "hazardous work" and the "unconditional worst forms of child labour" to be a definitional dichotomy consumed under the "worst forms of child labour" (p. 33). According to Article 3 of the 1999 ILO Worst Forms of Child Labour Convention (No.182), the "worst forms of child labour" consumes such areas as child prostitution, pornography, slavery, sale and trafficking, debt bondage, serfdom, forced or compulsory labor, forced or compulsory military recruitment, and illicit activities such as drug production and running as well as any other activity that will inherently result in harm to the child. The ILO (2002c), in its study estimating the extent of child labor, incorporates the more specific definition of "hazardous work" that was offered in the 1999 Worst Forms of Child Labour Recommendation (R190). Specifically, according to Article 2, Section 3, hazardous work includes

(a) work which exposes children to physical, psychological or sexual abuse
(b) work underground, under water, at dangerous heights or in confined spaces
(c) work with dangerous machinery, equipment and tools, or which involves the manual handling or transport of heavy loads
(d) work in an unhealthy environment which may, for example, expose children to hazardous substances, agents or processes, or to temperatures, noise levels, or vibrations damaging to their health
(e) work under particularly difficult conditions such as work for long hours or during the night or work where the child is unreasonably confined to the premises of the employer

Table 5.1   Type of Economic Activity by Age, 2000

Age Group	Type of Economic Activity			
	Nonhazardous Work/Labor		Worst Forms of Child Labor (WFCL)	
	Light Work	*Regular Work*	*Hazardous Work*	*Unconditional WFCL*
	<14 hours per week	≥14 hours per week & <43 hours per week	—exposure to abuse —underground/water —dangerous height —confined spaces —dangerous machinery —heavy loads —unhealthy environments —difficult work conditions ≥43 hours per week	—trafficking in children —slavery —serfdom —debt bondage —forced labor —forced military —prostitution —pornography —illicit activities
5–11	Child labor	Child labor	Child labor	Child labor
12–14	Child work	Child labor	Child labor	Child labor
15–17	Child work	Child work	Child labor	Child labor

Sources: ILO (2002); Minimum Age Convention (1973); Worst Forms of Child Labour Convention (1999); Worst Forms of Child Labour Recommendation (1999).

Tables 5.1 and 5.2 give concrete representation to the aforementioned overarching and specific conceptualizations related to child labor and the numbers associated with these categories. For example, table 5.1 shows that 12- to 14-year-olds who perform light work and 15- to 17-year-olds who perform nonhazardous work engage in types of economic activity that are viewed as positive and acceptable. Conversely, every other category is considered negative economic activity and "charted" for elimination. Table 5.2 illustrates that the total number of child laborers in 2000 was 245.5 million, or 69.8 percent of the 351.7 million economically active children.[7] Moreover, 170.5 million children (69.5% of child laborers) aged 5 to 17 years were employed in some form of hazardous work. The percentage of economically active children that are child laborers in hazardous work does become smaller as age increases. The corresponding figures for the 5–11, 12–14, and 15–17 age groups are 55.1 percent, 50.2 percent, and 42.0 percent, respectively.

Table 5.3 illustrates the same categories but only for female child laborers. The percentages are quite comparable to those found in

Table 5.2 Economically Active Children by Age and Type of Economic Activity, 2000

Age Group	Type of Economic Activity			Worst Forms of Child Labor	Economically Active Children
	Nonhazardous Work/Labor				
	Light Work		Regular Work	Hazardous Work	
5–11		49,200,000		60,500,000	109,700,000
12–14	24,500,000		25,800,000	50,800,000	101,100,000
15–17		81,700,000		59,200,000	140,900,000
Total		181,200,000		170,500,000 (69.5%)	351,700,000
Total Child Labor			245,500,000 (69.8%)		

Source: ILO (2002).

table 5.2, as 67.6 percent of female children who are economically active are classified as laborers, with 66.0 percent of laborers experiencing hazardous work. Moreover, the percentage of economically active females that are child laborers also decreases significantly with age: the numbers for the three aforementioned age groups are 55.8 percent, 41.7 percent, and 37.7 percent, respectively. Also worthy of note is that, in the 5–11 age group, females were just as numerous as males in hazardous work areas and nearly as numerous in nonhazardous areas.

The data on child labor has also illustrated a decidedly marked shift in terms of geographic location. Basu and Van (1998) make clear that the developed countries used to have a considerably larger problem with the practice (p. 414), but the current situation is different. According to the English and Wales census of 1851, 1.4 percent of 1,042,131 girls aged 5 to 9 years and 19.9 percent of the 949,362 girls aged 10 to 14 years were at work. This percentage increased to 65.2 for girls aged 15 to 19 years (Cunningham, 1990, pp. 140–145). Similarly, the U.S. Census of 1890 revealed that 9.0 percent of the 3,273,369 girls aged 10 to 15 years were at work in 1880. This rate hovered around 30 percent for the states of South Carolina, Georgia, Alabama, and Louisiana (Department of the Interior, Census Office, 1897, p. lxxxv).

By the latter twentieth century the geographical location of the majority of child labor was clearly in the developing world countries.

Table 5.3   Economically Active Female Children by Age and Type of Economic Activity, 2000

Age Group	Type of Economic Activity				
	Nonhazardous Work/Labor			Worst Forms of Child Labor	Economically Active Children
	Light Work		Regular Work	Hazardous Work	
5–11		23,600,000		29,800,000	53,400,000
12-14	13,300,000		14,900,000	20,200,000	48,400,000
15-17		41,000,000		24,800,000	65,800,000
Total		92,800,000		74,800,000	167,600,000
				(66.0%)	(47.7%)
Total Female Child Labor		113,300,000			
		(67.6%)			

Source: ILO (2002).

Table 5.4   Child Labor in the Unconditional Worst Forms of Child Labor, 2000

Unconditional Worst Forms of Child Labor	
Forced & Bonded Labor	5,700,000 (67.9%)
Armed Conflict	300,000 (3.6%)
Prostitution & Pornography	1,800,000 (21.4%)
Illicit Activities	600,000 (7.1%)
Total	8,400,000

Source: ILO (2002).

From 1980 to 2000, the number of economically active children went from 118.7 to 106.4 million in developed countries. Comparatively, the 1980 figure of 642.8 jumped to 782.9 million in 2000 for developing countries (ILO, 2006c).

Of the 211 million child laborers in 2000, 206.1 million (97.7%) were located in the developing world, with the Asia and the Pacific region having the highest number (127.3 million).[8] For a percentage of the total number of children aged 5 to 17 years, the sub-Saharan African region appears most problematic (31.9%), with Asia and the Pacific (25.4%), Latin America and the Caribbean (19.9%), and the Middle East and North Africa (18.7%) following close behind (ILO, 2002c, pp. 17–18). What is perhaps most alarming is that the problem becomes increasingly troublesome with age when the 5–9, 10–14, and 15–17 age groups are evaluated. The situation only becomes worse for the unconditional worst forms of child labor. Of the estimated 8.4 million children in this quandary, 7.9 million (93.7%) are located in the developing world, with 70 percent of these children subjected to forced or bonded labor in the Asia and the Pacific region (ILO, 2002c, p. 27). Table 5.4 breaks down the types of unconditional worst forms and their percentage makeup.

The regional differences in the developing world are accentuated by reporting on individual countries in the regions with the greatest numbers of child laborers. In India, according to Larson (2004, p. 103), an estimated 100 to 150 million 5- to 14-year-olds are economically active, with approximately half of them involved in hazardous work. Mehta (1994, p. 24) claims that India has 44 million children workers under age 13 and that 300,000 of them work in the infamous carpet industry. Moreover, Weissman (1997, p. 11) states that 15,000,000 child laborers are engaged in the practice of bonded labor. In sum, Arat (2002) contends that the child labor industry in India increased at an annual rate of 4 percent throughout the 1990s (p. 191).

Although India is arguably the largest employer of child labor in the region and the world, the issue is also quite problematic in neighboring countries. A 1994 U.S. Department of Labor study stated that there were an estimated 400,000 child rug weavers in India, and 150,000 and 1,000,000 in Nepal and Pakistan, respectively (Weissman, 1997, p. 11). Similarly, Silvers (1996) maintains that the number of child laborers aged 4 to 14 years in Pakistan is 11 million, with approximately half of these being under age ten and 0.5 to 1 million working as carpet weavers (pp. 80–81). A 2004 study by the Nepalese Ministry of Labor and Transport Management, however, suggests that the number of Nepalese child laborers is considerably lower at 2.6 million, with most of them being domestic laborers (55,600) and child porters (46,000). Interestingly enough, the ministry estimates the number of child laborers in the carpet industry to be only 4,200 ("Child Labour," 2004). Lastly, it is estimated that 18 percent of 5- to 14-year-olds in Bangladesh are child laborers resulting in an estimated 6.3 million children ("Child Labor," 2000).

While not many studies focus on the Latin America and the Caribbean region, there are enough to peruse some of the "trouble spots." Perhaps the most problematic country in the Latin American region is Mexico. According to Carey (2004), estimates of child labor in Mexico range from 400,000 to 11 million. Specifically, while UNICEF maintains that 8 million children (25.8%) younger than

15 work, the Mexican Statistics Institute states that the number is closer to 11 million (34.4%) (p. 125).

Traver (2004) reports that the number of 10- to 17-year-olds in Brazil is 7.5 million, with 2 million being under age 14. Moreover, the Brazilian Institute of Geography and Statistics claims that 11.6 percent of the Brazilian labor force is made up of child laborers, aged 11 to 14 years (p. 29). Patrinos and Psacharopoulos (1995) claim the existence of 7 million child laborers, of which 18 percent are aged between 10 and 14 years (p. 49). In a 1997 interview, the then director and president of the Foundation for Children's Rights in Sao Paulo, Oded Grajew, claimed that there were between 3 and 4 million child laborers below age 14 in Brazil ("Battling Brazil's Child Labor Brutality," 1997, p. 20).

Other parts of Latin America and the Caribbean region also suffer from great levels of child labor. Keys and DeFayette (2004) report that approximately 38 percent of Guatemalan children aged 7 through 14 (1.4 million) are child laborers (p. 80). Patrinos and Psacharopoulos (1995) state that 40 percent of 11- to 12-year-old female child laborers in Colombia are domestic workers (p. 49). It is also estimated that 150,000 to 200,000 Venezuelan children under age 14 are working, with girls starting to work at an earlier age than boys in such areas as washing and sewing (Marquez, 1996).

To conclude, it is undeniable that child labor, in its varied forms, continues to exist in great numbers throughout the world, although mostly in the developing regions. Moreover, the incidence of female child labor is at a par with male child labor, especially when those aged 5 to 14 years are considered. This holds true regardless of whether one is addressing the worst forms of child labor or the nonhazardous forms. Finally, it is quite conceivable that the most important group of child laborers today are females, who constitute the majority of child domestic workers, a form of child labor with the greatest potential for abusive behavior due to the laborer being "hidden" from society (IPEC, 2004b, p. 6; Pflug, 2002, p.8).

Specifics of the Practice

At ten-thirty in the evening, in a new high-rise flat in Dhaka, a little girl of about nine treads, noiseless and barefoot, on the cool marble floor. She sets a plastic tray on a table beside me, a plate of sweet bananas, biscuits and coffee. Catching my look of astonishment, my—a teacher—says "Shamina works for us. She is like our daughter."

His real daughter has been sleeping for more than an hour. Shamina
receives no wage. (Seabrook, 2000, p. 14)

Like her mother, 12 year-old Asiya spends her days and evenings
in a dim, dank garment factory in central Dacca, Bangladesh, where
cobwebs dangle from the ceiling and the only two exits are padlocked
or under guard around the clock. For the past two years, Asiya has
toiled six days a week in the factory, cutting fabrics and carrying piles of
shirts destined for Western markets. She earns $15 a month—about five
cents an hour—which her mother, Masuda, calls the difference between
comfort and hunger for her two children. But it is not a choice Asiya
makes willingly. "I don't like the work," the timid girl said matter-of-factly.
"I would prefer to go to school." (Stackhouse, 1996, p. 31)

The specific forms of female child labor are both numerous and
diverse. Consequently, past attempts at classification have been somewhat troublesome, in that different categorization schema have been
employed to address similar subjects. For example, the sixth item on
the agenda at the 86th session of the International Labour Conference
referred to the nature of child labor in terms of four components:
hazardous work, domestic workers, slavery and forced child labor, and
prostitution and the trafficking of children (ILO, 1998a). Moreover,
a UNICEF (1997) report on the dimensions of child labor identified domestic service, forced and bonded labor, commercial sexual
exploitation, industrial and plantation work, street work, work for the
family, and girl's work as the main categories of inquiry. Jaiswal (2000)
refers to four distinct categories, which include street children, those
who are bonded to their "employer," those who work in concert with
their family, and those who "work in factories, workshops and mines"
(pp. 36–37). Lastly, Murshed (2001) presented a continuum whereby
farm work and house chores were considered the least exploitative and
bonded labor the most exploitative type of child labor. Between these
extremes were types such as apprenticeships and wage labor.

The various issues within child labor that different international
bodies choose to emphasize illustrate the complexity of detailing the
specifics of the practice. For purposes of this inquiry, one must also
distinguish the types of labor that are more readily associated with
girls. Although difficult to accomplish, this differentiation will assist in
identifying potential resolutions. Finally, it is imperative to note that
the categorization schema typically utilized do not constitute mutually exclusive categories. For example, a female child domestic worker
might be classified under the general category of child labor but might

also be classified under the unconditional worst forms of child labor, depending on what she is subject to while serving in this capacity.

The course of action taken here will be to provide a more concrete idea about the types of "jobs" that characterize the general types of economic activity outlined in table 5.1: nonhazardous work, hazardous work, and the unconditional worst forms of child labor. In so doing, the extent to which girls are associated with a given activity will be noted. Again, while all categorization schemes can be brought into question, this particular approach appears to be most useful given the informational objective of this section.

Nonhazardous work or labor, as was mentioned earlier, can involve light work as well as regular work. Also important is the role that age plays in labeling. By convention, light work is permissible from age 12 unless it interferes with the education of the child. Light work can take on many forms, including what IPEC (2004b) refers to as "helping hands." As IPEC (2004b) states:

> In every country of the world, children lend a helping hand in their own home, maybe by preparing the meals or washing the dishes after dinner before going out to play. They may make the bed, for example, hang out the washing, mow the lawn, baby-sit a younger sibling, pick fruit on the family allotment, milk the goat or feed the chickens. In moderation and in particular as long as they do not interfere with the children's education or time to play, such "helping hand"-type tasks can be positive experiences. They help children to learn basic skills in preparation for the future and to feel that they are contributing to the family's tasks, thus raising their self-esteem. The children may grumble about it occasionally, but doing a few small jobs around the house will help them to learn about responsibility and sharing and to gain practical skills. This is not child domestic labour. (p. 5)

One might also make an argument that, in addition to the types of work listed by IPEC, cooking, gathering wood, gardening, collecting water, and going to the market might also constitute light work. For the most part these are chores that are outside of the formal economy and are not typically considered to be productive economic activity. As a consequence, it is not surprising to find that girls often outnumber boys in these types of enterprises. Moreover, the number of girls in these activities is probably underestimated because of formal surveys not taking unpaid economic activity into consideration (Ashagrie, 1998; ILO, 1996).

Light work is also assessed in terms of the age of the child and how many hours per week economic activity is performed. Light work that constitutes child labor is not only premised on the child being younger than 12 years but also involves the proposition that the child is working more than 14 hours per week. For those younger than 12 years, however, any light work would constitute nonhazardous child labor.

Regular work involves similar activities as outlined under "light work" and also considers age and hours of work. Moreover, almost any kind of work not found on the list of hazardous activities is likely to be found under regular work. Whether it constitutes child labor is dependent on whether the child is 15 (14 in countries with less well-developed economic and education systems). One must be older than this and work more than 14 but less than 43 hours per week for the economic activity to be considered nonhazardous work as opposed to child labor. If these stipulations are not met, for instance a child aged 13 years working 30 hours per week, then it is considered child labor, a practice subject to elimination.

Hazardous work involves more complex tasks and enterprises that are considered quite dangerous to the safety, morality, or health of the child worker (ILO, 1973). Consequently, there is no acceptable age at which a child (defined as an individual less than 18 years of age)[9] should be allowed to perform the activity. It is crucial to understand that the definition of "hazardous labor" is left up to the member nations via national laws and regulations.

To illustrate the potential differences between nations, it is instructive to both investigate how nations determine what constitutes hazardous child labor and explore the differences of opinion. The process by which nations determine what occupations and conditions constitute child labor is sixfold. The initial concern is with creating a framework by which major stakeholders, such as governments, labor unions, workers, and employers, are identified and included. This is followed by a concerted effort to gather all relevant information concerning international standards and current laws, as well as information pertaining to different types of labor. Most crucial at this point is to impose criteria for what constitutes "hazardous labor" and then construct a list of occupations and conditions and suggest ways to prohibit children from becoming involved in them.

Step four, identified in Article 4, Section 1, of the 1999 Worst Forms of Child Labour Convention (ILO, 1999), requires the "competent authority" to formalize the list. The promotion of the list to the general public and setting a timetable for action is also crucial. Concurrently, the collection of new information is instrumental in the final stage dealing with review of the list and implementation of any updates needed to the list or laws (IPEC, 2004a).

Moving through this process at a national level virtually guarantees that there will be differences not only in the criteria that identify hazardous labor but in the generated list of such economic activities and conditions as well. For example, one must be 18 years old in the United States to work in or with meat rendering, bakery, brick manufacturing, circular saws and dangerous machinery, construction and demolition, lifting machinery, excavation, forestry, mining, paper/printing, vehicle operation, and metalworking. Conversely, of these listed areas, India only has legal prohibition against working with circular saws and dangerous machinery, in construction and demolition, underground, and in vehicle operation. Of noteworthy difference, however, is the fact that the age for underground work and vehicle operation in India is 14 (ILO, 1991).

Hazardous labor is referred to as the conditional worst forms of child labor. More harmful, however, are the practices that constitute the unconditional worst forms of child labor, as were listed in table 5.1. Although several types exist, the focus here will be on forced labor. This is due to the large number of children that forced labor impacts and the fact that the typology of forced labor used here incorporates most of the other unconditional forms of child labor.

The ILO (2005, pp. 10–11) has recently put forth an alternative three-prong typology by which to classify forced labor. The first prong consists of the types of forced labor that are imposed by the State and includes, for example, prison labor, military conscription, and obligatory involvement in public works. The second prong consists of forced labor for purposes of sexual exploitation by private actors and includes the practices of prostitution and pornography.[10] The final prong covers forced labor for purposes of economic exploitation and includes bonded labor as well as child domestic workers and agricultural workers. The ILO estimates that there are a total of 12.3 million child victims of forced labor. Those who are economically exploited are most numerous (7.81 million, or 63.5%), while those who are victims of the State or military imposition number 2.49 million (20.2%). Finally, those who are sexually exploited number 1.39 million (11.3%), while an additional 610,000 (5.0%) are considered to cross over to more than one category (ILO, 2005, p. 12). What is perhaps most illuminating is that women and girls constitute 98 percent of those forced into sexual exploitation and 56 percent of those forced into economic exploitation (ILO, 2005, p. 15).

Economic exploitation takes on many forms. The definition of debt bondage and an associated form of forced labor is expressed in Article 1 of the 1956 Supplementary Convention on the Abolition of Slavery, the Slave Trade, and Institutions and Practices Similar to Slavery:

> Debt bondage, that is to say, the status or condition arising from a pledge by a debtor of his personal services or of those of a person under his control as security for a debt, if the value of those services as reasonably assessed is not applied towards the liquidation of the debt or the length and nature of those services are not respectively limited and defined.
>
> Any institution or practice whereby a child or young person under the age of 18 years, is delivered by either or both of his natural parents or by his guardian to another person, whether for reward or not, with a view to the exploitation of the child or young person or of his labour. (United Nations High Commissioner for Human Rights, 1956)

Forced labor in the form of debt bondage is critical in the sense that many children who experience this specific practice have a low probability of ever escaping. Debt bondage is pronounced in many economic enterprises, including the silk, carpet, beedi, agricultural, prostitution, and metalworking industries (Tucker, 1997, p. 573). The practice appears to be well entrenched in the cultures of many developing countries, but especially those in central Asia. The *chukri* system in Bangladesh and India typically require the girl prostitute to work for free for a year or longer in order to pay for necessities such as clothes, food, and other living expenses. Similarly, the *kamaiya* system in Nepal, although outlawed in 2000, continues to pass indebtedness through the family (i.e., intergenerational bondage) upon death or disutility of the person in bondage. The Pakistani *parchi charhana* system, mostly applicable to child domestic workers, maintains the indebtedness by forcing the child domestic to compensate her employer for items that she damages while "employed" (ILO, 2005, pp. 31–35; Weissman, 1997, p. 11).

Child domestic workers are the most vulnerable segment of the child labor population because the nature of their work is "hidden" from public view. The Dominicans call them *puerta cerrada,* or "closed door" servants (UNICEF, 1997b, p. 30). Because of this "invisibility," the child domestic worker is more likely to experience sexual as well as economic exploitation. Exploitation is also due to the inability of labor inspectors to investigate private homes that are outside their legal jurisdiction (ILO, 2005, p. 50; Jaiswal, 2000, p. 12).

The realm of child domestic work is disproportionately populated by girls. This is especially the case in the Asian region, where the perceived value of the girl child is, perhaps, the lowest of any developing region. Moreover, it appears that younger girls (aged 5 to 11 years) are more preferable than older girls (aged 12 to 14 years) to be a servant/maid. This becomes more pronounced when one looks at the urban as opposed to rural sector (Amin, Quayes, & Rives, 2004). One should note, however, that several Latin American nations also evince the same proclivity for girl child domestic workers. For example, the proportion of female child domestic workers in Brazil, Costa Rica, and Guatemala is 94.5 percent, 91.5 percent, and 90.4 percent, respectively (IPEC, 2004b, p. 20).

In general, female child domestic work is looked upon as a suitable alternative to educating a girl in a culture that is, in large part, inhospitable to the rights of the girl child. In essence, the value of the female child is relegated to secondary importance at best and is not regarded as a positive contribution to productive economic activity, something that domestic work is not considered to be. Female child domestic work is also seen as a "preparatory period" for marriage and the associated expectations of the girl's role in marriage. Given that the girl, in many cultures, will go to live with her husband's family, there is no reason for her family to formally educate her and lose the benefits of so-called education to another family.

Agricultural economic activity is the largest sector of child labor in terms of the absolute numbers of girls involved. One particular study indicates that a conservative estimate of child labor in the agricultural realm throughout the developing world is 230,000 (as cited in Arat, 2002, p. 180). A more recent ILO study indicates that 70 percent of child laborers work in agriculture, hunting, forestry, or fishing (as cited in UNICEF, 2005b, p. 22). Moreover, in a study of 26 countries, it was found that 75.3 percent of girls were involved in agriculture, hunting, forestry, or fishing (Ashagrie, 1998).

Regardless of the exact numbers, it is obvious that the vast majority of "identifiable" female child laborers work in agricultural enterprises. Moreover, it is often the case that girls are treated worse than boys in this particular sector. For example, girls will typically begin agricultural-related work at a younger age than boys. Because of the responsibilities associated with domestic considerations, girls also find themselves working considerably longer days than do boys (Arat, 2002, pp. 181–182; Ashagrie, 1998; ILO, 2002b, pp. 24–25; Jaiswal, 2000, p. 47). Much like their female domestic working counterparts, they too are often the victims of sexual abuse.

The agricultural tasks undertaken by girls are especially disturbing when the impact of this work on both their health and psyche is considered. Typically, the performance of certain tasks often exposes the child to biological, chemical, and carcinogenic agents; infections attributable to contaminated soil and water; and positional stress (ILO, 1998a, p. 11; ILO, 2002a, p. 24). Just as commonplace are irritations to the skin, eyes, and respiratory system (UNICEF, 1997b, p. 38). These particular types of health hazards are a consequence of coming into contact with a variety of chemicals such as fertilizers, pesticides, herbicides, and other toxic hazardous materials.

Perhaps the most well known type of forced labor that is imposed by the state is that of children "employed" by both government and antigovernment forces.[11] More specifically, the following definition of "child soldier" has been adopted by significant organizations such as UNICEF:

> any person under 18 years of age who is part of any kind of regular or irregular armed force or armed group in any capacity, including but not limited to cooks, porters, messengers and anyone accompanying such groups, other than family members. The definition includes girls recruited for sexual purposes and for forced marriage. It does not, therefore, only refer to a child who is carrying or has carried arms. (United Nations Children's Fund, 1997b)

It is estimated that the number of child soldiers is 300,000 worldwide. Regionally, Asia/Pacific and Africa are estimated to have 120,000 child soldiers each, whereas Latin American/ Caribbean (30,000) region, transition economies (5,000), and developed economies (1,000) are estimated to have considerably fewer (ILO, 2002c, p. 27). These are a conservative estimate, however, because of the inability to accurately count those children who "serve" combatants in indirect ways such as porters, cooks, and sexual slaves ("Kids without a Childhood," 2000).

Given that females are more likely to be abducted to fill the aforementioned roles, it is likely that estimates take too lightly the role that girls play among these forces. McKay and Mazurana's study (as cited in ILO, 2002b) indicates that of female child soldiers, 41 percent are fighters, 28 percent are sexual servants, 25 percent are porters, 21 percent are looters, 18 percent are camp followers, 13 percent are cooks, and 10 percent are used on suicide missions. Some of these girls are as young as 8 years old (ILO, 2002b, p. 34). Although Smolin (2000, pp. 964–965) states that this is an area that is outside the jurisdiction of the ILO, it is instructive to note that UNICEF (2005b, p. 28) believes that the incidence of this type of state forced labor appeared to have decreased by 2004.

CULTURAL RELEVANCE

Explanations for the practice of female child labor are as varied as the explanations given for the practice of prostituting female children. Moreover, while some cultural groupings (i.e., ethnic groups) exhibit similarities with respect to causation, many provide a diverse array of reasons for the continuation of the practice. What is common among most practicing cultures is that the explanation is multifaceted and draws on social and economic factors. Keeping in mind the likely possibility that the array of factors detailed herein will still represent—in a sense, cultural reductionism—we can proceed with clarifying the reasons for the practice.

While the practice of female child labor is largely an economic consideration, the factors addressed will be presented in terms of whether they are an expression of the supply side (i.e., "push" factors) or the demand side (i.e., "pull" factors) of the equation. The supply factors to be discussed relate to the general spheres of poverty, education, tradition and cultural norms, and vulnerability. The demand factors included revolve around childhood "characteristics" and globalization. The fact that these factors are separated into tidy categories for ease of presentation does not deny that there exists an extensive degree of overlap among the causal factors.

Given the pervasiveness of poverty among countries in the international system today, it is no wonder that its existence is usually associated with the rise of female child labor. Indeed, much of the scholarly literature on the subject views impoverishment as the primary (i.e., root) cause (Boonpala and Kane, 2001, p. 20; Pflug, 2002, p. 33; UNICEF, 1997a, p. 28; UNICEF, 2005b, pp. 12–13).

To state that poverty *necessarily* gives rise to female child labor, however, is to overstate the importance of general deprivation relative to other factors. For example, the southern state of Kerala in India and Cuba are among the poorest but have virtually eliminated the practice of child labor (Arat, 2002, pp. 200–201; ILO, 1998a, pp. 14–15). Likewise, Hasnat (1995) suggests that while poverty is the *basic* cause, it cannot be viewed as the *sole* cause (p. 419). Tucker (1997) proposes that the perception that poverty alone is responsible for child labor is one of the key myths associated with the practice (pp. 579–580). In essence, alternative factors are also important to understanding causation.

The manner by which the impact of poverty on female child labor is framed is of great consequence in terms of generating a program(s) for changing the practice. What is of similar importance is one's understanding of the concept of poverty. Often, those in the West look at poverty in an absolute sense. For example, if you have a family of four and earn an amount that falls below a designated "poverty line," you are in poverty. An alternative to this "absolutist" approach is to recognize that the concept of poverty is relative and multidimensional and differs from one family to the next. As IPEC (2004b) states:

> Poverty may be a state in which a family lives with no possessions at all and cannot afford to put food on the table. Or it may be a temporary situation where a family has entered into debt, for example by borrowing money it cannot afford to repay, or by acquiring goods (ranging for example from electronic equipment in an urban household to livestock or seeds for the family smallholding) and defaulting on repayments. (p. 17)

Moreover, the ILO (2002a, p. 50) indicates that not all households in "absolute" poverty resort to child labor while there are those households that are not in "absolute" poverty but still send their children to work. Given this structure, it is conceivable that a family may not be in poverty in an absolute sense, but still might be under sufficient economic pressure, relatively speaking, to promote female child labor.

The decision to employ one's children as labor is, in part, a result of the productivity and earnings of the household. Becker (1965) discusses the importance of time to productivity, suggesting that time spent in going to school, dining, or virtually any activity is time that is taken out of economic productivity (pp. 493–494). When families find themselves in poverty, whether in an absolute or relative sense, they are likely to reconsider the allocation of their children's time. Moreover, they might well consider how a reallocation of their time might serve to improve household earnings. The assumption underlying this is that households seek to optimally allocate the time of their children to produce the most effective economic outcome given the need. The most effective use of children's time is, in reality, born out of a cost-benefit calculus that is also employed in the family's decision on the number of children to have. Often, according to Becker and Lewis (1973), families will substitute quantity for quality. In essence, having more children may be a response to the, relatively, poorer quality of children.[12]

The actual importance of children to the earnings of the household can be quite large. Anker and Melkas (1996) indicate that child labor may range between 10 percent and 25 percent of total household income, with even a larger percentage for illegal activities. This is a substantial percentage, especially if one considers that the typical child's wage is considerably lower than an adult's. In essence, the child worker might well work for twice the time of an adult wage earner in order to receive similar outright wages.

A second supply side factor relates to the status of education in society. In large part, the lack of education is correlated highly with impoverishment. Moreover, the relationship is cyclical in terms of causation. An impoverished family will send the female children to work instead of spending this time on their education. This opportunity cost with respect to education results in a less educated child, which quite often results in future impoverishment. While this decision might be perceived as having a positive short-term outcome, the reality is that it will likely result in a long-term negative circumstance that completes the "catch 22" conundrum that relatively poor and uneducated households experience.

The lack of education can be presented in terms of a general lack of resources. For example, access to education, even at the primary level, is often limited because of the lack of an appropriate education infrastructure. Sometimes this is a result of governmental decisions to fund certain levels of education, such as the decision to primarily fund secondary and university education as opposed to primary education. The net effect of such a choice is to promote the education needs of the few over the education needs of the majority (Tucker, 1997, p. 577).

The relative lack of funding for primary education also results in fewer schools that are devoted to primary education. The low number of schools results in them being less accessible. Moreover, the costs associated with these schools, even for supposed "free" schools, are sufficient to turn families away from taking part. Conversely, not attending a "free" school may cost families up to one-third of their income, not to mention the cost of the time (i.e., income) that the child no longer has so as to help provide for the family (ILO, 1996). In discussing the reasons for not taking part in school, IPEC (2004b) summarizes the access component rather well:

> This may be because school was too difficult for them: school may have been so far away, for example, that the journey to and from school was unsafe, arduous or too expensive. There may not have been schools at the right level in the child's community. Even where schooling was available, it may have been too expensive. Often, even where "free" schooling is provided, there are related costs—for example for clothing, books, writing materials or meals—that push "free" school beyond the financial capacity of the child's family. (p. 23)

Access issues may also arise after the child has found the way to get to school. The lack of adequate instruction is often cited as a reason for dropping out. Students may not readily see the importance, in terms of it leading to practical application (i.e., future employment), of their formal education. Future employment may be impossible because of the insufficiency of one's education or come as a result of there being no jobs for which these children are preparing (Tucker, 1997, p. 577). Beyond this, access to a quality education is sometimes limited because of outdated teaching materials, the teaching of inappropriate skills, and the consistent absence, intoxication, or abusiveness of teachers (Boonpala and Kane, 2001, p. 21; IPEC, 2004b, p. 23; Murshed, 2001; UNICEF, 1997a, p. 29).

As was mentioned earlier the interplay between poverty and education is critical to understanding the practice of female child labor. Perhaps the easiest manner by which to understand this interface is to introduce the concept of the *luxury axiom* (López-Calva, 2001). In their effort to model the economics of child labor, Basu and Van (1998, p. 416) derived the *luxury axiom*. Plainly stated, the *luxury axiom* maintains that a family will only send children into the labor market if it cannot generate sufficient income without the utilization of child labor. In essence, families without child laborers that find their incomes insufficient to subsist cannot afford the luxury of not employing their children. When family income begins to increase, so too does the potential of the family to be able to afford the luxury of having children remain at home (Amin et al., 2004). Simply put, education can also be considered a luxury that those who are not impoverished are more readily able to take advantage of.

Tradition and cultural norms also factor into the supply side of the equation of female child labor. Not coincidentally, these norms are also correlated with the two supply factors mentioned earlier. The general impact that tradition and cultural norms have had on increasing the incidence of female child labor is widely noted in the literature (Boonpala and Kane, 2001, p. 22; "Campaign to End Child Labor," 1997, p. 74; Hasnat, 1995; ILO, 2005, p. 42.).

Although cultural norms are sometimes vaulted to prime importance (Weiner, 1991), the reality is that this factor is probably of less importance than the economic and education factors. It is entirely possible that the economic factor, in particular, weighs more heavily in the decision-making process. When substantial economic growth and development occurs, it is usually accompanied by multiple challenges to traditional norms and customs. In fact, one might well argue that those who are most impoverished may see fit to send their children into the labor market and justify the action by invoking long-standing cultural norms and traditions (Murshed, 2001).

One specific aspect of tradition and cultural norms is the implementation of practices that are steeped in a community's history.[13] These discriminatory practices may be related to the stratification of a society based on socioeconomic, racial, and ethnicity factors. Perhaps the most noted example of this discrimination are the families of the relatively disadvantaged scheduled castes/tribes and other backward classes[14] of India. Although sometimes argued to be a structured system of occupational differentiation, the reality is that one's position in the caste system virtually dictates one's future. Tucker (1997) maintains that in India, more than 98 percent of child bonded laborers either are *untouchables* (i.e., *dalits*,[15] meaning depressed) or come from indigenous tribes (i.e., *adivasi*, meaning aboriginals) that are equally discriminated against (p. 575). Moreover, the children from these two groups will begin work at an earlier age and most likely never attend school (UNICEF, 2005b, p. 14).[16]

Similar to the caste system in India, other communities have implemented discriminatory practices with respect to specific gender, ethnic, and indigenous minorities. As has been stated at length in other parts of this book, girls are more likely than boys to be discriminated against. The general attitude toward girls is one that encourages employment, at a younger age than boys, while discouraging education and personal advancement. Ethnic minorities are also more likely to be pushed into female child labor. According to a study reported by IPEC (2004b, p. 25) in 1998, 69 percent of children performing domestic work in Brazil were black, the racial minority. Similarly, lower castes and non-Muslims in Pakistan are discriminated against, so that they typically make up the majority of bonded laborers (ILO, 2005, pp. 30-31). Indigenous minorities are, likewise, the target of some of the most extreme exploitation due to traditional practices and cultural norms. Throughout many parts of Latin America, indigenous children begin work at earlier ages than their counterparts (UNICEF, 2005b, p. 14). Specifically, indigenous girls from isolated parts of Panama are considered "backward" and are often mistreated because of misunderstandings born out of language barriers (IPEC, 2004, p. 26). Perhaps UNICEF (1997b) summarized the situation best:

> The harder and more hazardous the jobs become, the more they are likely to be considered traditionally the province of the poor and disadvantaged, the lower classes and ethnic minorities. In India, for example, the view has been that some people are born to rule and to

work with their minds while others, the vast majority, are born to work with their bodies. Many traditionalists have been unperturbed about lower-caste children failing to enroll in or dropping out of school. And if those children end up doing hazardous labour, it is likely seen as their lot in life. (p. 31)

A fourth supply side factor involves the general notion of vulnerability. To be vulnerable is to be susceptible to physical injury or attack. Vulnerability may result from a number of sources, including, but not limited to, political conflict, natural disasters, family breakdown, and urbanization. The common denominator of these sources is that they typically result in a similar situation, whereby female children are "pushed" into labor in order to ensure the survival of the family or their own person.

Political conflict is all too commonplace in the world today. While the media typically concentrates on death tolls, it is equally important to consider those who have survived the carnage and how they adapt for survival. UNICEF (1995b) provides a good example of just this type of problem. While nearly 1 million innocents were murdered in the 1994 conflict in Rwanda, the reality is that over 40,000 households were left headed by female children. They were now responsible for the survival of other members of the family (p. 13). Political conflict can also lead to the migration of female children to areas thought to be more stable, even though employment cannot been found. The result is often that these children become victims of exploitative work. Other female children are taken during political conflict and are forced into many roles, including forced labor, soldiering, meeting the desires of soldiers, marrying high-ranking militia leaders, and so forth. This has been the case recently in several parts of the world—for example, the political conflict in the Sudan and the Lord's Resistance Movement of northern Uganda (ILO, 2005, pp. 44–45).

Natural disasters also result in extreme vulnerability to female children, often causing them to become involved in labor markets. Monsoon rains and floods repeatedly pelt already impoverished areas of such countries as Indonesia, Bangladesh, Sri Lanka, and India. The net result is that millions become instant refugees, who are often reliant on their central government as well as international good will. Quite often, families will be convinced to let their children leave to find survival opportunities elsewhere. This approach, however, heightens the potential vulnerability of female children to exploitative labor practices by employers (Boonpala and Kane, 2001, p. 22). Taking away the breadwinner of the family also results in increased child labor. The 2004 tsunami, triggered by an underwater earthquake in the Indian Ocean, is a case in point. One report estimated that 35,000 children from the Aceh province lost one or both of their parents. While they will become active laborers to support the family, the overwhelming concern is that gangs that traffic in the area will capitalize on the disaster and seize children to be sold into forced labor, sexual slavery, and so forth, in the neighboring Malaysia and Singapore ("Tsunami Children Lost, Vulnerable," 2005).

Events related to family breakdown can also serve to "push" female children into child labor. UNICEF (2005b) states:

> Families break down for many reasons, leaving the household short of income. Sometimes divorce leaves one parent looking after more children than she or he can afford to feed. Divorce is sometimes brought about by domestic violence, which also directly drives children to leave home when they are still young. . . . The result of premature death of one or both parents is that children take on the responsibility of seeking an income to support themselves and their younger brothers and sisters. In the case of HIV/AIDS, children often take on this role when their one surviving parent becomes seriously ill and is unable to work. (p. 13)

The breakdown of the traditional family might also be the result of political conflict, natural disaster, ethnic unrest, and changing social structures that reorient female children into child labor (Pflug, 2002, p. 33). The disruption that ensues, regardless of the source of said disruption, virtually ensures that female children will be increasingly pushed into labor markets in order to survive. These sources of vulnerability have an even greater impact on the most impoverished families of the community.

The last source of vulnerability to be discussed here is that which results from the migration of female children to urban centers. Many of the aforementioned vulnerabilities lend themselves to this migratory trend as families see the increased need to employ their daughters. Often, families, by sending their children to urban centers, are looking to cut family costs more than to increase family revenue. As a consequence, female children are often sent to work (i.e., given away) as domestics in urban centers. Because of the local calamity, many see an increased likelihood of success in urban centers. More often than not, however, female children who migrate to urban centers often find employment in unorganized sectors of the economy as well as in illegal labor (Jaiswal, 2001, pp. 59-60).

The other side of the equation that explains causation of female child labor deals with demand, or "pull," factors. At a minimum, these include reasons related to childhood "characteristics" and globalization.

Childhood characteristics relate to child specific qualities that represent an advantage, from the employer's perspective. One of these advantages is that children, females rather than males, represent a cheaper labor pool than adult workers (Arat, 2002, pp. 182–183; ILO, 1998a, p. 15; IPEC, 2004b, p. 36; Murshed, 2001; Tucker, 1997, p. 579; UNICEF, 2005b, p. 15). Related to wages, the *substitution axiom* proposes that the labor of children and adults is substitutable. Moreover, ceteris paribus, an employer will likely employ a greater number of child laborers, so that the "effective child wage" is less than the adult wage equivalent in a particular market (Basu and Van, 1998, pp. 416–417).

While some agree that ultimately cheap labor impacts the employers' decision, they argue that other advantages related to children give rise to the cheaper labor and hence increased demand. For example, children are less likely to benefit from collective bargaining and union membership, because they often work in "hidden" vocations and their work is largely illegal (Arat, 2002, p. 183; Murshed, 2001; UNICEF, 2005b, p. 15). Moreover, children are said to be easier to control (i.e., they are easily intimidated and hence are more obedient), do not receive benefits, and are often unaware of their rights (Murshed, 2001). The passages below are more pointed in making these arguments:

> Children may be paid lower rates than adults (if they are paid at all), but they are also generally less productive. The misperception that child labour is cheap labour persists largely because children are simply easier to abuse than adults: they are less assertive and less able to claim their rights; they can be made to work longer hours with less food, poor accommodation and no benefits. It is, in fact, these abuses that allow the employer to keep costs down. (Boonpala and Kane, 2001, pp. 19–20)

> Children are more amenable to discipline and control. They can be coaxed, admonished, pulled up and punished for defaults without jeopardizing relations. Children are not organized on lines of trade unions which can fight for their rights, not unionized and thus are paid a minimum wage to work for long hours. Children are paid substantially lower wages than their adult counterparts on the plea that they are less efficient, their requirements are less and they are learning the job. This keeps the cost of production low. (Jaiswal, 2001, pp. 50–51)

While the distinction about how these childhood characteristics are intertwined is important, the bottom line is that children, in particular females, represent a cheaper labor pool from which employers may draw.

Another childhood characteristic that receives a good deal of attention is the argument that children possess a set of irreplaceable skills that are advantageous to their employer. Perhaps a more apt manner by which to characterize "irreplaceable skills" is to refer to physical characteristics that are thought to be ideal given a certain task in the workplace. For example, the height of the child worker has been considered important depending on the type of job task to be performed. In Egyptian cotton fields, for example, female children are utilized not only because they are docile but because their height is appropriate for inspecting and picking the cotton. Height and physical dexterity are often behind the employment of female children in the hybrid cottonseed industry of India. Moreover, it is estimated that 85 percent to 90 percent of the workforce in this area is constituted by female children. Primarily, their work consists of emasculation and pollination work (Reddy, 2001).

Undoubtedly the more recognizable physical characteristic related to irreplaceable skills is the "nimble fingers" argument. Although generally regarded as not having acceptable supporting evidence, the argument maintains that (1) only children are able to perform certain job tasks, or (2) children perform certain job tasks better than adults because of their nimble fingers, supple hands, increased dexterity, and height (Arat, 2002, 183; ILO, 1996; Jaiswal, 2000, p. 23). This argument is furthered by the notion that female children are more likely to be employed in these particular tasks, because the tasks require them to sit for long periods of time and also require a certain temperament or docile behavior. For instance, traditionally the carpet industry in Asia was most appreciated, and so this argument might be utilized to justify female child labor in the beedi, silk, and silver industries, to mention but a few (Tucker, 1997, p. 579).

Regardless of evidence that refutes the justifications for the nimble fingers argument (Bachman, 2000), the practice continues. Many have come to refer to the argument as one of the great myths surrounding child labor (ILO, 1998a; Tucker, 1977, p. 579). UNICEF (2005b) maintains that the continuation of the myths, like the nimble fingers argument, strikes "a chord with local public opinion and come to be believed because they are repeated so often" (p. 16)

The second major demand side factor to be discussed is the impact that globalization has had on the demand for child labor. Admittedly, the topic of globalization conjures up a set of integrated economic relations between numerous nations. Although, in reality, "globalization" has taken on political and cultural connotations over time, the emphasis here is on the concept of economic globalization and the impact that it has on generating a need for female child labor.

The relatedness of economic globalization to child labor is caught up in the factors of production and maintaining a comparative advantage, so that international markets remain a viable avenue for economic growth and development. The rise of economic globalization, in the minds of many, has encouraged the use of child labor in order to cut the overall cost of production while concurrently ensuring an acceptable profit margin. To substitute adult labor for that of children may be the difference between having and not having a comparative advantage in the production process of a said good.

While some are unsure about the exact relationship (ILO, 2005, p. 18), others are quick to point out that unregulated competition involved in economic globalization is the culprit responsible for many producers in the developing world feeling as if they must employ child labor ("Campaign to End Child Labor," 1997; Weissman, 1997, p. 13). Murshed (2001) states the case more succinctly:

> Increasing globalization and the dependency of many developing countries on access to industrialized markets may link the vulnerability of an economy to child labor. On the one hand, increasing globalization makes national actors more vulnerable to external pressure from international movements. On the other hand, the increasing necessity to compete on the global market may compel industries to employ more children in an effort to reduce labor costs and gain a competitive edge. (p. 179)

Quite often, the export-oriented sectors of developing countries are cited as the potential employers of child labor. Weiner (1995) states that some industries in the export sector, such as carpets and gems, have seen an increase in child labor, which has allowed competitive access to world markets. Bachman (2000) suggests, however, that the numbers of child laborers are considerably higher in the domestic sector and that targeting the export sector illustrates misplaced emphasis. Indeed, it has been estimated that probably no more than 5 percent of child workers are actually employed in the export sector (UNICEF, 1997b, p. 21).

The employment of female child labor in export sectors, to the extent to which it occurs, has given many in the developed countries an opportunity to criticize child labor practices inasmuch as employing female child labor gives the competition an unfettered advantage in the world marketplace. The concept of "social dumping," it is argued, is responsible for this perceived unfair trade advantage. While an oversimplification of the concept, social dumping refers to using an unregulated labor market (e.g., child labor) in order to sell a product at an artificially lower price, which results in greater marketability of the product in global markets (Diller and Levy, 1997, p. 680). In conjunction with this, many suggest that increased unemployment in developed countries is related to the practice of social dumping of products (Hasnat, 1995, p. 422; López-Calva, 2001). The key aspect to the phenomenon, however, remains the fact that female children are employed in export sectors in order to increase the competitiveness of the product in world markets.

The Clash of Cultures

> Irrespective of what they do and what they think about what they do, the mere fact of their being children sets children ideologically apart as a category of people excluded from the production of value. The dissociation of childhood from the performance of valued work has been increasingly considered a yardstick of modernity. International agencies and highly industrialized countries now turn this yardstick into a tool to condemn as backward and undemocratic those countries with a high incidence of child labor. (Nieuwenhuys, 1996, p. 246)

The tradition of female child labor closely parallels prostituted female children, in the sense that both practices are not limited to non-Western cultures. Although both practices occur mostly in non-Western cultures, it would be dishonest to suggest that the West is exempt from the same criticisms that it is quick to hurl at those countries wherein female child labor is quite prevalent. The "culturally constructed lens" of the West, however, is focused not on the similarities that it shares with these countries but on particular differences that it views as obscene and a violation of the doctrine of the sanctity of life. Again, similarly to the practice of prostituting female children, the differences here are only with respect to the scope of the problem, the causal factors giving rise to the practice, and the manner by which girls are "brought into" the practice.

Perhaps key to understanding the criticism as well as the non-Western response is to assess the extent to which the evolution of cultural norms, with respect to child labor, is a significant factor in development. While it can be argued that considerations related to biological, physiological, and psychological maturation should be the chief determinants of the readiness of a child to become an economically productive member of society, one could just as easily suggest that cultural norms that consider the totality of societal conditions should be the primary consideration. In part, the allowance for child labor at an earlier age in the countries whose educational and economic systems are not well developed is, in effect, the recognition that the totality of societal conditions and how they bring acceptable cultural norms into being is an important factor in assessing the clash of cultures.

The realization that cultural norms between countries will be inherently different because of the diversity of factors that figure into the establishment of norms of behavior is a premise that many are cognizant of but fail to respect. The following selection speaks to the idea that Western notions of adulthood may be ill-conceived when one seeks to apply these standards to non-Western cultures.

> In reality, different societies have different thresholds for defining childhood. In some societies, fulfillment of certain social rites and obligations may be important in differentiating between "adult" and "child" status. In others, integration of childhood to adulthood may be so smooth and gradual that it may be virtually impossible to distinguish the different life phases. In still others, biological characteristics such as puberty or "when the boy is strong" or "when the girl is married" may be the sign of adulthood. Thus, what we have across societies is a social notion of childhood, not calendar-based childhood. (Hasnat, 1995, p. 423)

Likewise, Mahler (1997) recognizes that culture is as important as biology in determining the readiness of the individual and that doing what is best for the child "will likely take different forms, depending on the accepted values in a particular culture" (p. 82).

With respect to child labor, the "culturally constructed lens" of the West considers not only the importance of human rights (i.e., the moral argument) but also the impact that the practice has on the economic prowess of the Western world (i.e., the economic argument). More specifically, the argument is that the intended consequence of developing countries that greatly utilize the labor of children is greater (i.e., unfair) competitiveness in the global marketplace. This process of "social dumping" is deemed harmful to the economies of the Western world because of the loss of competitiveness, markets, and jobs. Alternatively, non-Western cultures maintain that the use of child labor today is no different than what the developed West did during its infancy in order to procure growth. As a past Pakistani Labor Ministry official once stated:

> Westerners conveniently forget their own shameful histories when they come here. . . . Europeans addressed slavery and child labor only after they became prosperous. Pakistan has only now entered an era of economic stability that will allow us to expand our horizons and address social concerns. Just as we are catching up with the West in industrial development, so we are catching up in workplace and social reforms. We are accelerating the pace of reform and have resolved to create viable welfare and educational structures that will eradicate child labor in the foreseeable future. (Silvers, 1996, p. 85)

This is really the basis for the clash of cultures with respect to female child labor. The apparent reality is that non-Western cultures are quick to emphasize the necessity of the economic argument winning out over the moral imperative, at least in the short term until economic stability is assured. Moreover, they appear justified in their indictment of the West for having followed the same path that it now so boisterously condemns.

The West is seemingly cognizant of its history regarding child labor and also understands the pressure that economic impoverishment throughout non-Western cultures has had on the incorporation of child labor as a cultural norm. It is readily understood that child labor is disproportionately procured from those inhabiting the lowest tiers of society with respect to economic and social status. From the Western perspective, however, the focus on the economic side of the coin cannot overcome the necessity of winning the moral argument and the resulting implementation of Western-defined human rights within non-Western cultures. In essence, the economic situation cannot excuse a culture from its moral (i.e., human rights) requirements with respect to children. Moreover, utilizing one's economic impoverishment as the basis for an argument legitimizing the use of female child labor may have the net effect of perpetuating cultural norms that might otherwise be unacceptable.

IMPLICATIONS FOR FOREIGN RELATIONS

The West typically criticizes the countries that have what are deemed to be problematic issues with respect to female child labor. Given that the primary locations in which the vast majority of injurious child labor practices occur are in the developing world, it is extremely important that this particular issue not stand in the way of financial flows from the West to the developing countries. While growth is not an isolated function of these flows, the Western funding is certainly an important consideration in the growth and development plans of many a developing country.

It goes without saying that countries that do not take action to curb the tide of female child labor are subject to a variety of implications that Western donors, lenders, and so forth choose to impose for noncompliance. The intended consequence of such actions, as seen by the Western countries and affiliated international organizations, is not to penalize the country in question by detracting from its ability to generate growth and development but to bring the said country into compliance with what is regarded by the West to be a human rights violation against female children. The elimination of female child labor is the explicit goal that countries should work toward if they are to benefit from the potential resource of international financial flows. Token support, in the form of legislation that outlaws the practice but is not enforced, is not recognized by the West as an adequate stance toward the acquisition of greater human rights for female child laborers.

To express more than token support for the Western goal of eliminating the practice of female child labor is a difficult proposition because of the relatedness of child labor to poverty. While certainly not the sole causal factor explaining female child labor, poverty provides a foundation on which other relevant causative factors are based. Given this relationship, it is difficult for an impoverished country that benefits domestically more than in export markets to value the long-term good over the short-term advantages of employing female child labor. After all, employment accentuates the short-term competitive position of the product in question. The consequence of short-term gains, however, is a potential decline in financial flows from the West as well as a heightened stigma that goes along with the perception held by others that your country abets the practice of female child labor, which is a human rights violation. Clearly, the Western perspective favors the elimination of female child labor regardless of the greater production costs and negative market consequences associated with this transition. The expectation is that this transition will be accompanied by increased financial flows to stimulate economic growth and development.

The Western countries, in general, have shown their willingness to be intricately linked to the process of eliminating the worst forms of female child labor. The United States, in particular, has played a primary role in exacting greater human rights for child laborers via a variety of methods including legislation. For example, Senator Tom Harkin has repeatedly introduced legislation, the Child Labor Deterrence Act (CLDA), in 1992, 1993, 1995, 1997, and 1999, that would prohibit any importation of goods produced through child labor. Moreover, both civil and criminal penalties may result from violations.[17]

The CLDA ultimately led to the then President Clinton's signing Executive Order 13126, *Prohibition of Acquisition of Products Produced by Forced or Indentured Child Labor*, in June 1999. Concurrent with these efforts has been the creation, in 1993, of the International Child Labor Program (ICLP). The ICLP was originally designed as a reporting mechanism by which Congress could be informed about the worldwide practice but has since expanded its mandate into other spheres (U.S. Department of Labor, 2006).

Perhaps the most important piece of legislation has been the 2000 Trade and Development Act. Although an amendment to the original legislation, the act requires developing countries to meet a set of criteria, including the implementation of ILO Convention 182. Refusal to take this step results in the elimination of trade benefits realized under the U.S. Generalized System of Preferences, the African Growth and Opportunity Act, and the Caribbean Basin Trade Partnership Act. Obviously, the implications related to this penalty would have a negative impact on both the short- and long-term development goals of these countries.

The United States has also shown its commitment to the elimination of the worst forms of child labor by assisting international programs and organizations with the necessary funding. For example, the ICLP program, since 1995, has contributed to the ILO/IPEC. Through 2006, appropriations for this program have totaled approximately $330 million, to be spent on technical assistance programs related to child labor. More recently, from FY2003 through FY2005, the United States has provided a total of $127,308,000 in funding to ILO/IPEC projects. Admittedly, however, the annual funding for this program has decreased annually, on average, by 5.3 percent over this time (United States Department of Labor, 2006).

In addition to funding ILO/IPEC, the United States also provides funds, via the ICLP, to programs such as its Child Labor Education Initiative (EI). Originating in 2001, the EI uses education to combat exploitative child labor practices around the world. Unlike the IPEC, however, funds are distributed via alternative nongovernmental organizations, such as the International Rescue Committee, Save the Children, CARE, World Vision, and Catholic Relief Services. Through FY2006, the U.S. government appropriated approximately $204,000,000 in support of this effort (U.S. Department of Labor, 2006).

The International Finance Corporation (IFC), an arm of the World Bank Group, recently reformed its Policy on Social and Environmental Sustainability and the associated performance standards that potential clients must meet in order to have IFC participation. Released in 2006, the new policy includes an entire section on IFC requirements regarding labor in general and child labor specifically. Performance Standard 2 speaks to the requirements concerning child labor and forced labor:

> The client will not employ children in a manner that is economically exploitative, or is likely to be hazardous or to interfere with the child's education, or to be harmful to the child's health or physical, mental, spiritual, moral, or social development. Where national laws have provisions for the employment of minors, the client will follow those laws applicable to the client. Children below the age of 18 years will not be employed in dangerous work. . . . The client will not employ forced labor, which consists of any work or service not voluntarily performed that is exacted from an individual under threat of force or penalty. This covers any kind of involuntary or compulsory labor, such as indentured labor, bonded labor or similar labor-contracting arrangements. (IFC, 2006)

New business projects that cannot meet the specifics of the performance standard in a reasonable amount of time will not benefit from IFC participation. Moreover, the new policy has an exclusion list of activities for financial intermediaries engaged in microfinance and trade finance. For purposes here, the most important consideration on the exclusion list is the "Production or activities involving harmful or exploitative forms of forced labor/harmful child labor" (IFC, 2006). Authorized capital of $2.45 billion coupled with only six members of the Western Group of Eight (the United States, Japan, the United Kingdom, Germany, France, and the Russian Federation) possessing 48.36 percent of voting power in the IFC can result in IFC financial flows being virtually nil if one does not comply with Performance Standard 2 (IFC, 2006).

The programs and policies of the U.S. Department of Labor and the IFC indicate a good deal of support for the elimination of the worst forms of child labor. Ineligibility for these sources of funds could hamper the growth and development efforts of many a developing country. Perhaps the greatest threat, however, is with the impact of linking the core standards of labor[18] with the World Trade Organization (WTO). For quite some time, the argument for doing just this has been made by those who are truly concerned with human rights considerations pertaining to child labor as well as by those who are interested only in the protection of their own markets from the social dumping that cheap child labor, in particular that of females, is said to facilitate.

Currently, the ILO is recognized as the dominant international organization in terms of formulating international labor standards and promoting what are internationally recognized human rights of laborers in general and child laborers specifically. Born in 1919, the ILO has produced many a convention and recommendations, but it has been extremely weak in enforcement with respect to those countries that have ratified the said conventions but violate their provisions with respect to child labor.

The relative lack of enforcement power is structural, in that Chapter II, Article 26, of the ILO constitution provides any member of the ILO the right to bring a complaint against a fellow member. The Governing Body may inquire with the accused party to find that the complaint is warranted and subsequently appoint a commission of inquiry. The recommendations of the commission are binding but may be appealed against by the accused party, in accordance with Article 29, to the International Court of Justice (ICJ). The problem here is that, regardless of whether or not a complaint is found by the commission of inquiry or the ICJ to have merit, there is no enforcement body within the ILO or the ICJ to ensure compliance with the recommendations (ILO, 2006a). At most, as was the case when the ILO Governing Body invoked Article 33 against Myanmar in 2000, members of the ILO and other international organizations can be encouraged to rethink their relations with the guilty party.[19]

This lack of enforcement capability is, in large part, the basis for arguing that the core standards of labor be placed under the purview of the WTO rather than the ILO. The WTO, after all, has great enforcement capability with respect to trade penalties for those found not in compliance with its rules and regulations. The frequency of trade sanctions, for instance, has been quite high since the first dispute settlement request under the WTO auspices in 1995. In part, this is due to the imposition of fixed timetables under the WTO, which leads to a situation where disputes cannot drag on for lengthy periods of time without any settlement. Granted, trade sanctions are typically applied within the same sector of the agreement in question, but they could be applied to other sectors in the same agreement or even to another agreement.

The proponents of linking child labor to the WTO are quite aware of the impact that this increased enforcement ability would have on countries that choose to forgo compliance with the decision of the WTO Dispute Settlement Body. Moreover, given that most international trade is now conducted within the confines of the WTO structure, the potential that this linkage would have to interfere with the development plans of many developing countries is great.

What is currently problematic, however, is the reluctance of the WTO to usurp power from the ILO and take the issue of child labor, as it did with intellectual property rights, under its structure. This hesitation was very clear at the 1996 Ministerial Conference of the WTO in Singapore when the WTO stated that while they wished to work closely with the ILO, they believed that the ILO had the mandate in the area of labor.

> We renew our commitment to the observance of internationally recognized core labour standards. The International Labour Organization (ILO) is the competent body to set and deal with these standards, and we affirm our support for its work in promoting them. We believe that economic growth and development fostered by increased trade and further trade liberalization contribute to the promotion of these standards. We reject the use of labour standards for protectionist purposes, and agree that the comparative advantage of countries, particularly low-wage developing countries, must in no way be put into question. In this regard, we note that the WTO and ILO Secretariats will continue their existing collaboration. (WTO, 1996)

The thought of being subject to WTO trade practices that include an agreement on child labor (i.e., a social clause) is one that many developing countries find objectionable. While the developing countries have routinely voiced their opposition to the potential WTO/ child labor linkage in favor of the ILO mandate, they have not seen fit to increase the enforcement capability of the ILO (Elliott, 2000, p. 1). Other opponents to linkage insist that the comparative advantage that many developing countries currently have would be undermined not to promote a universal notion of human rights with respect to child labor, but rather to promote the protection of a developed world economy (Brown, Deardorff & Stern, 2002; Elliott, 2004, p. 1).

Alternatively, the proponents of linkage (e.g., the European Union, Canada, the United States[20]) maintain that it would be an effective mechanism by which to force compliance by developing countries and achieve greater human rights for child laborers. Moreover, research also provides supporting evidence for the notion that respect for core labor standards is positively related to foreign direct investment (FDI), an important financial flow for developing countries. Moreover, it would appear that countries that are more economically developed are those that have received more FDI (Mattioli & Sapovadia, 2004, p. 63).

In sum, there appear to be both consequences in the present and the potential for much more in the future if linkage succeeds. To the extent that WTO linkage facilitates greater enforcement capability, developing countries will stand to lose considerably more than their developed counterparts as a result of the child labor issue. This prospect, combined with the aforementioned possibility of decreased financial flows from Western governments and international organizations, certainly illustrates the potential of child labor to have severe implications for foreign relations.

POTENTIAL RESOLUTIONS

Almost any potential resolution regarding the practice of female child labor will be tainted by whether or not one considers the practice to constitute a human rights violation. Western adherents to the concept of universal human rights will certainly maintain that the only conceivable resolution is to achieve total elimination of the practice. Cultural relativists, although cognizant that the demeaning labor practices committed with respect to female children are abominable, are not so quick to dismiss all aspects of this cultural behavior. Reasons exist that not only serve to explain the behavior but also suggest a certain degree of legitimacy. One might argue that the practice of female child labor, like the prostituting of female children, serves a function in some societies. While neither of the extreme positions on this issue is reconcilable with the demands of the opposition, there is perhaps a middle ground that would allow for both sides to achieve a compromise position. Although this position may not entirely suit either the adherents to universal human rights or the cultural relativists, the following is a first step, albeit in a somewhat revised form, in trying to eliminate the practice of female child labor while not impairing the ability of a culture to exist.

Those who argue for the application of universal human rights mostly desire the total elimination of female child labor. Because this practice is currently alive and well throughout most of the countries of the world, one might best label this as the revolutionary position.[21]

Although the revolutionaries have an arsenal of techniques at their disposal for achieving the goal of total elimination, they frequently attempt to legislate against the practice or utilize the IMF and the IBRD as "leverage," or use the ILO and IFC in an effort to further develop the country in question.

The attempt to legislate the problem away is not always successful. Legislation is, often, more in the service of expressing support for the cause as well as illustrating to the West that the country in question takes the issue seriously and is attempting to effectively deal with it. In reality, however, the target populations of legislative attempts to eliminate the practice are largely noncompliant. While legislative efforts are indeed indications to the West that the government in question takes seriously the ills associated with female child labor, it is a poor assumption that the laws in place in several countries are actually having an impact.

The ability to legislate the problem away is not necessarily a function of whether appropriate statutes exist. Statutes regarding female child labor abound and operate on at least three levels: intranational, supranational, and extranational (Basu, 1999, pp. 1091–1093). Extranational efforts are actions that are taken outside the target countries, most typically by other countries, and are designed to have an impact on female child labor in the target country. For example, the aforementioned ICLP and EI programs of the United States target the practice of female child labor around the globe. Supranational efforts take the form of international organizations, such as the ILO and the IFC, and their attempts to curb the use of female child labor. Intranational efforts primarily consist of governments, in countries where the practice is problematic, passing legislation to address the issue.

Efforts on all three levels, as is readily apparent, have their own weaknesses. Extranational efforts are typically inadequate in terms of resources devoted to the issue and most often come under attack as being instituted in order to protect markets and jobs. Supranational efforts often require the target country to sign and ratify a convention signifying that it intends to adhere to the new set of "rules." One should also point out that ratification of a convention does not mean that strict adherence is a guarantee. Of the current 178 ILO members, 144 have ratified Convention No. 138 while 160 have ratified Convention No. 182 (ILO, 2006b), but compliance appears to be considerably less. Moreover, supranational efforts are slow in coming, as they require their constituent members, some of whom drag their feet, to vote in favor of the new conventions and rules. Finally, funding is also an issue here with respect to being able to adequately address the educational and economic needs of the targeted population. Finally, while intranational efforts appear to illustrate to the West that the country is committed to change,[22] the reality is that enforcement is often problematic. Moreover, loopholes, weak enforcement, indifference to laws dealing with child labor, lack of female coverage in the legislation, inability to identify the age of the child, "invisibility" of domestic workers, lax penalties, lack of awareness, and inadequate resources all lead to the increased inability to legislate the issue of female child labor (ILO, 1998a, pp. 44–49; 2000, pp. 198–201; 2002b, pp. 83–84; Murshed, 2001, pp. 180–184). Perhaps Jaiswal (2000) summarizes it best while describing the problem as it applies to India:

> Weak enforcement machinery in the form of small inspectorates of laws related to child labour is another factor for the failure to implement such laws. The penalties are very light for transgression of laws. The offenders are not worried about deterrent punishment because they can always bribe the Labour Commissioners. When the employers get advance notice of the visit of Commissioners, they entrust "safe" jobs to the children. The law is also evaded due to non-awareness of the existence of laws, and illiteracy, of the people. . . . Protective labour legislations do not cover girls. . . . The work in domestic sectors, and other non-industrial sectors where the majority of children work, are excluded from labour legislations. . . . Another major fault is that the prosecution of the employer is possible only if the age of the child is established. In poor, illiterate families to which most child labourers belong, there is never any proof of age. (pp. 84–85)

Although many countries, such as Guatemala, Indonesia, Lesotho, and the Philippines (in 2003), and Jamaica and Thailand (in 2004), have either amended existing laws or passed new legislation, the practice of female child labor continues to flourish. The case of Haiti is especially telling of how new laws may not adequately deal with issues related to female child labor.

The reform of the Haitian Labor Code in May 2003 was in part designed to ban trafficking in persons and do away with the earlier version of the Labor Code that sanctioned child domestic labor. Many saw this reform as a way to bring Haiti into compliance with its obligations under the 1989 Convention on the Rights of the Child. Moreover, this revision of the Labor Code appeared to be part of a desired goal of the ILO/IPEC program, as the focus of the 2000–2003 program was on combating the exploitation of child domestics in Haiti.

The reality of this reform, however, was not considered to be of great significance. The perspective of the United States (which funded the three-year IPEC project) was that this new reform did not lead to the desired outcome. In its 2004 Findings on the Worst Forms of Child Labor report, the U.S. Department of Labor (2005) maintained that the 2003 Labor Code was not enforced:

> The Ministry of Labor and Social Affairs (MOLSA) is responsible for enforcing all child labor legislation, and the Institute for Welfare and Research (IBESR), which is part of the MOLSA, is charged with coordinating the implementation of child labor laws with other government agencies. However, child labor laws, particularly child domestic labor regulations, are not enforced. According to the government, the IBESR lacks the resources to adequately monitor the living conditions of child domestic workers, or to enforce protective measures on their behalf. (p. 225)

Not only was the reform viewed negatively, but the fact that Haiti still had not ratified Convention No. 138 or 182 did not indicate a strong desire to fully comply with the legislated reforms. As an aside, the recognition that Haiti did not devise a national plan of action in concert with the IPEC program and its goals might well have indicated the lack of sincerity with respect to the 2003 revision of the Labor Code.

There have been complementing efforts to legislate the problem away by using the IMF or the IBRD and thus try to boost the economic development of the country in question. The prevalent mode by which this is done is to tie financial programs to the ability of the country in question to reform its domestic economic and financial structures. The assumption is that these structural adjustment programs (SAPs) will result in greater economic stability and the ability to more fully participate in the international marketplace via trade, investment, and aid. While concerned with the long term, the unintended consequence is the promotion of child labor. Arat (2002) identifies the manner by which IMF and IBRD involvement leads to greater child labor:

> In the name of economic stability, these agencies require governments to implement measures of "fiscal discipline" which involve freezing wages, reducing government spending, and privatizing government enterprises. While the reduction in government spending typically means cutting down social expenditures (e.g., health and education) and eliminating government subsidies on basic goods, privatization

almost always results in major layoffs. Facing increasing unemployment levels, declining wages, and the increase in out of pocket expenditures for essential food items, utilities or transportation, the low income households in recipient countries find themselves tightening their belts more and more. Through the reduction of aggregate demand, the IMF may be successful in curbing inflation (although it has not been always as successful as expected even in meeting that objective), but it does so at the expense of poor households, which are likely to turn to child labor for addition income. (pp. 190–191)

In sum, efforts to legislate the problem away as well as IMF and IBRD attempts to further economic development via SAPs have met with questionable results. Moreover, it would appear that the primary means that were chosen by the West to try to eliminate the perceived human rights violation of female child labor were inadvertently serving to strengthen the practice.

At the other end of the continuum are the cultural relativists who, even though female child labor is often viewed as a practice more economically based rather than a consideration related to tradition, contend that the practice is an outgrowth of both culture and poverty. Consequently, the cultural relativists do not entirely agree with Western efforts (or the abolitionists) to immediately eliminate the practice. Moreover, it is a condition that for many countries now helps to define their sociocultural environment. In essence, the status quo position maintains that Western intrusion into this arena, under the guise of promoting the notion of universal human rights, is nothing more than cultural imperialism in the service of maintaining its privileged economic position in the international community. Although not necessarily the definitive answer, the following prescriptions on how to manage these two sides of the issue are not without some merit. Because they represent a "middle ground," however, they will undoubtedly come under attack from each of the dogmatic extremes. These prescriptions should also be prefaced with the knowledge that any potential satisfactory resolution to the practice of female child labor must start by addressing both the supply and demand factors mentioned earlier. While an admirable goal, an implicit assumption at this juncture is the notion that one will never be able to fully eliminate all of the supply and demand factors that aid the continuance of this practice.

First, one must recognize the central importance that impoverishment plays with respect to child labor. Although it is not *the* sole cause of female child labor, it is without question a foundational component giving rise to a host of other parameters that should also be factored into the equation. Poverty is reciprocally related to education, cultural status, birth registration, development, and, of course, child labor (Arat, 2000, p. 184; Baland & Robinson, 2000, pp. 665–667; Cigno et al., 2003, p. 6). To pinpoint which is the causal agent is less important than the realization that a "catch 22" situation exists, whereby once one finds oneself in this vicious circle, it is nearly impossible to exit without an external intervention. Moreover, it is critical to recognize the importance of the rural sector to child labor and target interventions accordingly.

This is exactly why the international community, extranational and supranational entities alike, must increase their commitment to interventionist programs that target the concerns giving rise to impoverishment. Discriminatory concerns, such as gender, caste, and class, result in greater poverty (Mattioli & Sapovadia, 2004, pp. 62–63) and need to be assigned special significance within the general framework. Select institutions, such as the IMF and World Bank Group, whose policies have historically focused on structural reform (i.e., austerity measures and SAPs) will need to become more cognizant of the impact that these policies have on select groupings, especially female children and education, and work to become more nurturing of the said groups in their development planning.

Placing all of one's resources into poverty alleviation projects would prove to be overly reductionistic, with failure proving to be the inevitable result (Bachman, 2000). Consequently, the second prong of this rural-focused strategy must focus on the role of education. While many countries already have mass literacy campaigns, they are typically insufficient if the goal is to reduce female child labor (Jaiswal, 2000, p. 65). Alternatively, educational programs need to be made compulsory for primary (5- to14-year-old) school children (Bachman, 2000). The importance of this was made known by the inclusion of this consideration in Article 28 of the 1989 Convention on the Rights of the Child. The emphasis on compulsory education is the key, but to be effective it must be accompanied by the following assumptions.

Above everything else there must be sufficient incentives for families to send their children, especially daughters, to school. Given that the education of a girl is generally considered a luxury good, and that girls are usually the first to be removed from schools in order to work (Arat, 2000, p. 191), an economic subsidy must be provided to the families so as not to worsen their condition (ILO, 2002a, pp. 100–101).

One must also recognize that child work and education are not mutually exclusive (Murshed, 2001, p. 183). In addition to their education, children are likely to work to the extent that it is viewed necessary in order to assist the family economically. In essence, one cannot assume that the provision of education alone will lead to the abolition of child work. Moreover, part-time (i.e. "non-formal" education) (UNICEF, 2005b, p. 55) may be preferable to full-time education if the doctrine of "gradualism" is acceptable.

Finally, one cannot assume that school attendance is highly correlated with learning (Anker, 2000). Relatively speaking, schools that are located in more impoverished centers may not provide the same quality of education that is found in a more financially stable area. Associated with this is the notion that a poorer education will result in less earning power. Moreover, there needs to be appropriate nurturance (funding, etc.) to ensure physical access (i.e., the physical presence of the school), the integrity of the academic curriculum, the quality of instruction, and whether academic objectives are being met. One particular study of World Bank lending suggests that many of these areas are being funded (Kaur, 2002, pp. 14–15).

While supply-side considerations are important, an emphasis on the demand side of the child labor equation must also occur. A controversial, yet important, consideration deals with the application of legal statutes that criminalize the practice. The troublesome areas in terms of enforcement of legal statutes, however, must be adequately funded. Placing emphasis on increasing the number of inspectors, providing them with an appropriate education relevant to their job tasks, and paying them commensurate with their status would go quite a distance in improving enforcement capabilities. While many believe that education alone will provide an adequate basis by which to thwart child labor—because children will be in school, where it is easier to ensure compliance (Basu, 1999, p. 1090)—it is quite plausible that the female children who are "non-formal" students will still be asked to help out the family.

A related demand-side item factoring into the enforcement of laws concerns birth registration. The ILO (2002a. p. 84) states that one-third (i.e., roughly 40 million) births go unregistered every year in developing countries. Because of the inability to determine age, this phenomenon increases the ability of those who employ child laborers to evade prosecution. The importance of registration is also vital to accessing other developmental services:

> Birth registration is a vital prerequisite to protecting all children from exploitation in child labour and to ensuring that they enjoy their rights as children. If a child is not registered at birth, it is impossible to know for certain her/his age, to pursue exploiters through the courts

when they exploit under-age children, to apply standards such as the minimum working age and to put in place registration and monitoring systems that not only trace the child's progress through school and work but also when the child or family relocates. Without an official status provided through birth registration, children are not guaranteed access to social services or schools. (IPEC, 2004b, p. 70)

Increasing funding to ensure birth registration will also allow countries to fulfill their obligations under such conventions such as the 1989 Convention on the Rights of the Child and the African Charter on the Rights and Welfare of the Child (Thompson, 1992, p. 435).

The final aspect related to demand-side considerations must concern the argument by some that the WTO must incorporate a "social clause" in order to ensure that child labor is not utilized in the production of goods. A country that is found to be in violation of a social clause would, in effect, be punished via trade sanctions. The incorporation of a social clause might well achieve the desired outcomes if one can ensure that all potential markets invoke the social clause against the perceived violator (Mansoor, 2004). The reality, however, is that trade sanctions will not end the majority of child labor. Trade sanctions would primarily impact the export sector of the country in question, a sector that may constitute 5 percent of all child labor. Moreover, adult employment opportunities would also be curtailed, resulting in the need to put one's children to work in order to manage.

In sum, the implementation of trade sanctions would not be beneficial if the goal is to stop child labor, either through a gradualist or abolitionist approach. Given that sanctions would result from the implementation of a social clause in the WTO, the argument in favor of the said clause must be set aside. It is premature at best to give this enforcement mechanism to the WTO. Alternatively, the ILO should remain the key organization to set the standards and enforce them.

In sum, one must approach change in the status quo by addressing both demand and supply factors that contribute to the continuation of the practice of female child labor. Moreover, one cannot expect change to occur in a short period of time. One can, however, expect that no substantive change will occur without the capital that fuels many of the program recommendations for lessening the extent of the practice throughout the world. Finally, the above recommendations are certainly favoring the revolutionary position, as described earlier. It is true, however, that the extremes of both universal human rights and cultural relativism will view these recommendations with hesitancy.

6

CONCLUSION: TOWARD
CROSS-CULTURAL UNIVERSALS

Cultural relativism, then, poses both theoretical and practical challenges. Theoretically, universal human rights imply, at a minimum, some set of "morally weighty" social norms that preempt, under all but the most exigent circumstances, other cultural value priorities. . . . But how can one set of values—international human rights—warrant universal acknowledgement as preemptory norms when, as a matter of social fact, highly divergent practices, morals, goals, and value hierarchies deeply divide the world's multiple and diverse civilizations? Practically, universal human rights must provide guidance about when and under what conditions international actors may intervene justifiably in the affairs of sovereign states to deter, terminate, or redress human rights violations. If, however, certain cultural traditions permit—perhaps even encourage—practices deemed morally abhorrent by other societies, by what criteria do we decide whether they violate "universal" standards that warrant international intervention?

Sloane (2001, p. 531)

A MODEST INQUIRY INTO THE IMPORTANCE OF
FUNCTIONALISM

This book began with an investigation into the nature of human rights. The conflicting concepts of universalism and cultural relativism were introduced in order to provide an adequate structural inquiry as well as to facilitate greater understanding about why the application of what are perceived to be universal human rights to specific cultural practices is such a tenuous proposition. Moreover, the focus on four particular cultural practices provided the necessary background by which to better understand this conflict. In so doing, greater understanding about the history and functions of these practices, and the evidence for the cultural relativist position, was acquired.

The case studies on female circumcision, infanticide, prostituting, and labor make readily apparent the difficulties encountered while trying to reconcile the differing beliefs associated with the proponents of universalism and those of cultural relativism. With respect to the concept of human rights, it would appear that these two positions have virtually no common ground. Moreover, the investigation of these two dogmatic extremes makes very clear the notion that a middle ground, with respect to the implementation of human rights for women and female children, is quite problematic. While adherents to universal human rights call for the abolition of what are perceived to be harmful traditional practices, the advocates of cultural relativism are swift to point out the manner by which these traditional practices provide a certain function (i.e., benefit) to the community.

Functionalism, as understood conceptually, does not necessarily entail value judgments regarding the various dimensions of the practice, and structure, or the practice itself. In reality, however, it is extremely difficult to divorce value judgments from our daily observations. When a practice is referred to as dysfunctional, for instance, the value implication is that the practice in question is harmful to the social structure and its stability. Consequently, while any or all of the aforementioned cases may also be distasteful to cultural relativists, they can often identify a concrete benefit that the practice contributes to societal stability. Conversely, adherents to universalism are apt to identify what they believe to be harmful consequences for both individuals and the larger society.

Perhaps the only point of agreement between these dogmatic extremes is the recognition that these practices are relevant to the cultures involved.[1] If viewed in terms of whether the practice has *manifest* or *latent* functions (Merton, 1968), it becomes easier to reconcile what appear to be irreconcilable beliefs and values. It may well be the case that in making their argument for the universal application of human rights, the proponents of the cause are only entertaining manifest functions: those that are almost inevitably viewed in the West as resulting in harmful consequences to both the individuals involved and the whole of the social structure. Cultural relativists, however, while not disagreeing that the practice may be distasteful, may well be focusing on the latent functions that result from the continuation of the practice. For example, the practice of female circumcision may well be dysfunctional in the sense that it is quite harmful to the girls involved, but it may also be functional in the sense that it provides a ceremonial atmosphere by which members of the community are brought together in a bonding experience.

The basic conflict between the application of universal human rights and cultural relativism, then, may well be an outgrowth of adherents to universalism making their argument based on the manifest functions of the practice in question, whereas the cultural relativists base their arguments more on the importance of latent functions. The importance of this is the realization that a middle ground may be found. As part of this compromise position, however, one cannot expect those observing the practice to abandon it unless an alternative practice is learned (i.e., becomes observed as part of the culture) that serves the same function as the practice abandoned. The implementation of the "substituted" practice would still weigh more favorably for the position of universalism as the targeted practice is also eliminated during the cultural transition.

THE FRAMEWORK EXPLORED: UNDERSTANDING CULTURAL SIGNIFICANCE

> The problem with an uncritical acceptance of cultural relativism lies within the resulting avoidance of examining the societal structure that creates the cultural norm. (Reichert, 2006, p. 29)

The position taken by the adherents to the uniform application of universal human rights is often better understood in the West because the said human rights are defined largely according to Western norms of behavior. Moreover, the four cultural practices that have been explored in this book are in large part alien to the "modern" experience of the West. As a consequence of this realization, it was important to provide a framework by which a more intrusive inquiry into each of the practices could take place. Accordingly, a sixfold framework was introduced that included an assessment of (1) the history of the practice, (2) the specifics of the practice, (3) the cultural relevance of the practice, (4) the clash between cultures, (5) the implications for foreign relations, and (6) potential resolutions. This framework has been instrumental in providing a deeper understanding of the functions that each respective practice provides to society as well as illuminating the various dimensions of the practice.

Within each part of the framework there exist some underlying commonalities. For example, it is quite apparent that the labor, prostituting, infanticide, and circumcision of female children have an exceptional storied history. While labor and circumcision practices date at least as far back as the sixth century B.C., the practices of prostituting and infanticide date back centuries earlier. It is also apparent that these practices were not geographically limited, as ancient Greece, Rome, Egypt, Phoenicia, China, Babylonia, Syria, Arabia, and so forth were all involved. Also of import is the notion that none of these practices is an outgrowth of one, and only one, religious orientation. Perhaps the most notable example is the errant belief that female circumcision originated as an Islamic practice, when in reality it was just as prevalent before the founding of Islam and Christianity. Finally, all of these practices indicate a great resilience in the face of external pressure.

The specifics of these practices also illustrate several points of resemblance. For example, attempts at defining what is meant by these four different practices are quite problematic. At first glance one would not think that this process would be that complex, but the reality is that the lack of definitional clarity is a consequence of the different types, or forms, of the practice. Unfortunately, the latter are quite varied and in terms of incorporation into a culture can be very distinct. In essence, different cultures often employ different "specific" forms of the same "general" practice, which leads to great consternation for cultural outsiders that are concerned with the application of universal human rights. With respect to female infanticide, for example, should universalism regard *active* and *passive* forms equally? Moreover, does prenatal sex selection (i.e., feticide) qualify as a human rights abuse, and should it be abolished?

Cultural relevance is another part of the framework in which each of the practices share similar characteristics. Each practice presents a plethora of potential explanations for its continual observance. While it is difficult to say with any degree of certainty which explanation is most important, it is certain that the following three explanations are essential. Tradition has, and will probably always be, the foolproof rationalization for the continuation of these practices. When social norms are established and instilled in the minds of societies' members, it is a virtually impossible task to inhibit its generational passing.

Given the focus on women and female children, it should come as no great surprise that patriarchy is another dominant and shared characteristic of these practices. So dominant is this gender- and hierarchically based institution that female children are in large part relegated to an abysmal existence from birth onward. Perhaps the key exception to this stark realization is when economic concerns are factored into the equation. Generally, poorer families are much more likely to have their daughters involved in these practices than are those from the higher economic strata of society. This is especially apparent with respect to the prostituting of female children and female child labor.

The implications for foreign relations are potentially severe for those countries continuing to practice what the West has labeled as

cultural practices that constitute human rights ʹ
speaking, the vast majority of countries where t
are economically impoverished. Many of them
foreign sources of capital for their development ɛ
with this is that the West continues to be in a priv
respect to aid flows and, as a consequence, is som
the necessary actions that these countries need
to these four practices. As was apparent in all of ɪ
United States, in particular, has wielded its influence over Western
international organizations such as the IMF and World Bank Group
to exert added pressure on these countries.

All of this continues to be in the service of abolishing these cultural practices and guaranteeing the universal human rights of all the
citizenry. This pressure is illustrated in all the cases but may prove to
be counterproductive if one believes the "economic" explanations
for the existence of these practices. In brief, people take part in these
practices because of impoverishment and relative deprivation. One
could very well argue that curtailing the potential for development by
limiting, or eliminating, sources of capital will only result in making
stronger the foundation on which the practice has been built.

Many commonalities also exist in the evaluation of the potential
resolutions to the basic conflict. For example, most countries have
tried to abolish the practice via legislation. The ineffectiveness of the
said attempts is also a shared experience with respect to each of the
practices covered here. In large part, this has been a consequence of
the inability, for a variety of reasons, to effectively enforce the relevant
statutes.

Education is mostly looked at as a critical component regardless of
whether one is approaching the matter from a position of abolition
or gradualism. Related to this is the prevalent notion that programs
should focus not on targeting the practice directly but rather con-
centrate its efforts on related considerations (e.g., literacy campaigns,
improving the status of females). This recognition gives rise, in all
four practices, to the idea that effective short-term solutions to
address the practice simply do not exist. In essence, while adherents
to the universal application of human rights might expect the abolition of these practices, they cannot expect it to occur immediately.

THE PROMOTION OF CROSS-CULTURAL UNIVERSALS

The cross-cultural approach begins by presuming that universal human
rights represent the desirable end-state. It then inquires how, in a

order characterized descriptively by cultural pluralism, one may
ctively establish conditions under which, more often than not, international human rights receive respect. The cross-cultural approach's
answer is to manipulate and redeploy each culture's internal resources
in the service of human rights. . . . Rather, the objective seems to reside
in amalgamating the most broadly-shareable mores of each society in
an effort to achieve an overlapping consensus of basic values that most
cultures will respect most of the time. (Sloane, 2001, p. 580)

As an artificial construct, paying reverence to the concept of human
rights is easily accomplished. The process of defining the characteristics and parameters of the concept and their application to the
real-world setting, however, has always been considerably more
difficult. While Western universalism continues to profess, through
its statutes, conventions, and so forth, that it knows precisely the
makeup of "human rights," cultural relativists are not as convinced.
Moreover, the West has continued to look at human rights in terms
of *absolute* as opposed to *general guidelines* that are relevant to a great
number of cultures. Likewise, adherents to cultural relativism have
been remiss in their overemphasis on the concept of tolerance. More
to the point, cultural relativists need to focus more on the extent to
which enculturation results in ethnocentric behaviors that presuppose
superior/inferior relationships when addressing questions pertaining
to the application of morality and human rights.

It was argued earlier that universalism and cultural relativism are
excessively dogmatic, and in most cases, a middle ground can be found
that, while not entirely satisfying to either extreme position, may represent a compromise that all cultures involved can accept. As it is used
presently, "middle ground" is defined in terms of identifying general
guidelines (i.e., *cross-cultural universals)* to which all can agree. Critical to the establishment and success of cross-cultural universals is the
acceptance of the proposition that all cultures, whether Western or
non-Western, suffer from ethnocentrism and a commitment to pre-
serving the values, beliefs, morals, and so forth that define one's own
culture. The conceptualization of *human rights universals,* and their
subsequent application to diverse cultures, is subject to this debilitat-
ing lack of recognition. The inability to incorporate those aspects
of human rights, which represent the *least common denominator*
of numerous cultures, into a framework of international human
rights to which all cultural groupings can, without qualification,
accept is the basis for the perennial conflict between universalism and
cultural relativism.

The ability to identify cross-cultural universals is also based on a better understanding of the factors giving rise to the cultural practices that, from a Western human rights perspective, have been called into question. This need has been the primary basis for the incorporation of the aforementioned case studies. Enhanced understanding of diverse cultures is a prerequisite not only for establishing the benchmark commonalities among diverse cultures but also as a basis to further understand the aforementioned functions that associated practices of non-Western cultures serve.

While the acquisition of greater understanding would facilitate the establishment of cross-cultural universals, many cultural relativists would contend that the forces of ethnocentrism are so prevalent as to render any supposed cross-cultural universal irrelevant. As Tilley (2000), a proponent of universalism, states in his refutation of the "ethnocentrism argument":

> Relativists are likely to revise the ethnocentrism argument so that it avoids our criticism. According to the new argument, even if universalists are not ethnocentric in the usual sense, any list of precepts they produce is bound to be culturally biased. This is ensured by the well-established thesis of *cultural determinism,* according to which all of our beliefs, concepts, and perceptions are culturally conditioned to such an extent that unbiased thoughts, choices, and inferences are impossible. (p. 540)

This countervailing view, similar to its universalist counterpart, must be reconciled in favor of a more balanced approach to the construction of cross-cultural universals. To do otherwise is to condemn the conflict between the extremes to perpetuity and to see as impossible any chance toward achieving a higher morality with respect to human rights universals.

THE ESTABLISHMENT AND IMPLEMENTATION OF CROSS-CULTURAL HUMAN RIGHTS UNIVERSALS: RECOLLECTIONS AND REALITIES

> Instead, cultures should evolve to accommodate human rights standards. How can this be accomplished? Certainly, education is an important ingredient in changing cultures. Important questions to ask are: Whose voices are being heard in a culture? Who defines culture, who has the power to define? Who benefits from the definitions of culture, who does not benefit? How can all voices be heard? How can education be designed so that those without power can be empowered? (Reichert, 2006, p. 29)

The case studies on female circumcision, infanticide, prostituting, and labor give rise to several recollections concerning cultural realities and the establishment and implementation of cross-cultural human rights universals to cultures that have practices deemed by the West to constitute human rights abuses. Given the proposition that the goal of the West should be to promote cross-cultural universals rather than universal human rights, the following points become very relevant to the process. Although presented separately, the reality is that the following ten considerations are not mutually exclusive. Moreover, the listing is far from an exhaustive enumeration of the many components that factor into the process of cultural transformation.

First, the greatest utility is to be found in the promotion of cross-cultural universals that serve to unite diverse cultures. The chief consideration at work here is the fact that universal human rights are unlikely to be defined or instituted in a manner that is suitable to virtually all governments as well as their citizenry. Consequently, the focus should be on those least common denominators related to values, beliefs, and morals that promise to give rise to evolutionary change.

Second, the West must recognize that *cultural development* occurs through evolutionary as opposed to revolutionary means. The abolitionist movement of the West, with respect to the cultural practices discussed herein, is ineffective because of the speed with which the proponents of change command cultural transformation. As the case studies make readily apparent, the historical development giving rise to these four cultural practices has been quite lengthy. Given this, the generational passing of tradition is not a driving force that can be readily discarded, especially if a functional vacuum is left in its place.[2]

Related to cultural development is the notion that *gradualism* as opposed to *abolition* must be the dominant operational mode of the West as well as those non-Western actors working for cultural change. Historical acceptance of these practices has become entrenched in the traditions and culture of those adhering to them. Moreover, the development of the international system, and associated norms of behavior, has been such as to cast a negative light on countries in the West that seek change via the promotion of what is in large part viewed as revolutionary change or imperialist rule. Conversely, if change is desired, the process of gradualism appears less forceful, although admittedly still *commanding* cultural change, than the alternative.

A fourth recollection involves the participants in the process of gradualism. History is replete with instances of where societal transition and cultural change have been more acceptable when the forces for change are primarily indigenous to the culture undergoing the said change. Although it could be argued, for example, that external factors were also responsible, the continuing transformation from communism to democracy and socialism to capitalism in modern-day Russia has been more successful than at any point prior to 1985 because of the internal recognition that change was needed. In sum, the success of gradualism requires acknowledging the fact that the sparks of cultural transformation will be relatively more successful in igniting the fire when applied by those closest to the pit.

A fifth recollection involves the relevance of *function*. Change for the sake of change is inherently a risky endeavor, as the process does not necessarily recognize the important functions that may have been served by the undesired cultural practices. Identification of these functions is a critical component to successfully understanding the practice and facilitating gradual transformation. Moreover, the success of the latter with respect to human rights universals will be dependent on the development of *functional substitutes* that will eventually aid in the displacement of the undesirable cultural practice.

Recognition must also be given to the fact that cultural practices have a tendency to succumb during the process of cultural evolution when they are no longer performing a necessary function in society. While one might wait for an intolerable practice to *naturally* die off, this can be an exceptionally long process. Alternatively, the implementation of functional substitutes may hasten the process within the framework of gradualism.

One must also observe the power of ethnocentric forces in society and their extraordinary potential to obstruct the process of identifying and implementing cross-cultural universals. Ethnocentrism, along with its cousin xenophobia, works at both the national and subnational level. A government, for example, may have signed and ratified an international covenant on human rights and even derived and implemented laws to guarantee these human rights. It is quite likely, however, that a subnational cultural group may disregard these statutes, as well as the international covenant, because it views its own customs and morality as culturally superior or it is fearful of cultural imperialism.

The dominant presence of patriarchy must also be incorporated into the realization that structural cultural components constitute predictable stumbling blocks to the incorporation of cross-cultural universals with respect to human rights. The power of patriarchy is perhaps greater than any other structural impediment to change. At its best it is a structured ordering of societal affairs. At its worst the reality of patriarchy is such that it severely infringes on the daily affairs of *all* members of society. From a Western perspective it encroaches on the basic freedoms associated with the doctrine of universalism (i.e., the universality of human rights). Undoubtedly, any construction and agreed-upon cross-cultural universals will have to have dealt effectively with patriarchy.

Building on the tenets of patriarchy, an eighth recollection involves an evaluation of how women and female children, specifically, have historically been oppressed by a plethora of cultural practices designed to perpetuate male dominance and status. The present investigation of four cultural practices has detailed the extent of this historical oppression. Moreover, it has illustrated the magnitude (the numbers affected, the geographical boundaries, etc.) as well as the present-day manifestations of the cultural practice in question. All of these variables are important in producing cross-cultural universals that seek to improve upon the human dignity of women and female children.

A ninth recollection surrounds the causal factors responsible for the cultural practice. One common denominator among each of the four practices discussed herein is the concept of poverty. As was discussed, many who have studied these cultural practices are quick to point to economic impoverishment as a critical, if not the most important, variable responsible for the persistence of these cultural practices. Others, however, give it no more importance than the role of myth, tradition, culture, and so forth. Perhaps the best manner to address the importance of economic impoverishment is to regard it as a predisposing factor that can easily trigger the incorporation of any of the cultural practices discussed here. As such it does have a position of relatively increased worth. Given this, however, it is extremely important to realize that economic impoverishment does not always lead to the incorporation of these cultural practices, as one can point to a goodly number of cultures that are poor but abstain from these practices.

The final recollection discussed here is to realize the positive impact that educational programs have in bringing about desired cultural changes. This involves education that focuses on specific aspects of the cultural practice in question. For example, it is critical to understand the relationship of rural/urban living to female child labor or that passing legislation dealing with a particular practice does not often result in compliance due to enforcement problems. Education must also be utilized to improve female literacy, as it correlates greatly with lowering the incidence of these cultural practices. Moreover, compulsory education programs will serve to lessen the prevalence of economic impoverishment, generally, resulting in diminishing the perception held by many that these four cultural practices must be preserved.

NOTES

CHAPTER 1

1. The proceedings from this panel were subsequently published in 1997 in the *Journal of Anthropological Research* 53 (4).
2. It is important to note that the concept of human rights and associated principles have been accepted in part or whole by some countries for over 200 years. The concept of universalizing these principles of human rights, however, has its origins in the immediate aftermath of World War II. Bennett and Oliver (2002) quote Louis Henkin in defining "universalization" of human rights as "their general acceptance by national governments, and he defines 'internationalization' of rights as the recognition that treatment of citizens in one country has become the business of other countries" (p. 372).
3. Admittedly, even Nussbaum (1995a) suggests that some basic human functional capabilities, such as living a life of normal length, must be "to some extent relativized to local conditions" (p. 83).
4. The Commission on Human Rights was one of two commissions constructed within the Economic and Social Council. The Commission on the Status of Women, which is relevant to the chapters that follow, was at first a subcommission of the Commission on Human Rights, but received full independent status in 1947.
5. Moreover, the Vienna Declaration and Programme of Action states unequivocally that "while the significance of national particularities and various historical, cultural and religious backgrounds must be borne in mind, it is the duty of States, *regardless of their political, economic, and cultural systems*, to promote all human rights and fundamental freedoms" (United Nations, 1993b).

CHAPTER 2

1. Cultural relativism dictates that not everyone will be happy with the use of the term "female circumcision" to describe the many forms of this practice. "Female circumcision" and "female genital mutilation" are most commonly used, but both are flawed from the viewpoint of cultural relativism. The use of "female circumcision," for instance, is read by some to imply that the distinctive forms of this practice are similar to

male circumcision. Most would agree that comparing male circumcision with infibulation or introcision would be extremely difficult.

Williams and Sobieszczyk (1997) point more precisely to the "jargon problem" when they state that "the use of the word 'circumcision' to describe the range of procedures performed on females is objectionable to some on the grounds that it suggests a less severe procedure. And the use of the term 'genital mutilation' to describe all forms of the practice is offensive to others, particularly in instances in which no permanent alteration of the genitalia occurs" (p. 968).

Hicks (1996, p. 1, note 1) uses the term "female genital operations" because of the belief that "female genital mutilation" implies a moral judgment while "female circumcision" is a misnomer because it does not sufficiently cover the wide range of operations that are performed today. While an admirable attempt to derive a more value-free concept, the use of "female genital operations" sounds sterile as if the varied procedures that are performed on women are done so in a modern facility with the best of equipment. The same can be said of "female cutting."

I have used "female circumcision" in the present analysis not because it is a far superior term than the others, but because it is more culturally sensitive to those on both sides of the present debate. Others have attempted to become more culturally sensitive to this jargon problem. Toubia (1993) has began to use both "female circumcision" and "female genital mutilation" on the basis of whether the practice includes the "cutting and removal of sexual organs." This distinctive use of the two terms is incorporated precisely due to her "recognition of the terms of reference of the communities where it occurs" (p. 9).

2. Debate does exist regarding the practice of infibulation by pharaonic Egyptians. Seligman (1913) indicates that very little evidence exists and suggests that "pharaonic circumcision" was actually practiced by the Egyptian pharaohs (p. 640).

3. Of particular note in the *hadith* is the suggestion that when the Prophet Mohammed was asked of his opinion on "female circumcision," he replied, "To circumcise, but not to destroy (the clitoris), for not destroying would be better for the man and would make the woman's face glow" (Althaus, 1997, p. 131). For greater elaboration on the extent to which the *hadith* "legitimates" female circumcision, see Abu-Sahlieh (1994).

4. In all fairness to the Jewish faith the incidence of female circumcision may be limited to the Falashas (i.e., Ethiopian Jews) who, because of persecution and isolation, may not have had adequate access to either "definitive Jewish texts or informed rabbinical sources" (Buff, 1995, p. 189).

5. It may be counterproductive to spend so much time on "the numbers." However, as will be shown shortly, there are several problems that may have led several researchers to overestimate the absolute number of females who have undergone some form of circumcision.

6. This is not an absolute indictment of Hosken's initial attempt to provide some clarity with respect to the numbers. Rather, she should be applauded for making the bold attempt so early on, when there were no surveys or health studies done in most of these countries. Moreover, many of her initial estimates are still utilized today for lack of clear survey data regarding the extent to which the practice occurs within any given population. The estimates that Dorkenoo (1994) utilizes are in large part Hosken's, with revisions for countries where survey data are available.

7. The data in Table 2.1 are based on the 2002 estimates of population and the 2000–2005 average population growth rates.

8. This number is derived by utilizing the Hosken numbers in the table. If one takes the overall number obtained by using the Hosken estimates, 125,464,714, multiplies it by the average percentage population growth rate of 2.61 percent, and adds them together, one would come up with 128,739,343, a number that is very close to that advanced by WHO but that understates the number of females in these African countries who have undergone circumcision.

9. I use the term "explanations" rather than "justifications" throughout the text. Many researchers and casual observers use the latter. The problem with "justifications" is that it implies that the culture being brought into question is wrong and that it must somehow justify its practices to outsiders. The use of the word "explanations" is perhaps more value-neutral as it tries to further the understanding about why a cultural practice exists. Indictments, if they are to be made, should only arise after one has acquired a thorough understanding of the practice in question.

10. Some, however, contend that initiation ceremonies have become more infrequent as many more operations are occurring in hospitals rather than in traditional settings (Thiam, 1983).

11. *Wanzo* is the element that is found in all humans that causes them to become "a confused, idiotic human being, which will cloud the intelligence and render one utterly useless to the community" (Montagu, 1995, p. 14). Moreover, it is commonly believed that *wanzo* prohibits both males and females from having sexual relations as well as from being able to speak with adults (Abdalla, 1982, pp. 77–78).

12. For more on the distinctiveness of the language used to depict the many forms of female circumcision and the implications with regard to cultural considerations, see Dixon (1997).

13. While it is true that the latter two indicators are included in the formula for HDI, it is also sometimes easier for one to obtain a more meaningful account of the poverty by looking at the raw numbers as opposed to an overall ranking such as the HDI and GDI.

14. See Billet (1993) for a detailed analysis of the positive impact that such financial flows as official development assistance (ODA), foreign direct investment (FDI), and foreign debt (DEBT) have on the economic growth and development of developing countries generally and African countries specifically.

15. This might well be due to the passage of the Vienna Declaration of the World Conference on Human Rights in June, 1993. Toubia (1994, p. 715) contends that because of the passage of this declaration, which holds that traditional practices (e.g., female circumcision) are a violation of human rights, most countries in the West will now outlaw the practice.

16. One might also argue that legalization of the removal of the prepuce of the clitoris is an acceptable practice given the acceptance of male circumcision in most Western cultures. Obviously, as in the United States, this would require an amendment to federal law.

Chapter 3

1. An immediate problem arises in terms of what female infanticide entails. As it is used here, infanticide is general and includes, but is not limited to, various cultural practices including neonaticide (death between 0 and 27 days), post-neonaticide (death from 28 days to 1 year old), infanticide (death coming after 1 year of age), and pre-natal sex selection (destruction of fetus). The killing of female infants has also been referred to in the literature as femicide and/or social femicide. Finally, "gendercide" is also becoming a referent to the practice (Jones, 2002).

2. There is no intention of negating the importance of male infanticide as it has occurred in the past and continues to occur today. Male infanticide is a most unusual circumstance today as most cases of infanticide are related to the perceived functions that males and females, respectively, perform in various societies (Williamson, 1978, p. 67). Moreover, systematic male infanticide is rarer yet (Miller, 1981, pp. 43–44). Rather, the intent is to highlight the plight of the "girl child" given the existence of patriarchal and patrilineal regimes that have been most dominant throughout history.

3. Other considerations are somewhat important in determining where the "missing girls" have gone and for what reasons. For instance, immigration and emigration figures may be an important aspect to consider, but is typically one that is considered relatively trivial (Coale, 1991, pp. 517–518). Moreover, demographers also suggest that some explanation can be gleaned from the underreporting of female newborns and post-natal mortality (Secondi, 2002).

4. Reliance on the secondary sex ratio alone also precludes any information regarding the number of female fetuses that have been intentionally killed.

5. TOTMISSFEM is calculated by taking the percentage difference between the FMR/GENPOP and the FMR/GENPOP for sub-Saharan Africa multiplied by MALEPOP.

6. TOTFEMPOT is arrived at by first calculating TOTFEMBIRTHS given TOTBIRTHS and FMR/BIRTH. The resultant number is multiplied

by the percentage difference between FMR/BIRTH and the FMR/ GENPOP for sub-Saharan Africa.

7. At least two studies, however, provide evidence for the argument that impoverishment isn't the "driving force" behind female infanticide (Banister, 2004; Croll, 2002, p. 18).

8. It is also possible, however, that for those who are considerably poor, the bridegroom's family may actually pay a small amount for the daughter recognizing that the daughter is of considerable worth to an extremely impoverished family (Hrdy, 1993, p. 645). In recognition of this, the Chinese government, in the mid-1980s, allowed families with only one female child to have a second child without penalty (Jones, 2002). Croll (2002, p. 28) has referred to this as China's "two child or single son policy."

9. Ironically, government efforts by China to curtail population, namely the 1979 One-Child Policy Act and the Household Responsibility System, are said to have led to greater female infanticide rates as families do not wish to be unduly penalized for having a girl while wishing to have a boy (Hom, 1992, pp. 263–275).

10. This implicitly refers to the birth order phenomenon that is present in many cultures that practice female infanticide. In short, the birth order phenomenon refers to the increased likelihood that a female baby will be killed if one female child already exists. Moreover, this likelihood increases for every female child that is already present in the family (Chunkath & Athreya, 1997, WS27–WS28; Kristof, 1991b).

11. Of obvious note here is the fact that great oil wealth among most of the west Asian countries serves to "mask" the true economic plight of many citizens residing in these countries.

12. Obviously other considerations aforementioned are important to recount here. Female infanticide, for instance, would be unlikely if the culture in question was not patriarchal and patrilineal in its social structure. Moreover, poverty coupled with a preference for male children also accentuates the possibility that female infanticide is more likely to occur.

13. This does not necessarily mean that the proponents of cultural relativism believe in the inherent worth of female infanticide and would personally like to see it continue. The current research did not uncover any statements to this effect, only statements that allow for the presence of female infanticide given its peculiar functional linkage to the socio-economic system.

14. One would be remiss not to note that it is not just the West that finds the practice of female infanticide abhorrent. Citizens of India also work very hard for the *elimination* of the practice (Muthulakshmi, 1997, p. 13). Moreover, some attempts, such as the Inter-Caste Marriage Assistance program, have been somewhat successful, on a small scale, in dealing with local populations (Social Welfare, Social Reforms and Vazhndhu Kaattuvom, 2001).

CHAPTER 4

1. The phrase "prostituting of female children" or "prostituted female child" is more preferable than "female child prostitution." The latter conveys a sense that somehow it is the choice of female children to engage in this vocation, while the reality is quite different. Moreover, the latter, perhaps inadvertently, suggests that it is the child that is the criminal (Hodgson, 1994, p. 512).

2. There is no intention of negating the importance of the prostituting of male children as it has occurred in the past and continues to occur today. The prostituting of male children, relatively speaking, is a practice that involves considerably fewer numbers than does the prostituting of female children. According to End Child Prostitution, Child Pornography and Trafficking of Children for Sexual Purposes (Boonpala & Kane, 2001, p. 23), the prostituted children are primarily female, although there is a particular preference for male children in Sri Lanka. The girls being in the qualified majority of those prostituted is a pattern recognizable in other regions as well. Consequently, the intent here is to highlight the plight of the "girl child" given the existence of patriarchal and patrilineal regimes that have been most dominant throughout the history of prostituted female children.

3. All females were made to, in essence, undergo a certain degree of sexual destruction by sitting on the knee of the statue of Mutinus.

4. The exclusion of countries outside the Asian and Central and South American regions does not mean that the prostituting of female children does not occur in other countries, including developed countries. For example, it is estimated that there are as many as 2.4 million prostituted children in the United States alone (Joseph, 1995, p. 8).

5. In all actuality the date of birth and death of Gautama Buddha is in great dispute. Generally, the West uses 563–483 B.C. The southern school uses 624 B.C., while the northern school employs numerous dates, which are typically around 300 years later than that used by the southern school. At a 1993 conference, however, there was general agreement that Buddha was probably born in the fourth-century B.C., but that the exact date could not be known (Bechert, 1993).

6. Obviously, this is not a "one-way" street. The number of children, in particular females, that are becoming infected with HIV-AIDS has been growing for some time (Hanenberg & Rojanapithayakorn, 1998, p. 69; Kristof, 1996, p. 18) and is particularly troublesome in the Asian region (Hodgson, 1994, p. 520).

7. Many pedophiles think that the prostitution of female children is an effective way to help alleviate some of the drastic poverty that is prevalent in these regions. On this point, see Nyland (1995, p. 549).

8. Two key issues are related to the concept of extraterritorial legislation. Specifically, countries must determine their stance on "double criminality" and "double jeopardy." Whereas the former refers to whether the offence

has to be criminal in both the home and host country, the latter refers to whether a national can be tried in the home country in addition to being tried in the host country.

9. One might assert that the trial and conviction of a 69-year-old man certainly suggests that Sweden is quite serious about this kind of activity. One should note, however, that while he could have received a four-year prison sentence, the court saw fit to sentence him to three months because of his age and physical health.

10. One should recall that a "child" was defined in this document as a person 18 years or younger unless majority is obtained earlier under the provision of an applicable law.

11. One should note that in her capacity as the U.S. delegate to the United Nations, Madeleine Albright signed this document on February 16, 1995. Ratification of the convention, under the Rights of the Child Act of 1997, would have required the United States to forgo assistance, under the Foreign Assistance Act of 1961, to any country that has not enacted and has not been enforcing laws against child prostitution, specifically, and the sexual exploitation of children, in general.

12. One might undoubtedly criticize the stance regarding decriminalization of adult prostitution on the basis that it disproportionately affects females in a negative manner while concurrently serving to further "enslave" them. One might respond, however, to say that the basic underlying assumption, regardless of how one might feel about the practice, is that the practice will continue with or without the blessing of society. Moreover, it is not entirely clear whether all prostitutes find themselves to be unwilling participants in this sector. While structural forces in society undoubtedly serve to "enslave" many who might otherwise be employed in alternative professions, this stance is also warranted to the degree that it is successful in decreasing female child prostitution.

CHAPTER 5

1. Although much of the literature pertinent to the issue of child labor uses the English spelling "labour," the spelling used throughout this chapter, except for direct quotes and citing titles, will be "labor."

2. While some will inevitably take issue with presenting the following in relation to slavery, as child labor and slavery can be presented quite distinctively, the fact is that it was quite difficult to distinguish between "freedwomen," "free women [i.e., citizen]," and "slaves." As Brock (1994) states, "In reality it will have been hard to deduce a woman's status simply from her occupation, except that if she did not work she was presumably a citizen, and if she was handling significant sums of money, she probably was not" (p. 345).

Additionally, one should note that the institution of slavery, at least from classical to late antiquity, was considerably different from the institution that exists today. Because manumission of slaves was frequent, there was incentive for slaves to work as if they were free laborers (Temin, 2004, pp. 526–528).

3. In fact, Boswell (1988) maintains that the "terms for 'child,' 'boy,' and 'girl,' for example, are regularly employed to mean 'slave' or 'servant' in Greek, Latin, Arabic, Syriac, and many medieval languages" (p. 27).

4. A brief note about "women" is necessary at this juncture. Often, a reference to "women" during antiquity was, in reality, a reference to older female children. It was preferable to marry by age 14 and to have children shortly thereafter (Pomeroy, 1975, p. 64).

5. In accordance with UNESCO practice, the bottom end of the age range is 5 years given the assumption that most children are not able to work or be schooled prior to this benchmark (ILO, 2002a, p. 29).

6. While Article 7 stipulates age 13 for light work and 15 for regular work, the reality is that the convention allows for many countries, mainly those whose education and economic systems are less well-developed, to substitute ages 12 and 14 for light and regular work, respectively.

   For purposes of statistical presentation, the ILO (2002) used 43 hours of work per week as the cutoff for "regular work" that a child ages 15 to 17 years could undertake without the economic activity being considered "child labour." The "normal" work week, depending on the country under investigation, is constituted by 35 to 46 hours. The cutoff used by the ILO (2002c) is an arbitrary "middle-ground" between 46 hours and what is considered to be the typical low end, 40 hours (pp. 33–34).

7. This number does not include the 8.4 million children estimated to be in the worst forms of child labor.

8. Comparatively, developing countries and countries in transition make up 2.5 and 2.4 million, respectively.

9. Also note, however, that the Minimum Age Convention (ILO, 1973) allows the minimum age to fall to 16 years if the safety, morals, and health of the child are adequately ensured.

10. The importance of prostituted female children was covered in a previous chapter. Given that pornography is closely related and often coupled with female child prostitution, these forms (i.e., forced labor for sexual exploitation) of forced labor will not be discussed here.

11. Given that, relatively, the number of girls affected by this type of state-forced labor is thought to be significantly greater than that of those impacted by prison labor, only female child soldiers will be discussed under this form of forced labor.

12. "Quality," as it is used here, refers to the education level of the child. There is said to exist an inverse relationship between quantity and quality.

13. Some beliefs that will not be covered herein include the belief that female child labor is a "community tradition" (Jaiswal, 2000) or that it is tradition for a child to follow in the footsteps of their parent (ILO, 1998a).

14. Other backward classes are constituted by populations that are characterized as criminals or have converted from Hindu to another religion. They make up roughly 50 percent of the present-day population of India,

whereas the scheduled castes and scheduled tribes make up roughly 15 percent and 7.5 percent of the population, respectively.

It is important to emphasize that none of these groups are considered to be part of the high castes. The latter are constituted by, in order of their significance, Brahmans (e.g., lawyers, doctors, engineers), Kshatriyas (e.g., landowners, rulers, warriors), Vaishyas (e.g., merchants), and Shudras (e.g., artisans and agriculturalists).

15. Mahatma Gandhi used to refer to this group as Harijan (i.e., the children of God) in an attempt to foster acceptance of the *untouchables.*

16. It is important to note that the government of India has implemented a "positive discriminatory" system to try to offset the ills that the untouchables experienced in the past. Unfortunately, this scheme has worked only in the more modern sectors of the country. The rural population, for all intents and purposes, still operates under a rigid caste system.

17. One should note that the earliest version of this legislation outlined the manner by which child labor was injurious to the American workers because of wage differences. Subsequent versions have highlighted the importance of the human rights questions rather than the economic question.

18. The core standards of labor are largely born out of ILO Conventions 29, 87, 98, 100, 105, 111, 138, and 182, and, as stated in the 1998 ILO Declaration on Fundamental Principles and Rights at Work, consist of the following:

  (a) freedom of association and the effective recognition of the right to collective bargaining;
  (b) the elimination of all forms of forced or compulsory labour;
  (c) the effective abolition of child labour; and
  (d) the elimination of discrimination in respect of employment and occupation. (ILO, 1998b)

19. One might argue that, to the extent that these other actors do reassess their relations with the guilty party, the invoking of Article 33 does result in stipulating that sanctions should be introduced. One might also note at this juncture that Article 33 has only been invoked once, in 2000, in the 87-year history of the ILO.

20. It should be noted here that the current Bush administration does not favor linkage.

21. Many label this the "abolitionist" approach, whereby nothing short of complete and immediate eradication of the practice is acceptable. Conversely, adherents to "gradualism" understand the negative sides of the practice but prefer a more gradual approach to bringing the practice in line with Western conceptions of human rights (Seabrook, 2000, pp. 13–14; Smolin, 2000, pp. 947–949).

22. The list of national laws and national plans of action is quite long. A very quick search of the ILO NATLEX Database turned up more numerous results than can be discussed here.

CHAPTER 6

1. Merton (1968) distinguished between three types of latent functions: those that are functional (i.e., beneficial), dysfunctional (i.e., harmful), and nonfunctional (i.e., not relevant). Adherents to universalism and cultural relativists would submit that these four practices are relevant to the respective societies in which they occur, but that "relevant" may entail a practice that is harmful or one that is beneficial.

2. One might challenge this assertion by suggesting that the Chinese practice of *footbinding* has a lengthy history, although dating only to the tenth century A.D. during the rule of Emperor Li Yu, and shared many characteristics with the four cultural practices detailed here. For example, there were different types of binding, different ages at which female feet were bound, sexual myths surrounding the practice, and a patriarchically structured society that condoned the practice. Unlike these practices, however, the anti-footbinding campaign was mostly internally derived following the 1911 nationalist revolution of Sun Yat-Sen. Internal forces, driven by revolutionary fervor, were in large part the reason for the quick demise of the practice. The key difference is that the West is not promoting revolutionary change in the form of national uprising in order to bring about immediate abolition of female child labor, prostituting, circumcision, and infanticide.

BIBLIOGRAPHY

Abdalla, R. H. D. (1982). *Sisters in affliction: Circumcision and infibulation of women in Africa*. London: Zed Press.

Abu-Sahlieh, S. A. (1994). To mutilate in the name of Jehovah or Allah: Legitimization of male and female circumcision. *Medicine and Law, 13*(7/8), 575–622.

Aird, J. S. (1990). *Slaughter of innocents*. Washington, DC: American Enterprise Institute Press.

Aldrete, G. S. (2004). Children. In J. E. Salisbury (General Ed.) & G. S. Aldrete (Vol. Ed.), *The Greenwood encyclopedia of daily life* (Vol. 1, *The ancient world*, pp. 50–61). Westport, CT: Greenwood Press.

Al-Khudairi, S. (1997). Female genital mutilation: Global and national perspectives. *Medicus: Journal of the Australian Medical Association, 31*, 21.

Althaus, F. A. (1997). Female circumcision: Rite of passage or violation of rights? *International Family Planning Perspectives, 23*(3), 130–133.

Amin, S., Quayes, M. S., & Rives, J. M. (2004). Poverty and other determinants of child labor in Bangladesh. *Southern Economic Journal, 70*(4), 876–892.

Amnesty International. (1997). *Female genital mutilation in Africa: Information by country*. Retrieved January 24, 2005, from http://www.amnesty.org/ailib/intcam/femgen/fgm9.htm

Anderson, J. W., & Moore, M. (1993, March 22–28). The burden of womanhood. *Washington Post National Weekly Edition*, pp. 6–7.

Anker, R., & Melkas, H. (1996). *Economic incentives for children and families to eliminate or reduce child labour*. Geneva: International Labour Office.

Arat, Z. F. (2002). Analyzing child labor as a human rights issue: Its causes, aggravating policies, and alternative proposals. *Human Rights Quarterly, 24*(1), 177–204.

Ashagrie, K. (1998). *Statistics on working children and hazardous child labour in brief*. Geneva: International Labour Office.

Asia Watch. (1993). *A modern form of slavery: Trafficking of Burmese women and girls into brothels in Thailand*. New York: Human Rights Watch.

Awanohara, S., Vatikiotis, M., & Islam, S. (1993, June 17). Vienna showdown. *Far Eastern Economic Review, 156*(24), 16–17, 20.

Bachman, S. L. (2000). A new economics of child labor: Searching for answers behind the headlines. *Journal of International Affairs, 53*(2), 545–572.

Baker, C. (1995). Child chattel lure tourists for sex beneath the palms. *Insight, 11*(11), 11–13.

Baland, J. M., & Robinson, J. A. (2000). Is child labor inefficient? *Journal of Political Economy, 108*(4), 663–679.

Banerjee, S. R. (1995). Child labor in India: Present status. *Indian Pediatrics, 32,* 403–408.

Banister, J. (2004). Shortage of girls in China today. *Journal of Population Research, 21*(1), 19–45.

Basu, K. (1999). Child labor: Cause, consequence, and cure, with remarks on international labor standards. *Journal of Economic Literature, 37*(3), 1083–1119.

Basu, K., & Van, P. H. (1998). The economics of child labor. *American Economic Review, 88*(3), 412–427.

Battling Brazil's child labor brutality: An interview with Oded Grajew. (1997, January/February). *Multinational Monitor, 18,* 20–21, 26.

Bechert, H. (1993). *The dates of Buddha.* Retrieved January 30, 2005, from http://www.buddhanet.net/e-learning/dharmadata/fdd8.htm

Becker, G. S. (1965). A theory of the allocation of time. *Economic Journal, 75*(299), 493–517.

Becker, G. S., & Lewis, H. G. (1973). On the interaction between quantity and quality of children. *Journal of Political Economy, 81*(2), S279–S288.

Bennett, A. L., & Oliver, J. K. (2002). *International organizations: Principles and issues.* Upper Saddle River, NJ.: Prentice Hall.

Berkman, E. T. (1996). Responses to the International Child Sex Tourism Trade. *Boston College International and Comparative Law Review, 19*(2), 397–422.

Beyer, D. (1996). Child prostitution in Latin America. In U.S. Department of Labor, *Forced labor: The prostitution of children* (pp. 32–40). Washington, DC: U.S. Department of Labor.

Billet, B. L. (1993). *Modernization theory and economic development: Discontent in the developing world.* Westport, CT: Praeger.

Birdsell, J. B. (1968). Some predictions for the Pleistocene based on equilibrium systems among hunter-gatherers. In R. B. Lee, & I. DeVore (Eds.), *Man the hunter* (pp. 229–240). Chicago: Aldine-Atherton.

Boonpala, P., & Kane, J. (2001). *Trafficking of children: The problem and responses worldwide.* Geneva: International Labour Office.

Boswell, J. E. (1984). *Expositio* and *Oblatio:* The abandonment of children and the ancient and medieval family. *American Historical Review, 89*(1), 10–33.

Boswell, J. E. (1988). *The kindness of strangers: The abandonment of children in Western Europe from late antiquity to the renaissance.* Chicago: University of Chicago Press.

Bower, B. (1994). Female infanticide: Northern exposure. *Science News, 146*(22), 358.

Bread for the World. (2004). *Are we on track to end hunger?* Silver Spring, MD: Bread for the World Institute.

Brock, R. (1994). The labour of women in classical Athens. *Classical Quarterly, 44*(2), 336–346.

Brothers, K. (2002). Covenant and the vulnerable other. *Medical Student Journal of the American Medical Association, 288*(9), 1133.

Brown, D. K., Deardorff, A. V., & Stern, R. M. (2002). *Pros and cons of linking trade and labor standards* (Discussion Paper No. 477). Ann Arbor: University of Michigan, School of Public Policy.

Bryk, F. (1934). *Circumcision in man and woman: Its history, psychology and ethnology.* New York: American Ethnological Press.

Buchanan, E. (Executive Producer). (1994). Girls: Children of a lesser God. *Primetime Live.* Washington, DC: ABC News.

Buddhanet. (1998). *The Buddhist schools.* Retrieved January 30, 2005, from http://www.buddhanet.net/e-learning/buddhistworld/schools1.htm

Budhos, M. (1997, March/April). Putting the heat on sex tourism. *Ms, 12*–17.

Buff, D. D. (1995, January 19). Female circumcision [Letter to the editor]. *New England Journal of Medicine,* p. 189.

Bunch, C. (1997). *The intolerable status quo: Violence against women and girls.* Retrieved January 26, 2005, from http://www.unicef.org/pon97/women1.htm

Burrhus-Clay, A. (1998). *Social implications of child prostitution.* Unpublished manuscript.

Burstyn, L. (1995, October). Female circumcision comes to America. *Atlantic Monthly, 276*(4), 28–35.

Butegwa, F. (1993). The challenge of promoting women's rights in African countries. In J. Kerr (Ed.), *Ours by right: Women's rights as human rights* (pp. 40–42). London: Zed Books.

Cairo Declaration for the Elimination of FGM. (2003). Retrieved February 8, 2005, from http://www.crlp.org/pdf/pdf_fgm_cairo2003_eng.pdf

Calcetas-Santos, O. (1996). *Rights of the child: Report of the special rapporteur on the sale of children, child prostitution and child pornography.* Retrieved January 30, 2005, from http://daccessdds.un.org/doc/UNDOC/GEN/G96/102/36/PDF/G9610236.pdf?OpenElement

Campaign to end child labor. (1997). *Women's International Network News, 23*(4), 74.

Carey, D., Jr. (2004). Mexico. In C. L. Schmitz, E. K. Traver, & D. Larson (Eds.), *Child labor: A global view* (pp. 79–90). Westport, CT: Greenwood Press.

Center for Reproductive Rights. (2005, February). *Female genital mutilation (FGM): Legal prohibitions worldwide.* Retrieved February 6, 2005, from http://www.crlp.org/pub_fac_fgmicpd.html

Central Intelligence Agency. (1996). *The 1996 world factbook.* Washington, DC: U.S. Government Printing Office.

Chandra, S. (1996). *SAFE—help educate girl children in India.* Retrieved January 26, 2005, from http://www.cse.nd.edu/~surendar/safe/

Chen, Y. (1980). *The dragon's village: An autobiographical novel of revolutionary China*. New York: Penguin Books.

Child labor. (2000, May). *Working children: An update* (Occasional Note No. 2). Washington, DC: World Bank.

Child labour to be eliminated by 2014. (2004, December 21). *The rising Nepal*. Retrieved March 10, 2005, from http://www.globalmarch.org/clns/clns-dec-2004-details.php#21-1

Child prostitution on the rise, report says. (2003, July 15). *Africa News Service*.

Chunkath, S. R., & Athreya, V. B. (1997). Female infanticide in Tamil Nadu: Some evidence. *Economic and Political Weekly, 32*(17), WS21–WS28.

Cigno, A., Guarcello, L., Lyon, S., Noguchi, Y., & Rosati, F. (2003). *Child labour indicators used by the UCW Project: An explanatory note*. New York: UNICEF.

Coale, A. J. (1991). Excess female mortality and the balance of the sexes in the population: An estimate of the number of "missing females". *Population and Development Review, 17*(3), 517–523.

Cole, S. G. (1981). Could Greek women read and write? In H. P. Foley (Ed.), *Reflections of women in antiquity* (pp. 219–245). New York: Gordon & Breach Science Publishers.

Colón, A. R., & Colón, P. A. (2001). *A history of children: A socio-cultural survey across millennia*. Westport, CT: Greenwood Press.

Croll, E. (1980). *Feminism and socialism in China*. New York: Schocken Books.

Croll, E. (2002). Fertility decline, family size and female discrimination: A study of reproductive management in East and South Asia. *Asia-Pacific Population Journal, 17*(2), 11–38.

Cunningham, H. (1990). The employment and unemployment of children in England c.1680–1851. *Past and Present, 126*, 115–150.

Cutner, L. P. (1985). Female genital mutilation. *Obstetrical and Gynecological Survey, 7*, 437–443.

Dare, F. O., Oboro, V. O., Fadiora, S. O., Orji, E. O., Sule-Odu, A. O., & Olabode, T. O. (2004). Female genital mutilation: An analysis of 522 cases in south-western Nigeria. *Journal of Obstetrics and Gynaecology, 24*(3), 281–283.

Das Gupta, M. (1987). Selective discrimination against female children in rural Punjab. *Population Development Review, 9*(1), 77–100.

Department of the Interior, Census Office. (1897). *Population of the United States at the Eleventh Census: 1890*. Washington, DC: U.S. Government Printing Office.

Dillard, H. (1984). *Daughters of the reconquest: Women in Castilian town society 1100–1300*. New York: Cambridge University Press.

Diller, J. M., & Levy, D. A. (1997). Child labor, trade and investment: Toward the harmonization of international law. *American Journal of International Law, 91*, 663–696.

Dixon, J. T. (1997). Bridging society, culture, and law: The issue of female circumcision. *Case Western Reserve Law Review, 47*(2), 263–274.

Doctor is convicted in death of a fetus after an abortion. (1989, June 13). *New York Times,* p. I18.

Dorkenoo, E. (1994). *Cutting the rose: Female genital mutilation— the practice and its prevention.* London: Minority Rights Group International.

Dorkenoo, E., & Elworthy, S. (1992). *Female genital mutilation: Proposals for change* (Minority Rights Group International Rep. No. 92/3). London: Minority Rights Group International.

Drèze, J., & Sen, A. (1989). *Hunger and public action.* New York: Oxford University Press.

Dugger, C. W. (1996, October 12). New law bans genital cutting in United States. *New York Times,* pp. A1, A28.

El Dareer, A. (1983). Epidemiology of female circumcision in the Sudan. *Tropical Doctor, 13,* 41–45.

Elliott, K. A. (2000, July). *The ILO and enforcement of core labor standards* (Policy Brief No. 00–6). Washington, DC: Institute for International Economics.

Elliott, K. A. (2004, March). *Labor standards, development, and CAFTA* (Policy Brief No. PB04–2). Washington, DC: Institute for International Economics.

Enactment of PROTECT Act against sex tourism. (2004). *American Journal of International Law, 98*(1), 182.

End Child Prostitution in Asian Tourism. (2005). *Countries with extraterri- torial legislation.* Retrieved February 20, 2005, from http://www.ecpat. net/eng/CSEC/faq/map.asp

Faerman, M., Kahila, G., Smith, P., Greenblatt, C., Stager, L., Filon, D., & Oppenheim, A. (1997). DNA analysis reveals the sex of infanticide victims. *Nature, 385*(6613), 212–213.

Female infanticide in the Bihar region of India. (1996). *Official Journal of the European Communities, 39,* 60.

Flores, R. (1996). Child prostitution in the United States. In U.S. Department of Labor, *Forced labor: The prostitution of children* (pp. 41–49). Washington, DC: U.S. Department of Labor.

Fluehr-Lobban, C. (1995). Cultural relativism and universal rights. *Chronicle of Higher Education, 41*(39), B1–B2.

Fourth World Conference on Women. (1996). *Beijing declaration and platform for action.* Retrieved January 26, 2005, from http://www.umn. edu/humanrts/instree/bejing4.htm

French, H. W. (1997, February 2). Africa's culture war: Old customs, new values. *New York Times,* pp. IV1, IV4.

Fuller, R. G. (1937). Child labor. In E. R. A. Seligman (General Ed.) & A. Johnson (Assoc. Ed.), *Encyclopaedia of the social sciences* (Vol. 3, pp. 412–424). New York: Macmillan.

Geis, G. (1993). Prostitution. In *Encyclopedia Americana* (Vol. 22, pp. 669–670). Danbury, CT: Grolier.

Giladi, A. (1990). Some observations on infanticide in medieval Muslim society. *International Journal of Middle East Studies, 22*(2), 185–200.

Gill, T. (1995). Prostitution law misses the target, say activists. Retrieved January 30, 2005, from http://www.geocities.com/CapitolHill/Senate/8931/dbt-gem1.html

Girish, U. (2005, February 9). For India's daughters, a dark birth day. *Chronicle of Higher Education*, p. 11.

Gordon, D. A. (1993). The unhappy relationship of feminism and postmodernism in Anthropology. *Anthropological Quarterly, 66*(3), 109–117.

Gruenbaum, E. (1996). The cultural debate over female circumcision: The Sudanese are arguing this one out for themselves. *Medical Anthropology Quarterly, 10*(4), 455–475.

Haines-Eitzen, K. (1998). "Girls trained in beautiful writing": Female scribes in Roman Antiquity and early Christianity. *Journal of Early Christian Studies, 6*(4), 629–646.

Hallett, J. P. (1984). *Fathers and daughters in Roman society: Women and the elite family.* Princeton, NJ: Princeton University Press.

Hanenberg, R., & Rojanapithayakorn, W. (1998). Changes in prostitution and the AIDS epidemic in Thailand. *AIDS CARE, 10*(1), 69–79.

Harris, W. V. (1999). Demography, geography and the sources of Roman slaves. *Journal of Roman Studies, 89*, 62–75.

Hasnat, B. (1995). International trade and child labor. *Journal of Economic Issues, 29*(2), 419–426.

Herskovits, M. J. (1972). *Cultural relativism: Perspectives in cultural pluralism.* New York: Random House.

Hicks, E. K. (1993). *Infibulation: Female mutilation in Islamic northeastern Africa.* New Brunswick, NJ: Transaction Publishers.

Hicks, E. K. (1996). *Infibulation: Female mutilation in Islamic northeastern Africa.* New Brunswick, NJ: Transaction Publishers.

Hobbs, S., McKechnie, J., & Lavalette, M. (1999). *Child labor: A world history companion.* Santa Barbara, CA: ABC-CLIO.

Hodgson, D. (1994). Sex tourism and child prostitution in Asia: Legal responses and strategies. *Melbourne University Law Review, 19*(3), 512–544.

Hom, S. K. (1992). Female infanticide in China: The human rights specter and thoughts towards (an)other vision. *Columbia Human Rights Law Review, 23*(189), 249–314.

Honeyman, K., & Goodman, J. (1991). Women's work, gender conflict, and labour markets in Europe, 1500–1900. *Economic History Review, 44*(4), 608–628.

Hornblower, M. (1993, June 21). The skin trade. *Time, 141*, 44–51.

Hosken, F. P. (1980). *Female sexual mutilation: The facts and proposals for action.* Lexington, MA: Women's International Network News.

Hosken, F. P. (1982). *The Hosken report: Genital and sexual mutilation of females*. Lexington, MA: Women's International Network News.

House Joint Resolution 302, 103d Cong., 1st Sess. (1993). Retrieved January 26, 2005, from http://thomas.loc.gov/cgi-bin/query/z?c103: H.J.RES.302.IH:

House Resolution 1849, 104th Cong., 1st Sess. (1995). Retrieved January 26, 2005, from http://thomas.loc.gov/cgi-bin/query/z?c104: H.R.1849.IH:

House Resolution 2047, 104th Cong., 1st Sess. (1995). Retrieved January 26, 2005, from http://thomas.loc.gov/cgi-bin/query/z?c104: H.R.2047.IH:

House Resolution 38, 103d Cong., 1st Sess. (1993). Retrieved January 26, 2005, from http://thomas.loc.gov/cgi-bin/query/z?c103:H.R.38.IH:

Hrdy, S. B. (1993). Infanticide. In *The encyclopedia of religion* (Vol. 2, pp. 644–648). New York: Macmillan.

Ilangovan, R. (2005, January 13). *Juvenile sex ratio falling, female foeticide rising*. Retrieved February 10, 2005, from http://www.hindu.com/2005/01/13/stories/2005011314610500.htm

India's disappearing females. (2004). *Futurist, 38*(2), 8.

Inter-African Committee on Traditional Practices affecting the Health of Women and Children. (1996). *Objectives and principles*. Retrieved January 24, 2005, from http://www.iac-ciaf.ch/

International Finance Corporation. (2006). *Environmental and Social Standards*. Retrieved May 10, 2006, from http://ifcln1.ifc.org/ifcext/enviro.nsf/Content/EnvSocStandards

International Labour Organization. (1973). *ILO Convention No.138*. Retrieved March 5, 2006, from http://www.ilo.org/ilolex/english/convdisp1.htm

International Labour Organization. (1991). Child labour: Law and practice. *Conditions of Work Digest, 10*(2), 48–54.

International Labour Organization. (1996). *Child labour: What is to be done?* Retrieved March 5, 2006, from http://www.ilo.org/public/english/standards/ipec/publ/policy/what/whatintro.htm

International Labour Organization. (1998a). *Child labour: Targeting the intolerable* (Report VI). Geneva: International Labour Organization.

International Labour Organization. (1998b). *ILO Declaration on Fundamentals and Principles at Work*. Retrieved May 10, 2006, from http://www.ilo.org/dyn/declaris/DECLARATIONWEB.INDEXPAGE

International Labour Organization. (1999). *ILO Convention No.182*. Retrieved March 5, 2006, from http://www.ilo.org/ilolex/english/convdisp1.htm

International Labour Organization. (2002a). *Action against child labour*. Geneva: International Labour Organization.

International Labour Organization. (2002b). *A future without child labour* (Report I). Geneva: International Labour Organization.

International Labour Organization. (2002c). *Every child counts: New global estimates on child labour.* Geneva: International Labour Organization.

International Labour Organization. (2005). *A global alliance against forced labour.* Geneva: International Labour Organization.

International Labour Organization. (2006a). *Constitution.* Retrieved May 10, 2006 from http://www.ilo.org/public/english/about/iloconst.htm

International Labour Organization. (2006b). *ILOLEX: Database of International Labour Standards.* Retrieved May 9, 2006 http://www.ilo.org/ilolex/english/docs/declworld.htm

International Labour Organization. (2006c). *Labour statistics database.* Geneva: International Labour Organization.

International Programme on the Elimination of Child Labour. (2004a). *Step by step: Examples of how countries determine hazardous child labour* [Brochure]. Geneva: International Labour Organization.

International Programme on the Elimination of Child Labour. (2004b). *Understanding child domestic labour and responses to it: Helping hands or shackled lives?* Geneva: International Labour Organization.

Irving, T. B. (1991). *The Qur'an: The noble reading* (Thomas B. Irving, Trans.). Cedar Rapids, IA: The Mother Mosque Foundation.

Jaiswal, P. (2000). *Child labour: A sociological study.* New Delhi: Shipra Publications.

James, S. A. (1994). Reconciling international human rights and cultural relativism: The case of female circumcision. *Bioethics, 8*(1), 1–26.

Jason, J., Gilliland, J.C., & Tyler, C.W., Jr. (1983). Homicide as a cause of pediatric mortality in the United States. *Pediatrics, 72,* 191–197.

Jehl, D. (1997, June 26). Egyptian court overturns ban on cutting of girls' genitals. *New York Times,* p. A12.

Jimmerson, J. (1990). Female infanticide in China: An examination of cultural and legal norms. *UCLA Pacific Basin Law Journal 8,* 57–62.

Johnson, K. E., & Rodgers, S. (1994). When cultural practices are health risks: The dilemma of female circumcision. *Holistic Nursing Practice, 8*(2), 70–78.

Jones, A. (2002). *Case study: Female infanticide.* Retrieved February 10, 2005, from http://www.gendercide.org/case_infanticide.html

Joseph, C. (1995). Scarlet wounding: Issues of child prostitution. *Journal of Psychohistory, 23*(1), 2–17.

Kaban, E. (1998). *United Nations body urges recognition of sex trade.* Retrieved January 30, 2005, from http://www.walnet.org/csis/news/world_98/reuters-980819.html

Kader, S. A. (1998). *One woman's view: Female infanticide.* Retrieved January 26, 2005, from http://www.metimes.com/articles/normal.php?StoryID=19980529-040622-5259r

Kaku, K. (1975). Were baby girls sacrificed to a folk superstition in 1966 in Japan? *Annals of Human Biology, 2,* 391–393.

Kangberee, S. B. (1994). Female circumcision [Letter to the editor]. *West Africa,* p. 1164.

Kaur, I. (2002). *A review of World Bank lending for children and its bearing on child labour.* New York: UNICEF.

Kelly, J. M. (1993). *Female genital mutilation: A search for its origins.* Unpublished doctoral dissertation, California State University, Fullerton, CA.

Kennedy, J. P., II. (1996). Keynote address. In U.S. Department of Labor, *Forced labor: The prostitution of children* (pp. 1–6). Washington, DC: U.S. Department of Labor.

Kenya struggles with child prostitution. (2003). *Reproductive Health Matters, 11*(21), 197.

Keuls, E. C. (1985). *The reign of the phallus: Sexual politics in ancient Athens.* New York: Harper and Row.

Keys, D., & DeFayette, A. (2004). Guatemala. In C. L. Schmitz, E. K. Traver, & D. Larson (Eds.), *Child labor: A global view* (pp. 79–90). Westport, CT: Greenwood Press.

Kids without a childhood. (2000). *Canada and the World Backgrounder, 66*(3), pp. 27–31.

Klain, E. (1999). *Prostitution of children and child-sex tourism: An analysis of domestic and international responses.* (National Center for Missing & Exploited Children). Alexandria, VA: National Center for Missing & Exploited Children.

Knott, L. (1996). Female circumcision in Britain. *Maternal and Child Health, 21*(5), 127–129.

Kopelman, L. M. (1994). Female circumcision/genital mutilation and ethical relativism. *Second Opinion: Health, Faith, Ethics, 20*(2), 55–71.

Kouba, L. J., & Muasher, J. (1985). Female circumcision in Africa: An overview. *African Studies Review, 28*(1), 95–110.

Kristof, N. D. (1991a, June 17). A mystery from China's census: Where have young girls gone? *New York Times,* pp. A1, A8.

Kristof, N. D. (1991b, November 5). Stark data on women: 100 million are missing. *New York Times,* pp. C1, C12.

Kristof, N. D. (1996, April 14). Asian childhoods sacrificed to prosperity's lust. *New York Times,* p. I1.

Kulkarni, M. L., Hebbal, K., Koujalgi, M. B., & Ramesh, M. B. (1996). Is female infanticide spreading to Karnataka? [Letter to the editor]. *Indian Pediatrics: Journal of the Indian Academy of Pediatrics, 33*(6), 525–526.

Lachmann, R. (1991). *The encyclopedic dictionary of sociology.* Guilford, CT: Dushkin.

Larson, D. (2004). India. In C. L. Schmitz, E. K. Traver, & D. Larson (Eds.), *Child labor: A global view* (pp. 101–112). Westport, CT: Greenwood Press.

Lee, W. (1993). *Possible causes and solutions of child prostitution in Taiwan.* Unpublished doctoral dissertation, Harvard University Law School, Cambridge.

Leheny, D. (1995). A political economy of Asian sex tourism. *Annals of Tourism Research, 22*(2), 367–384.

Lee-Wright, P. (1990). *Child slaves.* London: Earthscan.

Leonard, L. (1996). Female circumcision in southern Chad: Origins, meaning, and current practice. *Social Science and Medicine, 43*(2), 255–263.

Lester, D. (1986). The relation of twin infanticide to status of women, societal aggression, and material well-being. *Journal of Social Psychology, 126*(1), 57–59.

Lester, D. (1992). *Roe v. Wade* was followed by a decrease in neonatal homicide. *Journal of the American Medical Association, 267*(22), 3027–3028.

Levan, P. D. (1994). Curtailing Thailand's child prostitution through an international conscience. *American University Journal of International Law and Policy, 9*(3), 869–912.

Levine, P. (1993). Women and prostitution: Metaphor, reality, history. *Canadian Journal of History, 28*(3), 479–494.

Lewis, N. (1985). *Life in Egypt under Roman rule.* Oxford: Clarendon Press.

López-Calva, L. F. (2001). Child labor: Myths, theories, and facts. *Journal of International Affairs, 55*(1), 59–73.

MacCormick, C. P. (1993). Clitoridectomy. In *The encyclopedia of religion* (Vols. 3–4, pp. 535–537). New York: Macmillan.

Mackie, G. (1996). Ending footbinding and infibulation: A convention account. *American Sociological Review, 61*, 999–1017.

Madden, J. (1996). Slavery in the Roman Empire: Numbers and origins. *Classics Ireland, 3*, 109–128.

Magied, A. A., & Makki, A. (2004). Knowledge and attitudes of Sudanese youth towards female genital mutilation/female circumcision (FGM/FC). *Ahfad Journal, 21*(1), 29–40.

Maher, R. H. (1996). Female genital mutilation: The struggle to eradicate this rite of passage. *Human Rights, 23*(4), 12–15.

Mahler, K. (1997). Global concern for children's rights: The World Congress against Sexual Exploitation. *International Family Planning Perspectives, 23*(2), 79–84.

Maier-Katkin, D., & Ogle, R. S. (1997). Policy and disparity: The punishment of infanticide in Britain and America. *International Journal of Comparative and Applied Criminal Justice, 21*(2), 305–316.

Marquez, H. (1996, January 18). *Inter Press Service.* Retrieved March 10, 2005, from http://pangaea.org/street_children/latin/venez.htm

Mattioli, M. C., & Sapovadia, V. K. (2004). Laws of labor: Core labor standards and global trade. *International Trade, 26*(2), 60–64.

May, G. (1937). Prostitution. In *Encyclopedia of the social sciences* (Vol. 11, pp. 553–559). New York: Macmillan.

Mays, S. (1993). Infanticide in Roman Britain. *Antiquity, 67*(257), 883—888.

McGuire, M. R. P. (1967). Sacred Prostitution. In *New Catholic encyclopedia* (Vol. 11, pp. 881). New York: McGraw-Hill.

McKay, S., & Mazurana, D. (2000, September). *Girls in militaries, paramilitaries and armed opposition groups.* Paper presented at the International Conference on War-Affected Children, Winnipeg, Canada.

Mehta, P. S. (1994). Cashing in on child labor. *Multinational Monitor, 15*(4), 24–25.

Mensendiek, M. (1997). Women, migration and prostitution in Thailand. *International Social Work, 40*(2), 163–176.

Merton, R. (1968). *Social theory and social structure.* New York: Free Press.

Miller, B. D. (1981). *The endangered sex: Neglect of female children in rural north India.* Ithaca, NY: Cornell University Press.

Mixed news on female genital mutilation. (2004, August). *Contemporary Sexuality, 38*(8), 7–8.

Mohamud, O. (1991). Female circumcision and child mortality in urban Somalia. *Genus, 47*(3), 203–223.

Momoh, C. (2004). Attitudes to female genital mutilation. *British Journal of Midwifery, 12*(10), 631–635.

Monsoor, F. (2004). The WTO versus the ILO and the case of child labour. *Web Journal of Current Legal Issues, 11.* Retrieved May 8, 2006, from http://webjcli.ncl.ac.uk/2004/issue2/mansoor2.html

Montagu, A. (1995). Mutilated humanity. *Humanist, 55*(4), 12–15.

Morris, R. (1996). The culture of female circumcision. *Advances in Nursing Science, 19*(2), 43–53.

Moschovis, P. P. (2002). When cultures are wrong. *Medical Student Journal of the American Medical Association, 288*(9), 1131–1132.

Muecke, M. A. (1992). Mother sold food, daughter sells her body: The cultural continuity of prostitution. *Social Science and Medicine, 35*(7), 891–901.

Mulholland, L. (1992). Female circumcision: The view from Sudan. *Off Our Backs, 22*(11), 6–7.

Muntarbhorn, V. (1996). International perspectives and child prostitution in Asia. In U.S. Department of Labor, *Forced labor: The prostitution of children* (pp. 9–31). Washington, DC: U.S. Department of Labor.

Muntarbhorn, V. (1997, January/February). Sexual exploitation of children. *Childright,* pp. 8–9.

Murshed, M. (2001). Unraveling child labor and labor legislation. *Journal of International Affairs, 55*(1), 168–189.

Murtagh, J. M. (1967). Prostitution. In *New Catholic encyclopedia* (Vol. 11, p. 881). New York: McGraw-Hill.

Muthulakshmi, R. (1997). *Female infanticide: Its causes and solutions.* New Delhi: Discovery Publishing House.

Nagengast, C., & Turner, T. (1997). Introduction: Universal human rights versus cultural relativity. *Journal of Anthropological Research, 53*(4), 269–272.

Nardinelli, C. (1990). *Child labor and the Industrial Revolution.* Bloomington: Indiana University Press.

Nathan, G. (2000). *The family in late antiquity: The rise of Christianity and the endurance of tradition.* New York: Routledge.

Nicholas, D. (1995). Child and adolescent labour in the late medieval city: A Flemish model in regional perspective. *English Historical Review, 110*(439), 1103–1131.

Nieuwenhuys, O. (1996). The paradox of child labor and anthropology. *Annual Review of Anthropology, 25*, 237–251.

Noonan, J. T., Jr. (1965). *Contraception: A history of its treatment by the Catholic Theologians and Canonists.* Cambridge, MA: Harvard University Press.

Noonan, J. T., Jr. (1967). *Contraception.* New York: New American Library.

Nussbaum, M. C. (1995a). Human capabilities, female human beings. In M. C. Nussbaum & J. Glover (Eds.), *Women, culture and development: A study of human capabilities* (pp. 61–104). New York: Oxford University Press.

Nussbaum, M. C. (1995b). Introduction. In M. C. Nussbaum & J. Glover (Eds.), *Women, culture and development: A study of human capabilities* (pp. 1–34). New York: Oxford University Press.

Nussbaum, M. C. (1997). Capabilities and human rights. *Fordham Law Review, 66*, 273–300.

Nyland, B. (1995). Child prostitution, and the new Australian legislation on paedophiles in Asia. *Journal of Contemporary Asia, 25*(4), 546–560.

Oates, W. J., & O'Neill, E., Jr. (Eds.). (1938). *The complete Greek drama* (Vols. 1–2). New York: Random House.

O'Grady, R. (1992). *The child and the tourist.* Bangkok: End Child Prostitution in Asian Tourism.

O'Grady, R. (1994). *The rape of the innocent: One million children trapped in the slavery of prostitution.* Bangkok: End Child Prostitution in Asian Tourism.

Onadeko, M. O. (1985). Female circumcision in Nigeria: A fact or a farce? *Journal of Tropical Pediatrics, 31*, 180–184.

Oomman, N., & Ganatra, B. R. (2002). Sex selection: The systematic elimination of girls. *Reproductive Health Matters, 10*(19), 184–188.

Otero, J. F. (1996). Preface. In U.S. Department of Labor, *Forced labor: The prostitution of children* (pp. i–vii). Washington, DC: U.S. Department of Labor.

Parker, M. (1995). Rethinking female circumcision. *Africa, 65*(4), 506–523.

Patrinos, H. A., & Psacharopoulos, G. (1995). Educational performance and child labor in Paraguay. *International Journal of Educational Development, 15*(1), 47–60.

Perry, M. (1997). Are human rights universal? The relativist challenge and related matters. *Human Rights Quarterly, 19*(3), 461–509.

Petras, J., & Wongchaisuwan, T. (1993, March 13). Free markets, AIDS, and child prostitution. *Economic and Political Weekly*, pp. 440–442.

Pflug, B. (2002). *An overview of child domestic workers in Asia.* Geneva: International Labour Organization.

Piers, M. W. (1978). *Infanticide.* New York: W. W. Norton.

Pitt, S. E., & Bale, E. M. (1995). Neonaticide, infanticide, and filicide: A review of the literature. *Bulletin of the American Academy of Psychiatry and the Law, 23*(3), 375–386.

Pomeroy, S. B. (1975). *Goddesses, whores, wives, and slaves: Women in classical antiquity.* New York: Schocken Books.

Post, S. G. (1988). History, infanticide, and imperiled newborns. *Hastings Center Report, 18*(4), 14–17.

Prasad, S. (2004, November 5). *Fall in female infanticide, thanks to rise in awareness.* Retrieved February 10, 2005, from http://www.hindu.com/2004/11/05/stories/2004110507050400.htm

Ptolemy of Lucca. (1997). *On the government of rulers, with portions attributed to Thomas Aquinas* (J. M. Blythe, Trans.). Philadelphia: University of Pennsylvania Press. (Original work published circa 1300)

Rajan, V. G. J. (1996). *Will India's ban on prenatal sex determination slow abortion of girls?* Retrieved January 26, 2005, from http://www.hinduismtoday.com/archives/1996/4/1996-4-04.shtml

Reddy, C. P. (2001, June 21). Even multinationals employ girl children for a profit. *Financial Daily.*

Reichert, E. (2006). Human rights: An examination of universalism and cultural relativism. *Journal of Comparative Social Welfare, 22*(1), 23–36.

Reiman, J. (1996). Abortion, infanticide, and the asymmetric value of human life. *Journal of Social Philosophy, 27*(3), 181–200.

Ren, X. S. (1995). Sex differences in infant and child mortality in three provinces in China. *Social Science and Medicine, 40*(9), 1259–1269.

Renteln, A. D. (1990). *International human rights: Universalism versus relativism.* Newbury Park, CA: Sage.

Resnick, P. J. (1972). Infanticide. In J. G. Howells (Ed.), *Modern perspectives in psycho-obstetrics* (pp. 410–431). Edinburgh: Oliver and Boyd.

Rose, E. (1999). Consumption smoothing and excess female mortality in rural India. *Review of Economics and Statistics, 81*(1), 41–49.

Rosenthal, A. M. (1996, April 12). Fighting female mutilation. *New York Times*, p. A31.

Ruggiero, K. (1992). Honor, maternity, and the disciplining of women: Infanticide in late nineteenth-century Buenos Aires. *Hispanic American Historical Review, 72*(3), 353–373.

Rush, F. (1980). *The best kept secret: Sexual abuse of children.* New York: McGraw-Hill.

Rushwan, H. (1995, April-May). Female circumcision. *World Health: The Magazine of the World Health Organization, 48*, 16–17.

Sanger, W. W. (1972). *The history of prostitution.* New York: Arno Press.

Sarkis, M. (2003). *Female genital mutilation: An introduction.* Retrieved January 24, 2005, from http://www.fgmnetwork.org/html/modules.php?name=Content&pa=showpage&pid=1

Sartori, G. (1970). Concept misformation in comparative politics. *American Political Science Review, 64*(4), 1033–1053.

Scheper-Hughes, N. (1985). Culture, scarcity and maternal thinking. *Ethos, 13*, 291–317.

Seabrook, J. (2000, June 26). Invisible children of the south. *New Statesman, 129*, 13–14.

Secondi, G. S. (2002). Biased childhood sex ratios and the economic status of the family in rural China. *Journal of Comparative Family Studies, 33*(2), 215–235.

Seligman, C. G. (1913). Aspects of the Hamitic problem of the Anglo-Egyptian Sudan. *Journal of the Royal Anthropological Institute, 42*, 639–646.

Senate Concurrent Resolution 57, 105th Cong., 1st Sess. (1997). Retrieved January 26, 2005, from http://thomas.loc.gov/cgi-bin/query/z?c105:S.Con.Res.57:

Sentenced to life for female infanticide. (2004, October 20). Retrieved February 10, 2005, from http://www.hindu.com/2004/10/20/stories/2004102003250300.htm

Shahar, S. (1983). *The Fourth Estate: A history of women in the Middle Ages.* New York: Methuen and Company.

Sharma, D. C. (2003). Widespread concern over India's missing girl: Selective abortion and female infanticide cause girl-to-boy ratios to plummet. *Lancet, 362*, 1553.

Silvers, J. (1996, February). Child labor in Pakistan. *Atlantic Monthly, 277*, 79–92.

Simons, M. (1994, January 16). The littlest prostitutes. *New York Times Magazine*, p. 31.

Sitthirak, S. (1995). *Prostitution in Thailand: A north-south dialogue on neocolonialism, militarism, and consumerism.* Retrieved January 30, 2005, from http://www.signposts.uts.edu.au/articles/Thailand/ Tourism/353.html

Slack, A. T. (1988). Female circumcision: A critical appraisal. *Human Rights Quarterly, 10*, 437–486.

Sloane, R. D. (2001). Outrelativizing relativism: A liberal defense of the universality of international human rights. *Vanderbilt Journal of Transnational Law, 34*(3), 527–595.

Smith, P., & Kahila, G. (1992). Identification of infanticide in archaeological sites: A case study from the late Roman-early Byzantine periods at Ashkelon, Israel. *Journal of Archaeological Science, 19*, 667–675.

Smolin, D. M. (2000). Strategic choices in the international campaign against child labor. *Human Rights Quarterly, 22*(4), 942–987.

Snehi, Y. (2003). Female infanticide and gender in Punjab: Imperial claims and contemporary discourse. *Economic and Political Weekly, 38*(41), 4302–4305.

Social Welfare, Social Reforms and Vazhndhu Kaattuvom. (2001). Retrieved February 10, 2005, from http://www.tn.gov.in/per-budget-1999–2001/social-pb-e.htm

Stackhouse, J. (1996). Real-world solutions to child labor. *World Press Review, 43*(6), 31.

Sumner, W. G. (1911). *Folkways: A study of the sociological importance of usages, manners, customs, mores, and morals.* Boston: Ginn, Athenaeum.

Tasker, R. (1995, January 12). Alone in a man's world: Female governor fights child prostitution. *Far Eastern Economic Review, 158*, 28.

Taye Oberatu, J. (2004, November 24). 59 Nigerians arrested for child prostitution. *Africa News Service.*

Teklu, D. (2004, August 20). Child prostitution: "Rising problem with no due attention." *Africa News Service.*

Temin, P. (2004). The labor supply of the early Roman Empire. *Journal of Interdisciplinary History, 34*(4), 513–538.

Thiam, A. (1983). Women's fight for the abolition of sexual mutilation. *International Social Science Journal, 35*(4), 747–756.

Thompson, B. (1992). Africa's charter on children's rights: A normative break with cultural traditionalism. *International and Comparative Law Quarterly, 41*(2), 432–444.

Tilley, J. J. (2000). Cultural relativism. *Human Rights Quarterly, 22*(2), 501–547.

Togo: Child prostitution goes unchecked in Togo. (2004, April 16). *Africa News Service.*

Toubia, N. (1993). *Female genital mutilation: A call for global action.* New York: Women.

Toubia, N. (1994). Female circumcision as a public health issue. *New England Journal of Medicine, 331*(11), 712–716.

Tourism authority of Thailand. (2005). *Policy on prostitution: Penalty for the offender.* Retrieved February 26, 2005, from http://www.tatnews.org/ tat_news/detail.asp?id=1483

Traver, E. K. (2004). Brazil. In C. L. Schmitz, E. K. Traver, & D. Larson (Eds.), *Child labor: A global view* (pp. 27–38). Westport, CT: Greenwood Press.

Tsunami children lost, vulnerable. (2005, January 5). *CBS Evening News* [Television broadcast]. New York: CBS News.

Tucker, L. (1997). Child slaves in modern India: The bonded labor problem. *Human Rights Quarterly, 19*(3), 572–629.

United Nations. (1986). *Report of the world conference to review and appraise the achievements of the United Nations decade for women: Equality, development and peace.* Retrieved January 23, 2005, from http://www.un.org/ womenwatch/confer/nfls/Nairobi1985report.txt

United Nations. (1993a). *Report of the regional meeting for Asia of the world conference on human rights.* Retrieved January 23, 2005, from http://www.unhchr.ch/html/menu5/wcbangk.htm

United Nations. (1993b). *Report of the world conference on human rights: Report of the Secretary-General.* Retrieved January 23, 2005, from http://www.unhchr.ch/huridocda/huridoca.nsf/(Symbol)/ A.CONF.157.24+(PART+I).En?OpenDocument

United Nations. (1995). *Beijing declaration and platform for action.* Retrieved January 23, 2005, from http://www.un.org/womenwatch/ daw/beijing/platform/declar.htm

United Nations. (1996). *Human rights questions: Human rights questions, including alternative approaches for improving the effective enjoyment of human rights and fundamental freedoms.* Retrieved January 23, 2005, from http://www.unhchr.ch/huridocda/huridoca.nsf/%20(Symbol)/A.51.506.Add.1.En?OpenDocument

United Nations. (1998). *Charter of the United Nations.* Retrieved January 23, 2005, from http://www.un.org/aboutun/charter/

United Nations Children's Fund. (1997a). *Cape Town principles and best practices.* Symposium on the Prevention of Recruitment of Children into the Armed Forces and on Demobilization and Social Reintegration of Child Soldiers in Africa. Retrieved March 15, 2006, from http://www.unicef.org/emerg/files/Cape_Town_Principles.pdf

United Nations Children's Fund. (1997b). *The state of the world's children 1997.* New York: Oxford University Press.

United Nations Children's Fund. (2003, February 6). *UNICEF to governments: End female genital mutilation.* Retrieved February 6, 2005, from http://www.unicef.org/media/media_7553.html

United Nations Children's Fund. (2004). *Strategies for girl's education.* New York: United Nations Children's Fund.

United Nations Children's Fund. (2005a). *Convention on the Rights of the Child.* Retrieved January 30, 2005, from http://www.ohchr.org/english/law/pdf/crc.pdf

United Nations Children's Fund. (2005b). *End child exploitation: Child labour today.* New York: UNICEF.

United Nations Children's Fund. (2005c). *Optional protocols to the convention on the rights of the child.* Retrieved February 1, 2005, from http://www.unicef.org/crc/oppro.htm

United Nations Development Fund for Women. (1998). *About the trust fund: The trust fund in support of actions to eliminate violence against women.* Retrieved January 26, 2005, from http://www.unifem.org/support/trust_fund.php

United Nations Development Programme. (1991). *Human Development Report 1991.* New York: Oxford University Press.

United Nations Development Programme. (1995). *Human Development Report 1995.* New York: Oxford University Press.

United Nations Development Programme. (1999). *World Abortion Policies, 1999.* Retrieved January 26, 2005, from http://www.un.org/esa/population/publications/abt/abt.htm

United Nations Development Programme (2004). *Human Development Report, 2004: Cultural Liberty in Today's Diverse World.* New York: United Nations Development Programme.

United Nations Educational, Scientific, and Cultural Organization. (2004). *Convention on the Rights of the Child.* Retrieved January 30, 2005, from http://www.unicef.org/crc/crc.htm

United Nations General Assembly. (1993). *Declaration on the elimination of violence against women.* Retrieved January 24, 2005, from http://www.un.org/documents/ga/res/48/a48r104.htm

United Nations High Commissioner for Human Rights. (1956). *Supplementary Convention on the Abolition of Slavery, the Slave Trade, and Institutions and Practices Similar to Slavery.* Retrieved March 10, 2006, from http://www. ohchr.org/english/law/slavetrade.htm#wp1034270

United States Agency for International Development. (1996). *Update on activities toward the prevention and eradication of female genital mutilation.* Retrieved January 24, 2005, from http://www.fgmnetwork.org/html/ modules.php?name=Content&pa=showpage&pid=40

United States Department of Labor. (2005). *2004 findings on the worst forms of child labor.* Washington, DC: U.S. Department of Labor/Bureau of International Labor Affairs.

United States Department of Labor. (2006). *International Child Labor Program.* Retrieved May 10, 2006, from http://www.dol.gov/ilab/ programs/iclp/

United States Department of State. (1995). *Country reports on human rights practices for 1994* (Publication No. 86–839 CC). Washington, DC: U.S. Government Printing Office.

Venkatachalam, R., and Srinivasan, V. (1993). *Female Infanticide.* New Delhi: Har-Anand Publications.

Venkatram, S. (1995, September 6). Girl infanticide rife in India. *Nursing Standard,* p. 16.

Venkatramani, S. H. (1986, June 15). Female infanticide: Born to die. *India Today, 11*(11), 26–33.

Verzin, J. A. (1976). Sequelae of female circumcision. *Tropical Doctor, 5,* 163–169.

Vickers, J. (1993). *Women and war.* London: Zed Press.

Virgin territory. (1996, March 2). *Economist,* p. 37.

Voss, M. (1999). *The commercial sexual exploitation of children: An overview.* New York: ECPAT-USA.

Wallerstein, E. Circumcision. In *Encyclopedia Americana* (Vol. 6, p. 735). Danbury, CT: Grolier.

Weigel, G. (1995). Are human rights still universal? *Commentary, 99*(2), 41–45.

Weiner, M. (1991). *The child and the state in India: Child labor and education policy in comparative perspective.* Princeton, NJ: Princeton University Press.

Weiner, M. (1995). Children in labor: How sociocultural values support child labor. *World & I, 10,* 370–379.

Weir, R. (1984). *Selective nontreatment of handicapped newborns: Moral dilemmas in neonatal medicine.* New York: Oxford University Press.

Weiss, R. (1996, May 11). Anti-girl bias rises in Asia, studies show; Abortion augmenting infanticide, neglect. *Washington Post,* p. A1.

Weissman, R. (1997). Stolen youth: Brutalized children, globalization, and the campaign to end child labor. *Multinational Monitor, 18*(1), 10–17.

What's culture got to do with It? Excising the harmful tradition of female circumcision. (1993). *Harvard Law Review, 106*(8), 1944–1961.

Whitehorn, J., Ayonrinde, O., & Maingay, S. (2002). Female genital mutilation: Cultural and psychological implications. *Sexual and Relationship Therapy, 17*(2), 161–170.

Wiarda, H. (1981). The ethnocentrism of social science: Implications for research and policy. *Review of Politics, 43*, 163–197.

Wiedemann, T. (1989). *Adults and children in the Roman Empire.* New Haven, CT: Yale University Press.

Williams, L., & Sobieszczyk, T. (1997). Attitudes surrounding the continuation of female circumcision in the Sudan: Passing the tradition to the next generation. *Journal of Marriage and the Family, 59*, 966–981.

Williamson, L. (1978). Infanticide: An anthropological analysis. In M. Kohl (Ed.), *Infanticide and the value of life* (pp. 61–75). Buffalo, NY: Prometheus Books.

Winkel, E. (1995). A Muslim perspective on female circumcision. *Women and Health, 23*(1), 1–7.

Woolard, D., & Edwards, R. M. (1997). Female circumcision: An emerging concern in college healthcare. *Journal of American College Health, 45*(5), 230–232.

World Bank. (2004). *Country brief: India.* Retrieved January 26, 2005, from http://lnweb18.worldbank.org/SAR/sa.nsf/0/4F3233D642E4BB3985256B4A00706AA7? OpenDocument

World Bank. (2005). *Rural women's development and empowerment project.* Retrieved January 6, 2005, from http://www.worldbank.org.in/external/default/main?pagePK =64027221&piPK=64027220&theSitePK=295584&menuPK=295615&Projectid=P044449

World Congress Against the Commercial Sexual Exploitation of Children. (1996). *Draft declaration and agenda for action.* Retrieved January 30, 2005, from http://www.usemb.se/children/csec/declaration.html

World Congress Against the Commercial Sexual Exploitation of Children. (1998a). *Backgrounder 1: Prostitution of children.* Retrieved January 30, 2005, from http://www.usemb.se/children/csec/backgrounder1.html

World Congress Against the Commercial Sexual Exploitation of Children. (1998b). *Contributing factors.* Retrieved January 30, 2005, from http://www.usemb.se/children/csec/cfactors.html

World Congress Against the Commercial Sexual Exploitation of Children. (1998c). *Feature 3: Cambodia.* Retrieved January 30, 2005, from http://www.usemb.se/children/csec/feature3.html

World Congress Against the Commercial Sexual Exploitation of Children. (1998d). *Regional profiles.* Retrieved January 30, 2005, from http://www.usemb.se/children/csec/regional_pofiles.html

World Congress Against the Commercial Sexual Exploitation of Children. (1998e). *Scope of the problem.* Retrieved January 30, 2005, from http://www.usemb.se/children/csec/scope.html

World Health Organization. (1997). *Female genital mutilation: A joint WHO/UNICEF/UNFPA statement.* Geneva: World Health Organization.

World Health Organization. (2000). *Female genital mutilation—fact sheet N241.* Retrieved January 24, 2005, from http://www.who.int/mediacentre/factsheets/fs241/en/

World Trade Organization. (1996). *World Trade Organization: Ministerial conference, Singapore, 9–13 December 1996.* Retrieved May 10, 2006, from http://www.wto.org/english/news_e/pres96_e/wtodec.htm

Zechenter, E. M. (1997). In the name of culture: Cultural relativism and the abuse of the individual. *Journal of Anthropological Research, 53*(4), 319–347.

INDEX